Vita and Virginia

D1417293

VITA AND VIRGINIA

*The Work and Friendship
of V. Sackville-West
and Virginia Woolf*

SUZANNE RAITT

CLARENDON PRESS · OXFORD
1993

Oxford University Press, Walton Street, Oxford OX2 6DP

Oxford New York Toronto
Delhi Bombay Calcutta Madras Karachi
Kuala Lumpur Singapore Hong Kong Tokyo
Nairobi Dar es Salaam Cape Town
Melbourne Auckland Madrid
and associated companies in
Berlin Ibadan

Oxford is a trade mark of Oxford University Press

Published in the United States
by Oxford University Press Inc., New York

© Suzanne Raitt 1993

All rights reserved. No part of this publication may be reproduced,
stored in a retrieval system, or transmitted, in any form or by any means,
without the prior permission in writing of Oxford University Press.
Within the UK, exceptions are allowed in respect of any fair dealing for the
purpose of research or private study, or criticism or review, as permitted
under the Copyright, Designs and Patents Act, 1988, or in the case of
reprographic reproduction in accordance with the terms of the licences
issued by the Copyright Licensing Agency. Enquiries concerning
reproduction outside these terms and in other countries should be
sent to the Rights Department, Oxford University Press,
at the address above

This book is sold subject to the condition that it shall not, by way
of trade or otherwise, be lent, re-sold, hired out or otherwise circulated
without the publisher's prior consent in any form of binding or cover
other than that in which it is published and without a similar condition
including this condition being imposed on the subsequent purchaser

British Library Cataloguing in Publication Data
Data available

Library of Congress Cataloging in Publication Data
Raitt, Suzanne.
Vita and Virginia : the work and friendship of V. Sackville-West
and Virginia Woolf / Suzanne Raitt.
Includes bibliographical references.
1. Sackville-West, V. (Victoria), 1892–1962—Criticism and
interpretation.   2. Woolf, Virginia, 1882–1941—Criticism and
interpretation.   3. Sackville-West, V. (Victoria), 1892–1962—
Friends and associates.   4. Woolf, Virginia, 1882–1941—Friends and
associates.   5. Authors, English—20th century—Biography.
I. Title.
PR6037.A35Z84   1993
92–20159
823'.91209—dc20
ISBN 0–19–811249–1
ISBN 0–19–812277–2 (Pbk)

Typeset by Graphicraft Typesetters Ltd, Hong Kong
Printed in Great Britain
on acid-free paper by
Biddles Ltd, Guildford and Kings' Lynn

For Laura

Preface

THIS book is a study of the friendship between two women, of some of their various writings, and of the cultural context in which they lived and wrote. I conceived it originally as a study of varying accounts of women's sexuality and of 'femininity' —femininity not in the sense of how far these women were or were not 'feminine', in the everyday usage, but in the sense of how they experienced and lived their femaleness. I was prepared to use and to challenge psychoanalytic theory, cultural studies, any and every version of what a woman might be that I could lay my hands on. Central to my conception of the object of study was the idea of narrative, for I believe that all of us, self-consciously or not, live our lives as stories, piece ourselves together continually, find new explanations and rewrite our own histories as part of our daily lives and daily intimacies. I expected to think about narrative as I worked across the range of texts that Virginia Woolf and Vita Sackville-West produced: letters, diaries, autobiographical fragments, biographies, poems, and novels. In each genre I would look for the story, the process by which each one tried to find herself as a woman, or to find the shape of femininity itself. My idea was that it is through the forging and exchange of such narratives that intimacies develop. Life stories are endlessly reworked in response to the narratives and the confessions of other women. I wanted to identify that process, to understand how it is that women establish and maintain emotional and erotic identifications with one another.

This concept is still behind the book, and my curiosity about these matters is still the reason why I wrote the book. I wanted to evolve a way of writing about a variety of different kinds of texts all at once, and to understand what it means for women to produce that kind of diversity.

But inevitably over the years that I have worked on this project my own context has changed. One of the most significant changes has been the emergence, tentative at first, but now growing stronger, of lesbian and gay studies in universities and institutes of higher education in this country. As the book developed, I began to ask questions like: what is lesbian identity? what is identity? and I thought that Woolf and Sackville-West might suggest some answers. The book as it is now is more explicitly an intervention in debates about lesbianism than it was at first. I began to wonder what it meant to be a married lesbian, for example. I began to wonder what lesbian texts were, and whether we could say that Woolf or Sackville-West wrote them, either in their letters or diaries or in the works they wrote for publication.

One of the reasons that these questions started to form themselves more insistently than at first was the growing publicity surrounding Vita Sackville-West's life, and in particular her relationship with Violet Trefusis. First Sackville-West's *All Passion Spent*, and then Nigel Nicolson's *Portrait of a Marriage* were adapted for BBC TV. I first conceived my own project in 1985, in response to Victoria Glendinning's *Vita*, and to the publication of Vita Sackville-West's letters to Virginia Woolf.[1] In those days when I mentioned this project to people, several asked 'Peter Sackville-West? Who's he?' which did rather miss the point. Vita Sackville-West herself seemed to need introduction and explanation. Now, most TV viewers know at least something about her.

But few people have read her work. In order to grasp what was going on between Virginia Woolf and Vita Sackville-West, we need to know not just what went on between them (which was, in many ways, relatively little), but also what *else* was going on: what they were writing, thinking about, producing during those years that nourished and transformed their intimacy. This book is a study of Sackville-West's work, as well as of the contexts in which both women were living and writing. I have had to be selective about which of Sackville-West's texts I could include, and I have concentrated on her most popular books, and on the writing produced during the years of her intimacy with Virginia Woolf. There is another book to be written about all the Sackville-West texts I have had to leave out.

[1] Victoria Glendinning, *Vita: The Life of V. Sackville-West* (New York, 1983); and *The Letters of Vita Sackville-West to Virginia Woolf*, ed. Louise DeSalvo and Mitchell A. Leaska (New York, 1985).

Sackville-West and Woolf are not representative (whatever that means). They were both highly privileged and articulate women, who were rarely forced by economic need to do things that they did not want to do. Their stories are very specific, as all our stories are. At the same time, they were confronting just as much as any woman the problems of 'femininity', of sexuality, of narration. In understanding their narratives, and their ways of making narratives, we understand more about how any woman, under whatever kind of pressure, might forge her own identity, and those of other women.

The Introduction explores the apparent paradox of the married lesbian, and looks at the ways in which Woolf and Sackville-West negotiated their various positionings. The first chapter is an analysis of the writing of *Orlando*, and a study of its relation to the biographical style of the period. Chapter 2 looks at Sackville-West's writing at the time of Woolf's meeting with her, and demonstrates her and her culture's immersion in eugenic theory, an important context for 1920s accounts of lesbianism and sexual identity. Woolf's and Sackville-West's autobiographical writing, and the uses they made of it in building relationships to each other and to other women, are explored in Chapter 3. Chapter 4 is a reading of five of Sackville-West's best known texts, and suggests that she used conventional forms to say unconventional things, just as in her own life, she used marriage as a cover for her lesbianism. In Chapter 5 I offer an analysis of lesbian mysticism in the period, and show how Sackville-West's biographies of female saints challenge psychoanalytic interpretations of feminine mysticism, such as Lacan's. Chapter 6 is a reading of *The Waves* that examines its formal links with autobiography and biography, and suggests that it was the climax to Woolf's negotiations of images of maternity.

S.R.

August 1991

Acknowledgements

I AM most grateful to Nigel Nicolson for permission to quote from the Sackville-West and Nicolson papers held in the Lilly Library, Bloomington, Indiana, and from the published work of V. Sackville-West and Harold Nicolson. Professor Quentin Bell kindly gave permission to quote from Virginia Woolf's unpublished fragment, 'The tea table was the centre of Victorian family life', held in the Berg Collection, New York Public Library, Astor, Lenox and Tilden Foundations; and from Vanessa Bell's unpublished letters to Virginia Woolf, also in the Berg Collection. I am grateful to David Higham Associates for permission to quote from the unpublished letters of Ethel Smyth to Virginia Woolf, also in the Berg Collection.

This book is based on research done for a Ph.D. thesis at the University of Cambridge, and I am grateful to the British Academy, Jesus College, Cambridge, and Gonville and Caius College, Cambridge, for their support. Gonville and Caius College appointed me to a Research Fellowship, which allowed me to complete the research for the book. The staff of the University Library, Cambridge; the Lilly Library, Bloomington, Indiana; and the Berg Collection, New York Public Library, were unfailingly helpful.

Gillian Beer supervised the Ph.D. on which this book is based, and I owe her a special debt of thanks. Nigel Nicolson has been extremely generous in every way, allowing me free access to family papers at Sissinghurst Castle. Without his kindness and support this book would have been impossible. I am very grateful to Mary Hamer and Stephen Heath, who both read several drafts of the manuscript. Thanks also to: Isobel Armstrong, Caroline Ash, Liz Bellamy, Teresa Brennan, Mary Chadwick, Clare Crombie, Mary Lynne Ellis, Christine Fortin, Mandy Hetherton, Janet Hiddleston, Diana Hinds, Margaret Homans, Karla Jay, Jenny Kitzinger, Adam Lively, Elizabeth

Maslen, John Mullan, Noreen O'Connor, Kate Pahl, A.W. Raitt, Claire Raitt, Beverley Ross, Morag Shiach, Helen Small, Patricia Spacks, Simonette Strachey, Tony Tanner, Trudi Tate, Gill Thomas, and Kim Scott Walwyn. Becky Hall helped me through the final stages. This book is also for her.

Contents

Abbreviations

The correspondence between Vita Sackville-West and Harold Nicolson is held in the archive at the Lilly Library, Bloomington, Indiana. References to these letters in the text refer to unpublished material in this archive. References to the following works in the text are to these editions (the date of first publication is also given):

APS   V. Sackville-West, *All Passion Spent*, (London: Virago, 1983; 1st edn. 1931).

C   V. Sackville-West, *Challenge*, (New York: Bard Books, 1983; 1st edn. 1924).

D   *The Diary of Virginia Woolf*, ed. Anne Olivier Bell with Andrew McNeillie, 5 vols. (London: Hogarth, 1977–84).

DS   V. Sackville-West, *The Dragon in Shallow Waters*, (London: Collins, 1921).

E   V. Sackville-West, *The Edwardians*, (London: Virago, 1983; 1st edn. 1930).

FH   V. Sackville-West, *Family History*, (London: Virago, 1986; 1st edn. 1932).

G   V. Sackville-West, *The Garden*, (London: Michael Joseph, 1946).

H   V. Sackville-West, *Heritage*, (London: Futura, 1975; 1st edn. 1919).

JA   V. Sackville-West, *Saint Joan of Arc*, (London: Cobden-Sanderson, 1936).

L   *The Letters of Virginia Woolf*, ed. Nigel Nicolson and Joanne Trautmann, 6 vols. (London: Hogarth, 1975–80).

La   V. Sackville-West, *The Land*, 1926 (London: Heinemann, 1926).

MD   Virginia Woolf, *Mrs Dalloway*, (Oxford: World's Classics, 1992; 1st edn. 1925).

ND   Virginia Woolf, *Night and Day*, (Oxford: World's Classics, 1992; 1st edn. 1919).

O   Virginia Woolf, *Orlando*, (Oxford: World's Classics, 1992; 1st edn. 1928).

P   V. Sackville-West, *Pepita*, (London: Virago, 1986; 1st edn. 1937).

PM   Nigel Nicolson, *Portrait of a Marriage*, (London: Futura, 1974; 1st edn. 1973).

SP   Virginia Woolf, 'A Sketch of the Past', in *Moments of Being:*

Unpublished autobiographical writings, ed. Jeanne Schulkind (London: Triad Granada, 1978), 71–164.

SS   V. Sackville-West, *No Signposts in the Sea*, (London: Virago, 1985; 1st edn. 1961).

TTL   Virginia Woolf, *To the Lighthouse*, (Oxford: World's Classics, 1992; 1st edn. 1927).

W   Virginia Woolf, *The Waves*, (Oxford: World's Classics, 1992; 1st edn. 1931).

'You and I Alone Like being Married': Or, Having it Both Ways

VIRGINIA WOOLF wrote this account of Vita Sackville-West on 21 December 1925, a couple of days after they had first become lovers:

She shines in the grocers shop in Sevenoaks with a candle lit radiance, stalking on legs like beech trees, pink glowing, grape clustered, pearl hung. (*D*, iii. 52)

Her phrases shimmer with the luminosity of shared sexual pleasure. Earlier in the same diary entry she wrote:

These Sapphists *love* women; friendship is never untinged with amorosity. In short, my fears & refrainings, my 'impertinence' my usual self-consciousness in intercourse with people who mayn't want me & so on—were all, as L. said, sheer fudge. (*D*, iii. 51)

Her hesitancy apparently yielded to the incandescent delight of the first quotation. In the image of Sackville-West 'stalking' above her, legs like trees, Woolf recalls the unexpected angles from which the body of a lover is viewed. Her final phrases seem a kind of sexual tongue-twisting, rolling the words in the mouth: 'pink glowing, grape clustered, pearl hung'. Woolf's letters were sometimes even more explicit: 'you only be a careful dolphin in your gambolling, or you'll find Virginia's soft crevices lined with hooks!' (Woolf to Sackville-West, *L*, iii. 395, 4 July 1927). Sexual and linguistic play were intertwined.

In *A Room of One's Own*, published in 1929 soon after these passages were written, Woolf calls for a recognition of new possibilities, both emotional and textual. She imagines reading a new novel by a woman called Mary Carmichael. She comes upon the words 'Chloe likes Olivia' and immediately her imagination is fired. 'For if Chloe likes Olivia and Mary Carmichael knows how to express it she will light a torch in

that vast chamber where nobody has yet been.'[1] *A Room of
One's Own* is concerned with new kinds of fiction, and not with
new departures in private writing such as diaries or letters. But
it seems reasonable to link Woolf's call for the expression of
affection between women with her development, shortly before, of an erotic idiom in which she could court and flatter
Sackville-West in their unpublished texts. The possibility that
Chloe might like Olivia grew out of a certainty that Vita
already did like Virginia; and, even more surprisingly, that
Virginia found she had it in her to like Vita.

Sackville-West could not—or chose not to—match Woolf's
linguistic extravagance. But, already a self-identified and
experienced lesbian by the time she met Woolf, she was less
reticent about what she and Virginia had actually done, and
less romantic. She wrote to her husband Harold Nicolson:
'Virginia—not a muddle exactly; she is a busy and sensible
woman. But she does love me, and I did sleep with her at
Rodmell' (28 June 1926). It seems, then, that we are justified in
thinking of the women's relationship as a sexual one, in spite
of the fact that Sackville-West, later, drew back: 'I am scared
to death of arousing physical feelings in her, because of the
madness' (Sackville-West to Nicolson, 17 Aug. 1926). As we
saw, Woolf thought of Sackville-West as a 'Sapphist' (the first
citation of the word 'lesbian' in the *Oxford English Dictionary* is
in 1908—we will find Sackville-West herself using it in 1929).[2]
Explicit acknowledgement of sexual attraction was a part of
their relationship, and a decisive factor in their experiences of
one another.

Most critical and biographical accounts of the Sackville-West–
Woolf relationship concentrate either on the day-to-day de-

---

[1] Virginia Woolf, *A Room of One's Own*, (Oxford, 1992; 1st edn. 1929), 109. See
Jane Marcus, 'Sapphistory: The Woolf and the Well', in Karla Jay and Joanne
Glasgow (ed.), *Lesbian Texts and Contexts: Radical Revisions*, (New York, 1990),
164–79, for an analysis of the lesbian connotations of *A Room of One's Own*.

[2] For discussions of the development of ideas and vocabulary in the area of
lesbian sexuality see Blanche Wiesen Cook, '"Women Alone Stir My Imagination": Lesbianism and the Cultural Tradition', *Signs*, 4 (1979), 718–39; and
Catharine R. Stimpson, 'Zero Degree Deviancy: The Lesbian Novel in English',
Critical Inquiry, 8 (Winter 1981), 363–79.

tails of the involvement or on its effect on Woolf's writings.[3]
But Sackville-West was at least as prolific a writer as Woolf, and
certainly far more popular in their day. Her identity as a writer
was important to Woolf, perhaps specifically because of her
misgivings about Sackville-West's talent. 'Why she writes,
which she does with complete competency, and a pen of brass,
is a puzzle to me' (Woolf to Jacques Raverat, *L*, iii. 150, 26
Dec. 1924). Often in her letters to Sackville-West Woolf
acknowledged that writing was one of their common pursuits:
'as for the *mot juste*, you are quite wrong. Style is a very simple
matter: it is all rhythm' (*L*, iii. 247, 16 Mar. 1926). Sackville-
West's books were another way in to the body and the woman
Woolf found so compelling. After reading Sackville-West's
description of her journey across Persia, *Passenger to Teheran*
(1926), Woolf felt that she had found out all sorts of secrets
about her:

It is odd that now, having read this, I have picked up a good many
things I had missed in private life. What are they, I wonder, the very
intimate things, one says in print? There's a whole family of them. Its
the proof, to me, of being a writer, that one expresses them in print
only, and you do here. (Woolf to Sackville-West, *L*, iii. 291, 15 Sept.
1926)

Woolf's experience of Sackville-West as an author is central to
her gradual discovery of the woman she loves. Their friendship was self-consciously one between writers (Woolf was
Sackville-West's publisher), and the competitiveness that their
shared profession engendered—Sackville-West's admiration
of Woolf's writing, and Woolf's private disparagement of
Sackville-West's—was a hierarchy that structured elements of
their emotional as well as their professional relationship.

To ignore Sackville-West's writing in an account of their
relationship is to falsify the way in which they themselves

---

[3] See e.g. Quentin Bell, *Virginia Woolf: A Biography*, 2 vols. (London, 1972);
Nigel Nicolson, *Portrait of a Marriage* (1973; pbk. London, 1974); Louise A.
DeSalvo, 'Lighting the Cave: The Relationship between Vita Sackville-West and
Virginia Woolf', *Signs*, 8 (1982), 195–214; Joanne Trautmann, *The Jessamy Brides:
The Friendship of Virginia Woolf and V. Sackville-West* (Philadelphia, 1973); Phyllis
Rose, *Woman of Letters: A Life of Virginia Woolf* (Oxford, 1978); Victoria
Glendinning, *Vita: The Life of V. Sackville-West* (New York, 1983).

perceived their own intimacy. This book is as much a long overdue study of Sackville-West's work, as it is a reassessment of the Woolf–Sackville-West relationship as one between married lesbians. Examining the relationship between the two women in the context of Woolf's work alone gives us only half the picture. This distortion has affected our understanding both of the politics of women's writing in the early twentieth century, and of the history of sexual relationships between women.

Both Woolf and Sackville-West were married for most of their lives. It was a state with which both seemed more than reasonably content. 'In all London, you and I alone like being married', Woolf wrote to Sackville-West on 16 November 1925, a few days before their affair began (*L*, iii. 221). Earlier the same year she had identified her marriage as a haven of serenity and peace: 'I snuggled in to the core of my life, which is this complete comfort with L., & there found everything so satisfactory & calm that I revived myself, & got a fresh start; feeling entirely immune' (*D*, iii. 30, 14 June 1925). Woolf's belief in marriage as an institution—at least in the version that she and Leonard had agreed on—seems untroubled by her awareness of strong sexual feelings towards other women. Nowhere is there ever any suggestion of her leaving her marriage; and even if the letter to Sackville-West is deliberately provocative, even if Leonard *did* read the diaries, Woolf does not seem to have been fundamentally discontented with the idea of being someone's wife. Nor was Leonard, apparently, more than superficially uneasy about the situation with Sackville-West: 'rather a bore for Leonard, but not enough to worry him' (*D*, iii. 117, 23 Nov. 1926).

Sackville-West's marriage had suffered a much more severe crisis during her affair with Violet Trefusis. At times both she, and more rarely Nicolson, could see no way in which the marriage could survive. But, in the end, given the choice between life with Trefusis, and life with Nicolson, Sackville-West chose home and wifedom over an existence as an avowed lesbian (not that she was particularly secretive—Woolf did not want her to testify at the trial of *The Well of Loneliness* because '*your* proclivities are too well known' (Woolf to Sackville-West,

L, iii. 520, 30 Aug. 1928). From the upheaval with Trefusis, Sackville-West and Nicolson learnt how to reconcile homosexual feelings and heterosexual marriage. Sackville-West's return to Nicolson was an endorsement of marriage as a stable social institution, as well as the renewal of a private contract. Soon after Woolf's suicide, on 4 June 1941, Sackville-West wrote to Nicolson:

I was thinking 'How queer! I suppose Hadji [Harold Nicolson] and I have been about as unfaithful to one another as one well could be from the conventional point of view, even worse than unfaithful if you add in homosexuality, and yet I swear no two people could love one another more than we do after all these years.'
It *is* queer, isn't it? It does destroy all orthodox ideas of marriage? [*sic*]

In the midst of her intense grief for Woolf, Sackville-West found comfort in the contemplation of her marriage, which might subdue her sorrow. Loving Woolf, and being Nicolson's wife, were effortlessly continuous identities.

In the cases of Woolf and Sackville-West, then, lesbianism was not disruptive of marriage. There was no simple way in which, for them, unconventional sexual behaviour was inevitably either socially or politically subversive. Carroll Smith-Rosenberg has shown that intense erotic friendships between women in nineteenth-century America were tolerated and even encouraged by the fiancés and husbands of the women in question.[4] As she says:

There is every indication that these four women, their husbands and families—all eminently respectable and socially conservative—considered such love both socially acceptable and fully compatible with heterosexual marriage. Emotionally and cognitively, their heterosocial and their homosocial worlds were complementary.[5]

It is often suggested that this state of affairs ended with the greater visibility of lesbianism that resulted from the work of

[4] Carroll Smith-Rosenberg, 'The Female World of Love and Ritual: Relations between Women in Nineteenth-Century America', *Signs*, 1 (1975), 1–29.
[5] Smith-Rosenberg, 'Relations between Women', 8.

late nineteenth-century sexologists such as Krafft-Ebing and Havelock Ellis.[6] Sheila Jeffreys argues, for example:

Through looking at novels by and about women, we can see the effect which the sexological injunctions were having on women's relationships with each other. Once women's relationships might have spanned a continuum from casual friendship through intense emotional and physical involvement, to, in those cases where it seemed appropriate to the women concerned, relationships involving both lifelong commitment and genital sex. By the late 1920s a distinction had clearly been drawn between an acceptable level of friendship and lesbianism. The middle ground had been cut out. Women were no longer in a position to engage in passionate involvements with each other without being aware that they were on the edge of a precipice which might plunge them into the stigmatised world of the lesbian.[7]

But it seems that this was not quite true for Woolf and Sackville-West. They do not seem to have feared being overwhelmed by a new and difficult identity just because they went to bed with women. It is true that Sackville-West required initiation:

[Violet Trefusis] was far more skilful than I. I might have been a boy of eighteen, and she a woman of thirty-five. She was infinitely clever—she didn't scare me, she didn't rush me, she didn't allow me to see where I was going; it was all conscious on her part, but on mine it was simply the drunkenness of liberation—the liberation of half my personality. (*PM*, 106)

However, this initiation was not into a new way of life, but into an 'art of love' (*PM*, 107). This phrase marks the distance travelled between the women in Smith-Rosenberg's study, and lesbian women of the 1920s. Erotic relationships between women were no longer routine: they demanded the acquisition of a specialized sexual and emotional technique.

But women active as lesbians in the 1920s did not *have* to drop all other allegiances, any more than Carroll Smith-Rosenberg's women did. Lesbianism was not a political identity.

[6] For further discussion of this see Lillian Faderman, *Surpassing the Love of Men: Romantic Friendship and Love between Women from the Renaissance to the Present* (New York, 1981).

[7] Sheila Jeffreys, *The Spinster and her Enemies: Feminism and Sexuality 1880–1930* (London, 1985), 126–7.

In fact, it may not have been an *identity*, a place in which
the self was found, at all. Conceived as an intermittent sexual
or emotional orientation, it could flourish happily in the
interstices of heterosexual existence, hardly threatening it at
all. Biographers of Woolf and Sackville-West have assumed
that the two refused sexual relations with their husbands after
the initial years of marriage; but even of this there is no proof.
For Woolf and Sackville-West, the personal was *not* always
political. In most ways, both of them were anxious to protect
the heterosexual status quo, and this should cause us no
surprise.

Sackville-West was more concerned than Woolf with her
public image as a respectable married woman. In June 1929
she and Harold Nicolson gave a radio broadcast on marriage.
There was a certain irony—or defensiveness—in their agreeing to do so. Sackville-West was at the time sleeping with the
Director of Talks at the BBC, Hilda Matheson. Furthermore,
the scandal of Sackville-West's elopements with Trefusis had
spread far and wide: the listening public knew that the
Nicolson marriage had not been a smooth ride. In this
context, some of the conservatism of their conversation could
be seen as a defence, but it seems likely that they believed
most of what they said. (Their letters suggest that they took
the broadcast seriously. Nicolson wrote to Sackville-West: 'we
can do a long bit about men's and women's professions
clashing. It will be rather fun.'[8])

Their idea of the marriage relation is blandly liberal. 'In
marriage people ought to allow one another to remain themselves', announced Sackville-West.[9] But Nicolson offered a
confidently essentialist account of what those selves might be
like. 'I believe profoundly in the essential difference between
man and woman', he told Sackville-West. 'I believe that the
most virile woman is infinitely more feminine than the most
effeminate man.'[10] The sexual possibilities of what Eve
Kosofsky Sedgwick has called 'gender transitivity'—the blurring of the boundaries between what is masculine and what is

[8] Quoted in Glendinning, *Vita*, 215.
[9] V. Sackville-West and Harold Nicolson, 'Marriage', *Listener*, 1 (26 June, 1929),
900.   [10] Ibid.

feminine—were thus firmly evacuated from the discussion.[11] Sackville-West and Nicolson referred occasionally to the sexual side of marriage, but never to homosexuality or infidelity. Marriage, they agreed, served a biological necessity. To Nicolson's contention that 'the basic facts of generation place woman in a position of dependence', Sackville-West replied: 'that couldn't be denied even by the most extravagant feminist —which, by the way, I'm not.'[12] At no point does either of them suggest that marriage and child care arrangements are *social* matters, and therefore theoretically open to reform. Sackville-West's anxiety to repudiate feminist politics demonstrates her need, or her desire, to protect the institution of marriage, and her unwillingness to accept that it could be amended or even abandoned. The whopper on which the interview ends—'we have never seriously disagreed'[13]— reiterates one of the least tenable myths of heterosexual marriage: that within it radical differences are transcended or resolved. Sackville-West and Nicolson, in their lives and in this conversation, supported marriage as a social rather than a sexual contract; but they supported it none the less.

Sackville-West's and Woolf's lesbian feelings, then, seem not to have disturbed their fondness for marriage and heterosexual difference. *To the Lighthouse* (1927), published a couple of years before the Sackville-West–Nicolson broadcast, is at least as nostalgic for the beauties of Victorian marriage as it is critical of its shortcomings. Later in her life, when she came to write *Three Guineas* (1938), Woolf would modify her views somewhat, losing some of her patience with the more violent forms of masculine conservatism. But at this earlier date, the years of her love for Sackville-West, we see her celebrating the joys of marriage, both in her life and in her work.

Of course, Woolf and Sackville-West were not the only homosexuals of their time to hold conventional views on marriage and sexual roles. Vera Brittain, in her memoir of her companion Winifred Holtby, maintained that 'loyalty and affection between women is a noble relationship which, far from impoverishing, actually enhances the love of a girl for

---

[11] Eve Kosofsky Sedgwick, *The Epistemology of the Closet* (Hemel Hempstead, 1991), 1–2, 87–90.
[12] Sackville-West and Nicolson, 'Marriage', 899.   [13] Ibid. 900.

her lover, of a wife for her husband, of a mother for her children'.[14] Brittain was trying to redefine marriage in her own way as Sackville-West and Nicolson were in theirs. All were concerned to uphold the institution while finding ways, within its parameters, to fulfill their own specific needs. Radclyffe Hall, one of the period's best-known lesbians, is reported as saying: 'to be a good wife and mother is the finest work a woman can do.'[15] And John Addington Symonds, another of the era's better-known homosexuals, identified the continued demand for marriage among gay men in a letter to the sexual radical Edward Carpenter: '[homosexuality] does not interfere with marriage when that is sought as a domestic institution, as it always is among men who want children for helpers in their work and women to keep their households.'[16] Lesbians similarly could derive some advantage from marriage (financial and emotional security, respectability, status), if they were able to negotiate an acceptable version of it, as Woolf and Sackville-West did.

Lesbianism, then, was not always a radical force in terms of both social and sexual roles. As the Lesbian History group has noted, 'there can never be a fixed description of what it means to be a lesbian. The task for historians is to try to recreate the past as women then would have experienced it and to locate lesbians within it.'[17] In this book I shall try to re-create the particular political, historical, literary, and personal pressures which produced Woolf and Sackville-West as wives, as lesbians, and as writers. I am interested above all in the ways in which narratives of all kinds established and maintained their intimacy. My other interest is in the interactions of class, politics, and female sexual pleasure.

Sackville-West has been a problem for feminist critics, and particularly for socialist feminists. Not only did she publicize

---

[14] Vera Brittain, *Testament of Friendship: The Story of Winifred Holtby* (London, 1980), 2.
[15] Quoted in Michael Baker, *Our Three Selves: A Life of Radclyffe Hall* (London, 1985), 248.
[16] Quoted in Jeffrey Weeks, *Coming Out: Homosexual Politics in Britain, from the Nineteenth Century to the Present* (London, 1977), 56.
[17] Lesbian History Group, *Not a Passing Phase: Reclaiming Lesbians in History 1840–1985* (London, 1989), 14.

the joys of heterosexual marriage on national radio; she was also blatantly and unashamedly anti-working class; and very little of her published writing radically challenges conventional versions of femininity and female sexual pleasure (*All Passion Spent* (1931) is perhaps an exception). Nor did Sackville-West attempt literary innovation, like so many of her contemporaries. Her novels are unapologetically traditional in conception and execution. Woolf poses fewer problems for feminists. Her 'feminism' (like Sackville-West, she eschewed the label) was contradictory and at times highly reactionary (for instance in the areas of race and class), but she none the less *did* explore lesbian sexuality and relationships between women in her fiction (Mrs Ramsay and Lily Briscoe in *To the Lighthouse* (1927), Mrs Dalloway and Sally Seton in *Mrs Dalloway* (1925)); she *did* offer feminist critiques of culture and society in *A Room of One's Own* (1929) and *Three Guineas* (1938); and, although she remained married herself, she criticized elements of the institution of Victorian marriage in *To the Lighthouse* (1927).

When I first began work on this project, the traditional and feudalist nature of Sackville-West's attitudes and her work seemed problematic and incongruous in an age when, it has been claimed, 'if the conventions of syntax or of narrative technique must be abandoned, so too must the conventions of morality, behaviour and expectation'.[18] Sackville-West, after all, was far from conventional in her sexual and emotional life. But in fact, Sackville-West's politics, her attraction to Catholicism, her mysticism, and her traditionalist formal aesthetics were shared by many other literary lesbians of her time. Radclyffe Hall and Una Troubridge were keen to reproduce in their life together the country house atmosphere of Hall's childhood; Hall's prose and poetry are highly conventional in style; Hall and Troubridge were Catholic converts who believed in reincarnation, and held seances throughout their life together to communicate with Hall's dead lover, Mabel Batten.[19] Sylvia Townsend Warner and Valentine

[18] Gillian Hanscombe and Virginia L. Smyers, *Writing for their Lives: The Modernist Women 1910–1940* (London, 1987), 10–11.

[19] See M. Baker, *Our Three Selves*, for an account of their lives and a bibliography of Hall's writing.

Ackland, though they did not share Sackville-West's politics, were unconcerned with literary innovation, in their poetry at least; and Ackland too converted to Catholicism.[20] The failure to confront the interaction of lesbianism and social and aesthetic conservatism that Sackville-West's life and work dramatize, is a failure to confront all the possible political configurations of modernism and of lesbianism: configurations which Makiko Minow has suggested we call 'lesbian modernism'.[21]

Many of Sackville-West's texts are unashamedly romantic revisitings of a lost Edwardian idyll. Her most popular novel, *The Edwardians* (1930), is set in a large aristocratic estate highly reminiscent of her own childhood home at Knole. Anquetil, the rebel who comes to Chevron (the estate) to mock, is strangely discomfited by it: 'these two days have disturbed me more than I should have thought possible. I have perceived a certain beauty where I expected to find nothing but farce' (p. 91). At the end, Sebastian, new master of Chevron, is persuaded to go off travelling with Anquetil mainly because it will make him a better lord of the manor on his return. Sackville-West's Edwardian novels are a product of the literary and social crisis which Richard Sheppard has called the 'supersession of an aristocratic, semi-feudal, humanistic and agrarian order by one middle-class, democratic, mechanistic and urban'.[22] Sackville-West's writing fed the nostalgic and snobbish hunger of the middle-class reading public to revisit and to commemorate that decaying aristocratic order. None of Sackville-West's novels has an urban setting. *All Passion Spent* (1931), set in Hampstead, might just as well describe a small country house. Her most famous poem, *The Land* (1926)

---

[20] See Wendy Mulford, *This Narrow Place: Sylvia Townsend Warner and Valentine Ackland: Life, Letters and Politics, 1930–1951* (London, 1988), for an account of Warner's and Ackland's lives; and Valentine Ackland, *For Sylvia: An Honest Account* (London, 1985), for an account of Ackland's conversion. See Joanne Glasgow, in 'What's a Nice Lesbian Like You Doing in the Church of Torquemada? Radclyffe Hall and other Catholic Converts', in Karla Jay and Joanne Glasgow (ed.), *Lesbian Texts and Contexts*, 241–54, for an analysis of the attraction of the Catholic Church for lesbians of the period.

[21] Makiko Minow, 'Versions of Female Modernism: Review-Article', *News from Nowhere*, 7 (1989), 67.

[22] Richard Sheppard, 'The Crisis of Language', in Malcolm Bradbury and James McFarlane (ed.), *Modernism*, (Harmondsworth, 1976), 325.

is a pseudo-Virgilian epic celebrating the 'timeless' rhythms of rural life and agriculture. Her work, in fact, testifies to what Raymond Williams has called the persisting 'cultural importance of rural ideas' long after the agricultural economy had been marginalized.[23] Her country house novels, as I shall show, are 'the pretty seat . . . of unconscious reaction, and . . . of that conscious reaction which was . . . a militant resident Toryism'.[24]

A return to nature, and to rural existence, was characteristic not only of the literary conservatives of the time, but also of the homosexual community. Edward Carpenter, sexual radical and social reformer, retreated to the country in search of the kind of organic social unity towards which he had been working in his personal and professional life. Sylvia Townsend Warner and Valentine Ackland based themselves in Dorset; Radclyffe Hall and Una Troubridge lived for a while on a country estate called 'Chip Chase', and eventually moved to Rye; and Sackville-West herself rarely left her country home at Sissinghurst after she and Nicolson acquired it in 1930.[25] Sackville-West's conservative pastoralism is typical of the homosexual subculture of the 1920s and 1930s.

The retreat was away from society and into sex. Sackville-West's writing, and in particular her poetry, like that of Sylvia Townsend Warner and Radclyffe Hall, reimagined the natural world as a space in which sexuality could be renegotiated and enjoyed in seclusion and safety. Hall, Warner, and Sackville-West all looked to the rural setting for images of an originary or Edenic relationship. In their poetry, the innocent countryside is the kind of sensuous world that all these women, as they grew away from the protected environs of childhood, were trying to re-create, or in some cases, such as that of Valentine Ackland, create for the first time.[26] Images of a lost paradise also accommodated their fantasies of a pastoral social stability that the multiple crises of the early twentieth century

---

[23] Raymond Williams, *The Country and the City* (London, 1985), 248.
[24] Ibid. 254.
[25] Information in this paragraph is derived from Weeks, *Coming Out*; Mulford, *This Narrow Place*; M. Baker, *Our Three Selves*; and Glendinning, *Vita*.
[26] In *For Sylvia*, Ackland describes the difficulties of her relationship with her mother.

had apparently destroyed. It almost goes without saying that
this use of the rural world was a profound historical
falsification, as Raymond Williams has pointed out.[27] The
eroticism of these poems is profoundly apolitical, deliberately
dreamlike and Utopian. Lesbian pleasure, and the love of
women, are imaged as part of a nostalgic golden world, pre-
war, Edwardian. It was perhaps this softness of focus that got
many of these poems past the censor at exactly the time when
The Well of Loneliness (1928) was being prosecuted and banned
for obscenity.

Sackville-West's explicitly lesbian poetry was published in a
collection called *King's Daughter* (1929). Its style is unadventurous: 'If in my arms she soft as peaches lie, / Why then, I'll
simply say, "How happy I!" '[28] Some of the poems have a male
persona; but some, addressed to a woman, do not. Although
Sackville-West published under the name 'V. Sackville-West',
her gender (and her sexual choices) were well known. It is an
open question whether or not we are justified in calling an
erotic text 'lesbian' because it is written by a woman and
addressed to a woman, even when the author in the poem is
sexually neutral. Sackville-West and Nicolson certainly feared
that *King's Daughter* (published by the Woolfs at the Hogarth
Press) would be read as homosexual verse, although their
exchanges in letters about the poems are strangely ambiguous
and contradictory. Sackville-West wrote to Nicolson, on 11
August 1929, initially for advice on whether to publish
(although when Nicolson *did* ask her to suppress the collection, she had to confess that it was already in production):

You see they are love poems, and purely artificial at that,—I mean,
very artificial, rather 17th century most of them, and although I
should have thought this would be sufficiently obvious (that they
were just 'literary', I mean,) it has since occurred to me that people
will think them Lesbian. I should not like this, either for my own
sake or yours.

This rigid separation of the technical and the emotional was
not a view the two always subscribed to. Sackville-West

---

[27] Williams, *The Country and the City*, 258.
[28] V. Sackville-West, *King's Daughter* (London, 1929), p. 30. Further references
in the text will be to this edition.

described some of the sonnets in *King's Daughter* as 'a sort of catharsis to a great many pent-up feelings' (Sackville-West to Nicolson, 2 Dec. 1927): they were written during her affair with Mary Campbell. From the reader's point of view, it is hard to maintain an absolute separation between author and persona when no distinct narrator is constructed within the text itself. Sackville-West's caveat ('the only thing which made me pause was that they are frankly to "she" and "her"' (Sackville-West to Nicolson, 15 Aug. 1929)) suggests that the pronouns are marginal to the poem's address. In fact, of course, they are the poles of its utterance. A similar evasiveness characterizes Nicolson's response. He asked that the poems be suppressed not for personal but for artistic reasons: he thought they were not good literature and would damage Sackville-West's reputation (Nicolson to Sackville-West, 26 Aug. 1929). Even in private letters, it seems, Sackville-West and Nicolson were reluctant to acknowledge or discuss homosexual identity.

Many of the poems in *King's Daughter* have an almost pre-Raphaelite flavour to them. Women wander in meadows, by lakes, among trees; their hair tends to be long, and their faces pale. Almost all of the love poems set the loved one up as a spectacle, spying on her and even intruding on her dreams ('How shall I haunt her separate sleep' (pp. 15–16)). 'If I might meet her in the lane' (pp. 9–10) has a series of possible visions: the woman astride 'a raven horse / That trailed his golden halter loose'; the woman playing her harp by the lake, or singing 'in the reeds'; and finally, the woman gliding away 'into the fir-trees' night'. The woman is wild, romantic, alone; her horse has broken free of its harness; she leads a nomadic existence. At the same time she is traditionally domestic, with her little harp and her songs. The focus is on the woman observed rather than on the observer/poet, and the woman is conventionally feminine, fragile, and enigmatic. The lesbian gaze constructs her as a mistress to be courted, protected, and interpreted: 'Then should I know that I had read / Her changeling soul aright' (p. 9). 'Changeling' could signify a hidden shift into lesbian desire.

At times, the poet enlists the help of a male mediator. 'Goosey, goosey gander' (pp. 12–13) imagines a lady 'whiter than the candle-wax / Whiter than the rose' into whose bedroom 'goosey' is urged to penetrate: 'Goosey, goosey gander, / Will you be my spy?' The lesbian gaze shares the vision of a masculine eye, but is distinguished from it by virtue of appealing to it for help. An erotic space is opened up in which the spectator is both masculine and feminine: a woman sharing a perspective usually identified as heterosexually masculine (watching the woman undress), and thereby unsettling conventional sexual positioning. But the poet's call for assistance to a masculine collaborator also functions to hold heterosexual structures firmly in place. Sexual access to the woman is dependent on the co-operation of a man, even if it is a man who is willing to ally himself with a lesbian ('How shall I haunt her separate sleep?' (p. 16)):

> And one shall pause beside her couch,
> And bend and whisper low
> Some music of a foreign tongue,
> But what, she shall not know;
>
> Only, some echo of his speech,
> Melodious on the air,
> Shall tremble still against her heart,
> My lovely messenger.

An unfamiliar sexual message is brought by the man, but transformed by the heart of the woman into something that she *can* understand, a pleasure of her own. The secrecy which recalls the taboo on lesbian activity could also suggest the privacy of lesbian experience itself, inaccessible to men and largely unacknowledged. Yet in these poems, as in Sackville-West's and Woolf's lives, the space for lesbian experience is provided by men: in the poems by 'goosey' and his confederates, and in their lives, by supportive and understanding husbands. In the diary entry with which this introduction opened, Woolf suggests that it was Leonard who encouraged her to overcome her hesitations and to act on her feelings for Sackville-West: 'partly thanks to him (he made me write) I wound up this wounded & stricken year in great style' (*D*, iii. 51–2, 21 Dec. 1925).

Woolf and Sackville-West acted on lesbian feelings, intermittently in Woolf's case, and more regularly in Sackville-

West's, with the help of the men who were their husbands—a process dramatized in the poems of Sackville-West herself. Woolf and Sackville-West, like all of us, lived their sex as a coincidence and sometimes as a conflict of various and varying roles: wife, lesbian, writer. Femininity for them was not a stable condition, or a reliable constellation of qualities and behaviours. Rather, it was a site of continuing negotiation and adaptation with each other, with their husbands, with their memories, as I shall show in the next chapter. The nostalgia, even the mourning, which Woolf and Sackville-West shared for a maternal femininity which was apparently lost, and which could be re-created only in the secret space of lesbian sexual pleasure, coexisted with feelings of restlessness and impatience. The idea that lesbian energy originated in a past golden age, either pastoral or pre-Oedipal, meant that it could be deployed as often to resist change, as to encourage it. Sackville-West, and more particularly Woolf, *did* at times express anger at the oppression of women, and seek to ameliorate it through social and political change. But in remarking on this, we must also acknowledge that such indignation was accompanied by a certain reluctance. Woolf was *forced* to anger by repeated frustrations. Her desire for a world (and an art) without feminist rage, expressed so trenchantly in *A Room of One's Own*, had its profoundly conservative side. For I shall show that it was in essence a wish for a world before heterosexual injustice began, for a world of pastoral—and perhaps lesbian—innocence. Woolf's image for the mind that has transcended the oppressions of gender, 'pluck the petals from a rose or watch the swans float calmly down the river',[29] echoes the pastoral imagery of one of Sackville-West's lesbian love poems: 'If I should see the ebon swan / With scarlet beak sail by' (*King's Daughter*, p. 9). The locus for the creation of authentic art is the delicate riverside idyll of lesbian desire, innocent of the ugliness of heterosexual anger and oppression. If Chloe liked Olivia, the women hoped, then life and writing might return to a state of Edenic and apolitical simplicity, before the unlucky arrival of Adam.

[29] Woolf, *A Room of One's Own*, 136.

CHAPTER 1

Gallivanting with Campbell:
Orlando and Biography

ON 14 March 1927, Virginia Woolf announced in her diary the genesis of a new book.

Although annoyed that I have not heard from Vita by this post nor yet last week, annoyed sentimentally, & partly from vanity—still I must record the conception last night between 12 & one of a new book. (*D*, iii. 130–1)

Her thoughts about it developed slowly. That seed of disappointed irritation with Sackville-West grew first into a compensatory fantasy about 'two women, poor, solitary at the top of a house ... Also old men listening in the room over the way ... Sapphism is to be suggested. Satire is to be the main note' (*D*, iii. 131, 14 Mar. 1927). As the year progressed, Sapphic fantasy was joined by inspirations about a new form for biography: 'it might be a way of writing the memoirs of one's own times during peoples lifetimes' (*D*, iii. 157, 20 Sept. 1927). Then, on 5 October 1927, Woolf decided to write 'a biography beginning in the year 1500 & continuing to the present day, called Orlando: Vita; only with a change about from one sex to another' (*D*, iii. 161). *Orlando* was intended to function in several related ways: as a panoramic historical portrait of England through the ages; as an exploration of female friendship and of men in relation to women's sexuality ('old men listening' in another room); and finally as a celebratory commemoration of Vita Sackville-West, Woolf's friend and, for some time, lover.

The idea of *Orlando* had a peculiarly personal resonance for Virginia Woolf. From the very beginning, the writing of the book was bound up with her desire for Sackville-West. Its conception was a response to Sackville-West's immediate absence (she was in Teheran, visiting her husband Harold Nicolson), and it can be read now as a testimonial to Woolf's intimate knowledge of, and love for, her subject. Nigel Nicolson has called *Orlando* the 'longest and most charming love-letter in literature' (*PM*, 201), and Woolf saw it as a personal communication as well as a public piece (she dedicated it to Sackville-West, and made her a present of the original manuscript.[1] The writing of *Orlando* injected a new energy and tension into their relationship, sustaining it and in a way *becoming* it. As Sackville-West's biographer, Woolf gained a new hold over her friend, and Sackville-West discovered a new narcissistic delight in Woolf's company. However, as this chapter will show, Woolf's hold over Sackville-West was far from innocent. Beneath the desire to compliment and to flatter, so evident in *Orlando*, lay a more sinister impulse to punish and to hurt. The sexual and emotional ambivalence that was characteristic of their relationship is worked out in the text of *Orlando* itself, and in the conditions of its writing.

Orlando is not an easy text, for all that Woolf conceived it as 'a writer's holiday' (*D*, iii. 177, 18 Mar. 1928). J. J. Wilson calls her essay about it 'Why Is *Orlando* Difficult?'[2] Her answer is that *Orlando* is not easily identifiable. Is it a novel? A biography? A fantasy? Or is it just a joke? J. J. Wilson suggests finally that we should see it as an 'anti-novel', along the lines of Sterne's *Tristram Shandy*.[3] Critics have called it many other names: a satire, a fantasy, a fairy-tale, a love-letter, a caricature, a parody, and a 'very bad book'.[4] Woolf herself seems to have seen *Orlando* more as a biography than as a work of fiction. The original dust cover of the book, published by the Woolfs themselves, shows the title as *Orlando: A Biography*. Woolf wrote to Sackville-West, in the letter in which she first described to her the project of *Orlando*, 'I could revolutionise biography in a night' (*L*, iii. 429, 9 Oct. 1927); and later, after Leonard had

---

[1] Details of the intricate weaving of facts about Sackville-West's life and ancestry into the narrative and images of *Orlando* can be found in Frank Baldanza, '*Orlando* and the Sackvilles', *PMLA* 70/1 (1955), 274–9; David Green, '*Orlando* and the Sackvilles: Addendum', *PMLA* 71/1 (1956), 268–9; and in Frederick Kellermann, 'A New Key to Virginia Woolf's *Orlando*', *English Studies*, 59 (1978), 138–50.

[2] J. J. Wilson, 'Why is *Orlando* Difficult?', in Jane Marcus (ed.), *New Feminist Essays on Virginia Woolf* (London, 1981), 170–84.   [3] Ibid. 173.

[4] Delia Donahue, *The Novels of Virginia Woolf* (Rome, 1977), 149. For various different descriptions of *Orlando* see John Graham, 'The "Caricature Value" of Parody and Fantasy in *Orlando*', *University of Toronto Quarterly*, 30 (1961), 345–66.

read the manuscript, and pronounced it 'very original', Woolf was relieved 'to be quit this time of writing "a novel"; & hope never to be accused of it again' (*D* iii. 185, 31 May 1928). She was concerned, however, that its ambiguous status was affecting sales:

We may sell a third that we sold of The Lighthouse before publication—Not a shop will buy save in 6es and 12es. They say this is inevitable. But it is a novel, says Miss Ritchie [the traveller at the Hogarth Press]. But it is called biography on the title page, they say. It will have to go to the Biography shelf. I doubt therefore that we shall do more than cover expenses—a high price to pay for the fun of calling it biography. And I was so sure it was going to be the one popular book! (*D*, iii. 198, 22 Sept. 1928)

Orlando's place in the biographical tradition of the 1920s has been given little critical attention. But, as we have seen, Woolf thought of it this way, and took care to give it all the trappings of Victorian biography: a preface, dates, photographs (of Sackville-West herself, and of some of the Knole portraits), and an index. An understanding of this context is essential to any analysis of the way the text and its writing functioned as a communication between Woolf and Sackville-West.

Woolf herself was highly conscious of the history and conventions of biography. Her father, Leslie Stephen, was principal editor of the *Dictionary of National Biography* until the early 1890s. The weight of her father's achievements had a paralysing effect on Woolf. She wrote in her diary, on 28 November 1928, soon after the publication of *Orlando*: 'Father's birthday. He would have been 1928–1832/96 96, yes, today; & could have been 96, like other people one has known; but mercifully was not. His life would have entirely ended mine. What would have happened? No writing, no books;—inconceivable' (*D*, iii. 208). Yet the form for which she reached when it came to commemorating her extra-marital lesbian affair was exactly that which had shadowed her own past: Leslie Stephen spent Woolf's childhood years worrying and complaining about the burden of the *DNB*. *Orlando* reached back into individual and familial traditions as well as into literary ones. In a way Woolf's task in *Orlando* paralleled her father's in the *DNB*.

What was the *DNB* trying to do? Sidney Lee, Leslie Stephen's successor as editor, described its aims as follows: 'national biography, we have seen, commemorates within the limits of one literary cyclopaedia the men and women who have excited the nation's commemorative instinct.'[5] The construction of the dictionary was, like the writing of *Orlando*, a piecing together of national culture. The *DNB* condenses and defines tradition by telling over again the stories of distinguished men and women, and makes national achievement visible by placing it between the covers of many large and impressive volumes. It is supposed 'to leave no room for doubt in the mind of posterity, what was the nature of the achievements or characteristics that generated in the nation the desire of commemoration. It should, in fact, offer to future ages a plain justification for its existence.'[6] Leslie Stephen hoped it would be, for future generations, 'a confidential friend constantly at their shoulder', directing their research, containing their knowledge with 'a summary of the knowledge of antiquaries, genealogists, bibliographers, as well as historians, upon every collateral point which may happen for the moment to be relevant'.[7]

The idea of the 'great man', or more rarely, 'great woman', embodied in much Victorian biography, and particularly in the *DNB*, could be profoundly oppressive. Woolf and her friends are famous for their impatience with Victorianism. But eagerness for change, in the wake of the First World War, was not confined to the Bloomsbury group. Gone was the reverence with which nineteenth-century biographers had approached their subjects. Biography in the 1920s assumed a certain equality between the readers of a biography, its writer, and its subject. These new methods spoke to new ideas about community and democracy. Virginia Woolf described the change:

If we open one of the new school of biographies its bareness, its emptiness make us at once aware that the author's relation to his

[5] Sidney Lee, 'National Biography', *Cornhill*, NS, 24 (1896), 265.
[6] Ibid. 258.
[7] Leslie Stephen, 'National Biography', in *Studies of a Biographer*, 2 vols. (London, 1898), i. 20.

subject is different. He is no longer the serious and sympathetic companion, toiling even slavishly in the footsteps of his hero. Whether friend or enemy, admiring or critical, he is an equal.[8]

Others too noticed this new relationship. Mark Longaker, writing in 1934, attributed the contemporary growth of interest in biography to the increased loneliness and strain of twentieth-century life. Modern readers of biographies, as opposed to their nineteenth-century forebears, were encouraged to understand, even to live with, those they read about. Longaker suggests that this had a therapeutic effect, reassuring nervous twentieth-century readers, and offering them models for comprehending and organizing their own life stories.[9] In this belief, he is, of course, taking his cue from psychoanalysis, which was gaining in popularity as a clinical practice in Britain at exactly this period. Freud's publication of his case studies, and his extrapolation of developmental models from individual histories, encouraged biographers to see differences between people as insignificant in the face of a fundamental structural similarity between human psyches.

Not only were 1920s biographies more accessible than earlier works, they were also noticeably shorter (and in this, of course, they paralleled changes in the contemporary novel). Gamaliel Bradford, an American imitator of Lytton Strachey, invented a new form for biography, the 'psychography', which relied on the reader's identification with the subject. The psychography was a short work, which condensed the essence of a life or personality, or even of a work like Pepys's diaries, into a few pages. As Bradford himself put it: 'What gives [Pepys's diary] at once immortal worth and also a certain sacredness is the tremendous identity of human hearts, the fact that when the diarist records his inmost secrets he is recording your secrets and my secrets as well as his own.'[10] Any notion of the commemoration of unique achievement, so dear to the nineteenth-century image of the 'great man', has disappeared. As Ralph Denham says in *Night and Day* (1919):

[8] Virginia Woolf, 'The New Biography', in *Collected Essays*, 4 vols. (London, 1966–7), iv. 231.

[9] Mark Longaker, *Contemporary Biography* (Philadelphia, 1934), 12–14.

[10] Gamaliel Bradford, *Samuel Pepys: The Soul of a Man* (London, 1924), 13.

' "No, we haven't any great men," Denham replied. "I'm very glad that we haven't. I hate great men. The worship of greatness in the nineteenth century seems to me to explain the worthlessness of that generation" ' (p. 15). Woolf's mistrust of that generation and their traditions urged her to try her hand at a biography that would upset all those Victorian preconceptions. Her idea was to use those preconceptions as a vehicle for 'Sapphic fantasy': to speak a relationship for which Victorian convention had no name.

This sense of equality between reader, writer, and subject emerging in the 1920s opened up fresh possibilities for biography, and more particularly for biography as a transaction between women. As long as commemoration of greatness was the aim of biography, a distancing of the reader from the subject was inevitable. But as the new century progressed, the field of biography widened and the gap between the reader and the subject narrowed. Identification and recognition became the primary psychical operations involved in the reading of biographies. This had a profound effect on the ways in which women in particular could both read and write life narratives. Elizabeth Abel contends that identification, rather than differentiation, should be seen as the paradigmatic mode of relationships between women. Evidence from both novels and psychoanalytic theory, in her view, shows that 'identification replaces complementarity as the psychological mechanism that draws women together'.[11] In particular, Abel cites the passage from *To the Lighthouse* in which Lily leans her head on Mrs Ramsay's knee: 'For it was not knowledge but unity that she desired, not inscriptions on tablets, nothing that could be written in any language known to men, but intimacy itself, which is knowledge, she had thought, leaning her head on Mrs Ramsay's knee.' (p. 70). Lily Briscoe desires not simply to *know* Mrs Ramsay, but almost to inhabit her body with her: to become her. Woolf deliberately confuses the pronouns in the passage to emphasize the potential interchangeability of the two women.

All this she would adroitly shape; even maliciously twist; and, moving over to the window, in pretence that she must go,—it was dawn, she

---

[11] Elizabeth Abel, '(E)merging Identities: The Dynamics of Female Friendship in Contemporary Fiction by Women', *Signs*, 6 (1981), 415.

could see the sun rising,—half turn back, more intimately, but still always laughing, insist that she must, Minta must, they all must marry, since in the whole world whatever laurels might be tossed to her (but Mrs Ramsay cared not a fig for her painting), or triumphs won by her (probably Mrs Ramsay had had her share of those), and here she saddened, darkened, and came back to her chair, there could be no disputing this: an unmarried woman has missed the best of life. (p. 68)

Which 'she' is which? It takes some thought, and a little re-reading, to disentangle all those 'hers'. The language achieves a fluidity that longingly enacts that peculiarly female process of intimacy that Lily craves. The ending of the passage—suddenly emphasizing the difference between the unmarried Lily and the married Mrs Ramsay—militates against the pronominal identification of the two women by showing that that identification is enacted on the level of language only, as a kind of erotic and linguistic game: a fantastic story.

Orlando is the most fantastic story of all. Biographies traditionally agree on a basic shape for their narratives. Like lives, they have their own specific rites of passage: birth, marriage, ageing, death. Mrs Ramsay's condemnation of spinster-hood suggests that Lily does not have any authentic story of her own femininity to tell. One of *Orlando*'s most important functions is to unsettle expectations about the structure of lives, and to ridicule rituals, such as marriage and birth, which appear to guarantee sex. Orlando is not only a 'great man', the stuff of Victorian biography: he is also a woman, and biographical conventions shift unstably around her. Orlando's rite of passage is neither birth, marriage, nor even death, but a fantastic and ridiculous experience of transsexualism. *Orlando* suggests that it is the central ambiguity of gender which displaces all sorts of other certainties:

We must snatch space to remark how discomposing it is for her biographer that this culmination to which the whole book moved, this peroration with which the book was to end, should be dashed from us on a laugh casually like this; but the truth is that when we write of a woman, everything is out of place—culminations and per-orations; the accent never falls where it does with a man. (pp. 297–8)

Gender, exposed here as 'just a joke'—its 'casual laughter'—seems to mock biography's solemnities, so that narratives are differently inflected, an alternative system—or anti-system —of values implied.[12] Gillian Beer suggests that it is through Orlando's change of sex that even death, the ultimate rite of passage, is banished from the text. Orlando, instead of ageing, becomes a woman: 'death, it seems, finds its way in, at least in fantasy, by the separation of male and female. Orlando skirts death by changing dress.'[13]

Jokes about gender are used in *Orlando* for subversive purposes: to mock biography, mock history, mock the rules and rites of Western society. Marriage is an institution which, while endorsed by the text (Orlando and Shelmerdine get married), is yet up for grabs: 'She was married, true; but if one's husband was always sailing round Cape Horn, was it marriage? If one liked him, was it marriage? If one liked other people, was it marriage? And finally, if one still wished, more than anything in the whole world, to write poetry, was it marriage' (p. 252)? Orlando, driven to marry by the bodily inscription of a social imperative ('a ring of quivering sens- ibility about the second finger of the left hand' (p. 229)), sees marriage as an exercise in speculation—as did both her author and her original. The spume of *Orlando*'s prose celebrates marriage as an adventure with a stable base: some- thing that at once frees Orlando from and at the same time anchors her in, the past and the traditions of her society. *Orlando* uses the conventional stresses of biography—mar- riage, death—to question life's and biography's terms. It is peculiarly appropriate that Woolf should have chosen to use biography, so quintessentially respectable a form, to explore new ways of writing lives and inscribing half-concealed relationships. For it was the obvious respectability of her married state that allowed her, under its protection, to explore her own sexuality as she had experienced it with another woman. The material and emotional stability of her marriage allowed her the kind of adventure to which the playful prose of *Orlando*—closely allied to the erotic idiom of her diary, which I quoted in the Introduction—bears

---

[12] Judith Butler, *Gender Trouble: Feminism and the Subversion of Identity* (London, 1990), discusses gender as parody, 137–41.
[13] Gillian Beer, 'The Body of the People in Virginia Woolf', in Sue Roe (ed.), *Women Reading Women's Writing* (Brighton, 1987), 99.

such eloquent witness. Virginia Woolf was exploiting new biographical methods as a way of inserting women into the tradition on their own terms. The gradual acceptance of identification as an intrinsic element in the reading process for biography meant fresh opportunities for female self-expression. The 'great man', who had had an influence on national history, became, in *Orlando*, the woman whose greatness derived from the depth and intensity of her effect on her lovers.

Orlando is the story of a private love. But it is also the story of one of the most public families, and one of the most notorious women, in the country. It teases at the ambiguity of all biographies, which dramatize a concealed and usually unacknowledged relationship between writer and subject, alongside the public—and often the private—doings and events of the subject's life. Biographies must always be associated with the establishment of community and with the definition of public and private—what can be disclosed and what must be held back. This definition was changing during the 1920s and 1930s following the publication of Woolf's friend Lytton Strachey's *Eminent Victorians* (1918), *Queen Victoria* (1921), and *Elizabeth and Essex* (1928).

Queen Victoria created a tremendous stir. Unlike Victoria's official biographer, Sidney Lee, whose book came out in 1902, Strachey is intent on the personality of the queen and the way she combined her roles as wife and as monarch. Indeed his main interest is in her marriage, and he is concerned with her as sovereign just in so far as her public role affected her private life. The tragedy of the prince consort's life is drawn with consummate sympathy.

For in spite of everything he had never reached to happiness. His work, for which at last he came to crave with an almost morbid appetite, was a solace and not a cure; the dragon of his dissatisfaction devoured with a dark relish that ever-growing tribute of laborious days and nights; but it was hungry still.[14]

This kind of imaginative empathy with the private tragedies of people obliged to live like kings and queens is quite absent

[14] Lytton Strachey, *Queen Victoria* (Harmondsworth, 1971), 168.

from Sidney Lee's biography. He, on the contrary, is acutely concerned with Victoria as monarch and with the history of her participation and intervention in government. He breathes not a word about marital tensions caused by Victoria's public role: 'the union realised the highest ideal of which matrimony is capable'.[15] Lytton Strachey, of course, has no qualms about puncturing the myth of the perfect marriage: 'he was not in love with her', he says.[16] Lee makes no mention of clashes between Victoria and her mother at the time of her accession, where for Strachey they are the main focus of interest; and Lee portrays Victoria's relationship with Melbourne as purely professional, where Strachey fills it with all the romance of which he was capable. For Sidney Lee, the interface between public and private is strictly taboo, and this leads him to present the two areas as entirely distinct, almost as if Victoria the queen (who is occasionally hectored and criticized by the avuncular Lee) has a *doppelgänger* (above criticism) who is Victoria the wife.

Strachey's biography allows a coy reference to the prince's sexual hold over the queen: 'every day his predominance grew more assured—and every night.'[17] Freedom to mention such matters was partly pioneered by Strachey, but it was also part of a wider post-war frankness that we see exemplified in the lives and conversations of the Bloomsbury group themselves. Readers of biographies began to feel that they might have not only common emotional experiences with the famous, but even common sexual experiences.[18] However, this 'seduction' of readers by ever more explicit biographers was of course resisted in some quarters, and viewed as a literary neurosis.

Strachey's collection of brief, ironic sketches in *Eminent Victorians* (1918), for example, was unlike any biography that had been written before. Critics claimed that Strachey had altered, even invented the facts, to support interpretations which were closer to fantasy than to history. Under Freud's

[15] Sidney Lee, *Queen Victoria* (London, 1902), 118.
[16] Strachey, *Queen Victoria*, 88.   [17] Ibid. 102.
[18] For a discussion of the changing sexual atmosphere of the 1920s see Sheila Jeffreys, *The Spinster and her Enemies; Feminism and Sexuality 1880–1930* (London, 1985); and Ann Snitow, Christine Stansell, and Sharon Thompson (ed.), *Desire: The Politics of Sexuality* (London, 1984). Woolf describes the downing of 'all barriers of reticence and reserve' in *Moments of Being*, ed. Jeanne Schulkind (London, 1978), 200.

influence, critics were now producing symptomatic readings of biography, and one contemporary reviewer read *Elizabeth and Essex* as an indication of Strachey's own sexual disturbance. 'The author shows himself preoccupied with the sexual organs to a degree that seems almost pathological. So these two volumes exhibit the development of a sense of humour not, perhaps, utterly remote from that of the nameless scribblers who deface the walls of public lavatories.'[19] The mistrust of fantasy in the sense of groundless speculation coincides with a condemnation of fantasy in the sexual sense. Published historical fantasies are to be disapproved of exactly because they look too much like more personal rhapsodies. The boldness of the biographer whose evidence is too slender to stand up to scrutiny, implies an ethos of permissiveness and self-indulgence: fantasy, self-gratification, the graffiti artist. For symptomatic readings like the above, the public lavatory is a bizarre symbol of the domain of Stracheyan biography. At once public and private, it is a common space used for a secret and intimate purpose. Strachey is accused of undermining the public–private divide by using biographical space for idiosyncratic sexual fantasy, and of invading the reader's privacy by forcing him or her to witness something unexpected and unsolicited.[20] If she had been any less circumspect, Woolf herself might have experienced the same kind of criticism for *Orlando.*

For biography roused passions in the 1920s (as, indeed, it does today). In the 1920s and 1930s there was a flood, not only of biographies, but also of essays, books, articles, and lectures on the status of biography—discussion of its methods and of its status.[21] James Clifford, compiling a collection of

[19] Charles Smyth, 'A Note on Historical Biography and Mr. Strachey', *Criterion,* 8 (1929), 659.

[20] Strachey did in fact write a great many unpublished pornographic poems and stories with a strong scatological tendency. See Michael Holroyd, *Lytton Strachey and the Bloomsbury Group: His Work, Their Influence* (Harmondsworth, 1971), 61–3 and 375–8.

[21] See e.g. Gamaliel Bradford, 'Confessions of a Biographer', in *Wives* (New York, 1925), 3–14, and *Samuel Pepys*; Longaker, *Contemporary Biography*; Emil Ludwig, *Goethe: The History of a Man,* trans. Ethel Colburn Mayne (London, 1928); André Maurois, *Aspects of Biography* (Cambridge, 1929); Harold Nicolson, *The Development of English Biography* (London, 1927), and *Some People* (London, 1927); Lytton Strachey, *Books and Characters: French and English* (London, 1922), and *Portraits in Miniature and Other Essays* (London, 1931).

extracts about the art of biography, concluded that biography as a literary genre became a prominent topic in critical discussions only in the 1920s. 'Not until our day has there been any widespread discussion of the complex psychological and artistic problems involved in the re-creation of character. It is surely significant that almost half of the present collection is made up of selections from the past forty years.'[22] The period after the First World War saw a new self-consciousness among biographers, which was reflected in a growing tendency to experiment with, and reflect on, their art.

Of course, experiment, as always, meant imitation as well as innovation, and among the many new biographers of the 1920s there were a significant number who simply aped Strachey's style—Emil Ludwig, for example. But there were also those who developed their own methods. The work of André Maurois, for example, friend and translator of Virginia Woolf, was translated during these years: his *Ariel* in 1924, *Disraeli* in 1927, and *Byron* in 1930. *Ariel*, a novel based on the life of Shelley, is characterized, like *Orlando*, by a homoerotic romanticism that plays with the Victorian concept of the great man so that we are drawn into the narrative through the barely sublimated desire of the author. 'It was impossible for Harriet to oppose a demi-god with flashing eyes, a shirt-collar open on a delicate throat, and hair as fine as spun-silk.'[23] Erotic fantasies (delicate throats and silken hair) are thinly disguised (they appear with much less apology in *Elizabeth and Essex*) as admiration for Shelley's semi-divine intellectual genius. Reader and biographer identify with Harriet's feminine perspective, and Maurois's casting of the biography in the form of a novel constitutes his audience as predominantly female, bringing the best-selling biographer alongside the romantic woman novelist.

His methods changed somewhat in *Disraeli*. He no longer assumes omniscience. A mood of conjecture comes in, a hesitation. Many thoughts are imputed to Disraeli on slack evidence, and the tone is one of inference, rather than of report, as in *Ariel*.

[22] James L. Clifford (ed.), *Biography as an Art: Selected Criticism 1560–1960* (London, 1962), p. x.
[23] André Maurois, *Ariel: A Shelley Romance*, trans. Ella d'Arcy (London, 1924), 16.

He was fifteen years old, and facts had proved that school was dangerous for him; would he find at the university, if he went there, the same prejudices, the same hatreds? What was to be done? But first of all, what did he want? With the turmoil of the little schoolboy world, the memories of his intrigues, his triumphs, his miniature wars, had come glimpses, as through scattering clouds, of clear and vivid landscapes.[24]

The text lacks the certainty of a fictional world. Instead, it is haunted by an unease that is expressed syntactically in the insistent use of questions. The biography is cast as the incessant interrogation of a silent source. *Disraeli* dramatizes biography as a *demand* ('my questions about your past can wait till you're in London', wrote Woolf to Sackville-West (*L*, iii. 433, 21 Oct. 1927)).

Sackville-West's husband, Harold Nicolson, biographer of Byron, Tennyson, and Swinburne, also played with the relation between fantasy and fact in a collection of stories about people he had known, *Some People* (1927). Woolf was thinking about *Orlando* as she read and reviewed *Some People*. Its epigraph runs: 'many of the following sketches are purely imaginary. Such truths as they may contain are only half-truths.'[25] Woolf was enchanted by this idea. '*Some People* is not fiction because it has the substance, the reality of truth. It is not biography because it has the freedom, the artistry of fiction.'[26] It is likely that Woolf's reading of *Some People* had some influence on the final form of *Orlando*. She felt that Nicolson had solved the central problem of biography—'on the one hand there is truth; on the other there is personality'—by legitimizing a controlled form of fantasy as a means for the transmission of personality.[27]

Some People is a comic book. Part of the reason for its flirtations with the truth was to protect itself, and those characters whom it mocked, from the dangers of libel. *Orlando* too was meant to be comic. Woolf, in her diary, called it a 'joke' (*D*, iii. 177, 18 Mar. 1928), and its subtitle, as she remarks in the above quotation, was simply a piece of 'fun'. But it had its more solemn side: 'I want (& this was serious) to give things their caricature value' (*D*, iii. 203, 7 Nov. 1928). It

---

[24] André Maurois, *Disraeli: A Picture of the Victorian Age*, trans. Hamish Miles (London, 1927), 16. [25] Nicolson, *Some People*, p. vi. [26] V. Woolf, 'The New Biography', 232. [27] Ibid.

was intended to be simultaneously light-hearted comedy, and more serious-minded satire.

Woolf was worried about its ambiguous tone. 'It may fall between stools, be too long for a joke, & too frivolous for a serious book' (*D*, iii. 177, 22 Mar. 1928). A couple of months later she was surprised by Leonard's reaction to it: 'L. takes *Orlando* more seriously than I had expected. Thinks it in some ways better than The Lighthouse; about more interesting things, & with more attachment to life, & larger. The truth is I expect I began it as a joke, & went on with it seriously. Hence it lacks some unity' (*D*, iii. 185, 31 May 1928). If it is a joke, it is not entirely humorous. Of course, no jokes are. Freud's analysis suggests that joking is a fundamentally aggressive act.[28] But I believe that biography, notorious raiser of relatives' temperatures, is similarly hostile; and that Woolf's choice of a 'joke' form for her biography of the woman with whom she was so intimately and ambivalently involved, was more than a simple coincidence. It expressed the desire to hurt, as well as the desire to love.

Freud, in *Jokes and their Relation to the Unconscious*, stresses the centrality of agency and control to the process of the joke. A joke is a judgement, he says, and it relies on the active behaviour of a subject in relation to an object. The person who is the 'butt' of the joke is effectively silenced: she or he is taken possession of by the joker, who is concerned to set up a structure of communication that excludes the object of the joke: 'Generally speaking, a tendentious joke calls for three people: in addition to the one who makes the joke, there must be a second who is taken as the object of the hostile or sexual aggressiveness, and a third in whom the joke's aim of producing pleasure is fulfilled.'[29] In the same way, the biographer takes hold of her or his material, arranges it, and offers to the reading public ('in whom . . . the aim of producing pleasure is fulfilled') his or her own version of the life that was lived. The subject of the biography, like the butt of the joke, is usually in no position to answer back, since traditionally, biographers waited until their subjects were dead. In Sackville-West's case,

---

[28] Sigmund Freud, *Standard Edition of the Complete Psychological Works*, viii. *Jokes and their Relation to the Unconscious*, ed. and trans. James Strachey (24 vols.; London, 1966–74).   [29] Ibid. 100.

contributions were not invited—she never saw the manuscript during writing—and she was presented with a *fait accompli*, a published book (see *PM*, 206). Her participation was strictly contained by Woolf's insistent and specific questioning of her: 'Is it true you grind your teeth at night? Is it true you love giving pain? What and when was your moment of greatest disillusionment?' (*L*, iii. 430, 14 Oct. 1927). Trapped as she was in the structure of the joke/biography, 'taken as the object of the hostile or sexual aggressiveness', Sackville-West could not complain. Was there an ambivalence behind the affectionate joke of *Orlando*, a desire to silence Sackville-West? *Orlando*'s humour became Woolf's alibi: any aggressiveness in it was 'only a joke'.

Freud notes also that jokes have the aim of momentarily bewildering their audience. 'The word that is the vehicle of the joke appears at first simply to be a wrongly constructed word, something unintelligible, incomprehensible, puzzling. It accordingly bewilders. The comic effect is produced by the solution of this bewilderment, by understanding the word.'[30] The joke derives its effect from the resolution of a hesitation to produce *meaning*. It produces sense from nonsense, understanding from bewilderment.

Tzvetan Todorov uses similar terms to discuss the fantastic as a genre. In fantasies, he says, something happens which cannot be explained according to familiar laws, 'something unintelligible, incomprehensible, puzzling'. The person in the fantasy to whom it happens, or who witnesses (reads) it, can choose between two possible interpretations of this changed environment. Either she or he is the victim of an illusion, and the laws of the universe are unchanged; or 'the event has indeed taken place, it is an integral part of reality—but then this reality is controlled by laws unknown to us'.[31] According to Todorov, 'the fantastic occupies the duration of this uncertainty. Once we choose one answer or the other, we leave the fantastic for a neighbouring genre, the uncanny or the marvelous'.[32] Both jokes and fantasies depend on hesitation and puzzlement, but the essence of fantasy *is* that hesitation,

---

[30] Ibid. 13.
[31] Tzvetan Todorov, *The Fantastic: A Structural Approach to a Literary Genre*, trans. Richard Howard (Ithaca, NY, 1975), 25.   [32] Ibid.

where the essence—the punch-line—of a joke lies in the resolution of bewilderment and the re-establishment of a familiar world. Fantasies can opt for the unfamiliar, 'controlled by laws unknown to us', and can be profoundly destabilizing; or, like jokes, they can reaffirm the world we know. Such reaffirmation usually entails disappointment as well as relief. Jokes, on the other hand, resolve in a way that surpasses relief and creates an excess pleasure expressed in laughter. The irresolute nature of *Orlando*'s ending—it offers neither punch-line nor explanation—indicates that it opts neither for joke nor fantasy.

Orlando hesitates. We recognize in it elements of biography, but at the same time we do not absolutely recognize it *as* biography; we catch glimpses of Sackville-West's likeness in its pages, and at the same time we know that Orlando is not quite like her, is far from historically specific. *Orlando* fantasizes a world without genre (Woolf wants at the same time to sell it as a novel, and not to be accused of having written one). It also fantasizes a world where endless jokes are possible, a world in which humour endures without needing a comic resolution, so that the moment of the joke coincides with the moment of fantasy instead of lagging behind and depending on an ending. What Woolf needed was a joke without the shock of end and loss. So *Orlando* became a fantasy about jokes and yearned after a world which could hover on the brink of laughter without ever revealing its punch-line. Orlando herself, like the androgynous circus clown, alternates between the two sexes and postpones resolution for ever. Woolf finally conceded that *Orlando*, like Orlando, was not even a joke, but rather a 'freak': a moment of bewilderment whose antecedents and descendants are uncertain.[33]

Even the timing of its writing was confusing. The composition of *Orlando* before, rather than after, Sackville-West's death, called into question many Victorian assumptions about the function of biography and its role as the public face of mourning (some Victorian relatives of great men felt it to be

---

[33] See e.g. 'Orlando, which is a freak' (*D*, iii. 180, 21 Apr. 1928), and 'freakish and unequal' (*D*, iii. 184, 31 May 1928).

their duty to write their biographies, for instance).[34] Great stress was laid on the necessity, both ethical and aesthetic, of the subject's death before the biography was written. Sidney Lee was particularly emphatic: 'Death is a part of life and no man is fit subject for biography till he is dead. Living men have been made themes of biography. But the choice defies the cardinal condition of completeness ... The living theme can at best be a torso, a fragment.'[35] Images of damage and fragmentation—inevitably present when the subject is dead—intrude strangely into Lee's well-regulated prose. It seems that the integrity of the living body actually prevents the body of the biography from taking shape. Moreover, the continued existence of the living body can set all kinds of desires in motion that quite disrupt the smooth writing of the biography. Biographies of the living are more likely to be read in the wrong way, says Lee. They might appeal to idle curiosity, or savour 'either of the scandal or of the unbalanced laudation'.[36] The biography and the living subject become like a pair of threatening doubles, always encroaching on each other's territory, squabbling, betraying each other, distracting people's attention. The luminous eroticism of Orlando/Vita's body is central to *Orlando*'s prose: 'as if all the fertility and amorous activity of a summer's evening were woven web-like about his body' (p. 19). His sensations—the sensations of a living body—are part of the texture of the book, 'that riot and confusion of the passions and emotions which every good biographer detests' (p. 16). The erotic distractedness which Orlando's vitality provokes in his biographer (and perhaps also in his readers) is signalled in the text.

Directly we glance at Orlando standing by the window, we must admit that he had eyes like drenched violets, so large that the water seemed to have brimmed in them and widened them; and a brow like the swelling of a marble dome pressed between the two blank medallions which were his temples. Directly we glance at eyes and forehead, thus do we rhapsodise. Directly we glance at eyes and

---

[34] See e.g. Francis Darwin, *Life and Letters of Charles Darwin*, 3 vols. (London, 1887).
[35] Sidney Lee, *The Principles of Biography* (Cambridge, 1911), 12.   [36] Ibid.

forehead, we have to admit a thousand disagreeables which it is the
aim of every good biographer to ignore. (p. 15)

The biographer of the dead probably ignores them rather
more successfully than the biographer of the living, and the
curious coincidence of Vita's name and the Italian word for
life led Woolf to think of her as, above all else, a vital source of
pleasure and energy. 'Life, life!' was one of Woolf's favourite
refrains: 'but life, life! How I long to take you in my arms &
crush you out!' (*D*, ii. 238, 6 Mar. 1923) she wrote in her diary
shortly after meeting Vita. In *Orlando* the same chant gains
added resonance from the affair the text commemorates:
'then they come here, says the bird, and ask me what life is;
Life, Life, Life!' (p. 258). In a letter only days after their first
sexual encounter, Woolf had rung the same triple note of
triumph: 'we walk through the clods together talking, first one
and then another, of Vita Vita Vita as the new moon rises and
the lambs huddle on the downs' (*L*, iii. 225, 23 Dec. 1925).

But the writing of *Orlando* does inscribe absence: the
absence of infidelity rather than of death, as in conventional
biography. Woolf wrote the first lines in response to news
of Sackville-West's new affair with Mary Campbell, as she
describes in a letter to Sackville-West: 'its all about you and the
lusts of your flesh and the lure of your mind (heart you have
none, who go gallivanting down the lanes with Campbell)'
(*L*, iii. 429, 9 Oct. 1927).[37] A week later she was able to use
Orlando as a threat: 'if you've given yourself to Campbell, I'll
have no more to do with you, and so it shall be written,
plainly, for all the world to read in Orlando' (*L*, iii. 431, 14
Oct. 1927). *Orlando* was bound up with Woolf's experience of
loss, as well as of power. In writing Sackville-West's life, she
established her own claim to it. By writing Sackville-West's life
for her, Woolf recaptured Sackville-West. It was as though she
had actually *become* her. But in celebrating Sackville-West,
Woolf also obliterated her. *Orlando* at once mourned the

---

[37] For an account of *Orlando* as Woolf's revenge for Sackville-West's infidelity
see Jean O. Love, '*Orlando* and Its Genesis: Venturing and Experimenting in Art,
Love and Sex', in Ralph Freedman (ed.), *Virginia Woolf: Revaluation and Continuity*
(Berkeley, Calif., 1980), 189–218.

death of Sackville-West's fidelity and punished her by ousting her from the centre of her own life.

More conventional biographies, whose subjects are dead, were more straightforwardly part of the work of mourning, especially when they were written, as so often, by close relatives of the deceased. Vera Brittain in her autobiography describes the reaction of her fiancé's mother to his death on the front:

Two or three weeks after Roland's death, his mother began to write, in semi-fictional form, a memoir of his life, which she finished in three months, as well as replying at length to letters of condolence from friends and readers all over the country. At the end of that time she had a short breakdown from shock and overwork, and was in bed warding off serious heart trouble for several weeks.[38]

The writing of the biography is at once part of mourning (written immediately after Roland's death), but also a way of postponing grief, a fantasy of Roland's survival ('in semi-fictional form'). In Chapter 6 we shall see Woolf having a similar fantasy of the survival of her brother Thoby after his death. Orlando does the opposite, grieving for Sasha as if she were dead when in fact what he mourns is her survival in a transformed state. Orlando, in fact, has the experience that Woolf, watching Sackville-West fall in love with someone else, was going through herself. Woolf forces Orlando/Sackville-West to suffer what she herself was suffering. Meeting Sasha again after her infidelity (and now both of them, significantly, are women), Orlando barely recognizes her:

'Oh, Sasha!' Orlando cried. Really, she was shocked that she should have come to this; she had grown so fat; so lethargic; and she bowed her head over the linen so that this apparition of a grey woman in fur, and a girl in Russian trousers with all these smells of wax candles, white flowers and old ships that it brought with it might pass behind her back unseen. (p. 289)

Emotional estrangement from Sasha is translated by the process of ageing into a physical estrangement and the blankness

[38] Vera Brittain, *Testament of Youth: An Autobiographical Study of the Years 1900– 1925* (London, 1979), 250.

of at once knowing and not knowing her. The shock of seeing her is close to the shock of seeing one's own reflection
unexpectedly, or for Sackville-West, of reading *Orlando*: at
once recognizing, and yet feeling alienated from, one's own
body and one's own life. The simultaneity of the life and the
biography, Sackville-West living her life as fact while Woolf
is writing it as fantasy, established an unusual dependency
between the two women. The two activities, writing and living,
sustained each other, nourished each other as if for ever. So
Woolf wrote to Sackville-West on 14 October 1927:

I make it up in bed at night, as I walk the streets, everywhere. I want
to see you in the lamplight, in your emeralds. In fact, I have never
more wanted to see you than I do now—just to sit and look at you,
and get you to talk, and then rapidly and secretly, correct certain
doubtful points. (*L*, iii. 430)

The writing of the biography turned their friendship into
a game of the watcher and the watched, giving to Woolf a
strange and atavistic power over Sackville-West of which she
at least was aware. When *Orlando* was finished, she wrote to
Sackville-West: 'did you feel a sort of tug, as if your neck was
being broken on Saturday last at 5 minutes to one? That was
when he died—or rather stopped talking, with three little dots
. . .' (*L*, iii. 474, 20? Mar. 1928). Although the book ends not
with the death of Orlando, but with the return of Shel and the
vision of the wild goose, there is also a sense—a desire?—for
Woolf in which she has ended Sackville-West's life—death by
hanging (the traitor?). Perhaps the apparently unconscious
change of gender—'he died', when Orlando is female at the
end of the book—is compensatory, a way of saying, Vita, it
wasn't really you that I killed.

But *Orlando* is affectionate and protective as well as murder-
ous. If Woolf felt that the end of *Orlando* would bring
Sackville-West's life to an end, then as long as she was writing
the book, and describing an immortal Orlando, she was
protecting Sackville-West and keeping her death—and the
possibility of standard biography—at bay. *Orlando* can then be
seen as a biography offered in place of biography, a text that
actually precludes the conditions on which its production
would normally depend. *Orlando* is not a biography: it is

simply *like* a biography. In this way its basic enterprise depends on the figure of simile, one thing like another.[39] Yet it is haunted by a sense of the impossibility, the disjuncture at the heart of a figure that depends on likeness, approximation rather than identity. So Orlando, writing, stares out of the .window:

In order to match the shade of green precisely he looked (and here he showed more audacity than most) at the thing itself, which happened to be a laurel bush growing beneath the window. After that, of course, he could write no more. Green in nature is one thing, green in literature another. Nature and letters seem to have a natural antipathy; bring them together and they tear each other to pieces. (p. 16)

It is from that despair at the impossibility of representation that *Orlando* develops as fantasy. For Woolf, despite her enjoyment of biographies, was fundamentally sceptical about them (hence, presumably, *Orlando*'s unorthodox form). She wrote in her diary just before starting on *Orlando*: 'I have never forgotten . . . my vision of a fin rising on a wide blank sea. No biographer could possibly guess this important fact about my life in the late summer of 1926: yet biographers pretend they know people' (*D*, iii, 153, 4 Sept. 1927). The pain of mere approximation is bound up with Woolf's own self-consciousness about her femininity, and her feeling that her own version of it is somehow inadequate (see Chapter 6).

Woolf's experiments with biography in *Orlando* were linked to a more general concern of biographers in the 1920s: where could biography possibly go, in the shadow of Strachey's influence? Writers were also uneasy about the blurring of boundaries and the mixing of genres. In 1911, Sidney Lee could state categorically that 'biography rules a domain of its own; it is autonomous—an attribute with which it is not always credited'.[40] But the work of Lytton Strachey, and particularly of André Maurois, seemed to bring the novel and the biography ever closer together. In *Ariel* they had apparently

---

[39] Morris Philipson discusses the literalization of simile in *Orlando* in 'Virginia Woolf's *Orlando*: Biography as a Work of Fiction', in Dora B. Weiner and William R. Keylor (ed.), *From Parnassus: Essays in Honour of Jacques Barzun* (New York, 1976), 246. [40] Lee, *The Principles of Biography*, 18.

merged. It began to look as though biography was increasingly losing its autonomy as a literary genre at just the time when it was becoming increasingly popular. Harold Nicolson forecast an immense amount of diverging activity in the field. Scientific biographies would be like case histories: 'there will be medical biographies—studies of the influence on character of the endocrine glands, studies of internal secretions.' On the other hand, there would be the literary biographies, characterized mainly by their emotional tone: 'we may have some good satirical biographies, we may even have invective: I can well envisage the biography of hate.'[41]

Is *Orlando* that biography of hate? Beneath its affection and its charm, as we have seen, runs a darker vein of hostility and pain. What is hate, anyway? For Woolf, in an earlier text, it was to do with the desire to humiliate. Miss Kilman, with her 'hatred of Mrs Dalloway' (*MD*, 163), has 'an overmastering desire to overcome her; to unmask her' (*MD*, 163). *Orlando* unmasks Sackville-West, despite its high-spirited masquerade; it overcomes her, taking over the telling of her story and allowing her no quarter. And already in *Mrs Dalloway* hatred is being linked to sexual obsession. Miss Kilman loves Elizabeth, Mrs Dalloway's daughter, and feels a need to overwhelm her: 'if she could grasp her, if she could clasp her, if she could make her hers absolutely' (p. 142). Her need is made vividly present through images of her greed with food: 'it was her way of eating, eating with intensity, then looking, again and again, at a plate of sugared cakes' (p. 170). Hate and love are both manifestations of appetite: the overwhelming need to consume.[42] In *Orlando* Sackville-West is absorbed into Woolf's mind and body in a complex manœuvre that speaks of both hate and love.

Katherine Mansfield, one of Woolf's closer friends and rivals, also pointed out the inextricability of appetite, love, and hatred. The following letter was written to Mansfield's husband Middleton Murry during the winter of 1919–20, which she spent in Italy with her lifelong companion and probably lover, Ida Baker.

[41] Nicolson, *The Development of English Biography*, 16.
[42] Many writers have commented on the complex relationship in Woolf's own life between food and sexuality. See Roger Poole, *The Unknown Virginia Woolf* (Cambridge, 1978).

Christ! To *hate* like I do. It's upon me today. You don't know what hatred is because I know you have never hated anyone—not as you have loved—equally. That's what I do. My deadly deadly enemy has got me today and I'm simply a blind force of hatred. Hate is the *other* passion. It has all the opposite effects of Love. It fills you with death and corruption, it makes you feel hideous, degraded and old, it makes you long to DESTROY. Just as the other is light, so this is darkness. I hate like that—a million times multiplied. It's like being under a curse. When L. M. [Ida Baker] goes I don't know what I shall do. I can only think of breathing—lying quite still and breathing. Her great fat arms, her tiny blind breasts, her baby mouth, the underlip always wet and a crumb or two or a chocolate stain at the corners—her eyes fixed on me—fixed—waiting for what I may do that she may copy it. Think what you would feel if you had consumption and lived with a deadly enemy![43]

Here, sexual love and hatred are seen as the two limits to physical and emotional relationship. They are equally obsessive, equally tend towards sexual fantasy (the lingering over parts of the body associated with eroticism—the arms, the breasts, the mouth), and equally sustaining. Some of Mansfield's compulsion derives from an enforced identification, the constant threat of the double ('waiting for what I may do that she may copy it'). There is in the very name of Mansfield's disease an image of draining and engulfment. She is being 'consumed', eaten away inside both by TB and by Ida's insistent copying, and her life will finally end with a literal draining, a flow of blood from the lungs.[44]

To say that love and hate are close together is a truism. I am more concerned here to show that Nicolson's 'biography of hate' marks an end to the possibility of sexual fantasy beyond which fantasy—and biography—cannot go. It was at that limit that *Orlando* was written. It is a limit which complements the orgasmic intensity of more typical sexual fantasies with an intensity determined particularly by preoccupation with doubling, the desire for and the fear of separation. Strange desires are set in motion by the genesis of *Orlando* from the sexual intensity between Sackville-West and Woolf. 'The question now is, will my feelings for you be changed? I've lived

[43] *The Letters and Journals of Katherine Mansfield: A Selection*, ed. C. K. Stead (Harmondsworth, 1977), 152, 20 Nov. 1919.

[44] See Antony Alpers' description of her death in *The Life of Katherine Mansfield* (Oxford, 1982), 383.

in you all these months—coming out, what are you really like? Do you exist? Have I made you up?' asks Woolf as she finishes *Orlando* (*L*, iii. 474, 20? Mar. 1928). Sackville-West, consumed and transformed by Woolf's identification with her, is frightened for her own physical and sexual reality. 'I feel like one of those wax figures in a shop window, on which you have hung a robe stitched with jewels.'[45] She feels immobilized, her own body nullified by the deceptive presence of another, a textual body that purports to tell all the truth. It seems to her that Orlando now takes priority over Vita. And yet: 'you have invented a new form of Narcissism,—I confess,—I am in love with Orlando—this is a complication I had not foreseen.'[46] As they did for Katherine Mansfield, fear of the double and identificatory sexual love come together in a figure of self-recognition—narcissism, 'waiting for what I may do that she may copy it'—that is often used in descriptions of sexual relations between women.[47] Identification and images of doubling can structure both erotic desire and fantasies of hate. The two come together in a complexity of the sexual which is exploited in *Orlando* both through the role it plays in the relationship between Woolf and Sackville-West, and through the imagery of the text itself: an opulence of compliment alongside a fantasy of destruction.

[45] *The Letters of Vita Sackville-West to Virginia Woolf* ed. Louise DeSalvo and Mitchell A. Leaska (New York, 1985), 288, 11 Oct. 1928.

[46] Ibid. 289, 11 Oct. 1928.

[47] See e.g. Djuna Barnes, *Nightwood* (New York, 1937), 143: 'a man is another person—a woman is yourself, caught as you turn in panic; on her mouth you kiss your own.' See also Kate Millett, *Flying* (London, 1974), 482–3.

CHAPTER 2

'Moral Eugenics': The Working-Class Fiction of V. Sackville-West

SACKVILLE-WEST'S political and class allegiances have always been a stumbling block for her feminist admirers. This chapter will argue that she was already profoundly, and publicly, reactionary, by the time Woolf met her. In 1942 Sackville-West was enraged by the Beveridge Report, as we shall see; but her hostility to the working class is obvious already in her earliest published fiction. The woman with whom Woolf fell in love was, among other things, an unashamed eugenicist, and her extensive knowledge of the subject shapes the narrative of, and the assumptions behind, two of her earliest popular novels, *Heritage* (1919) and *The Dragon in Shallow Waters* (1921). Sackville-West's early novels were also unwitting exposés (unwitting because Sackville-West herself reproduces them) of the misogynist attitudes lying at the heart of the Darwinian and eugenic sciences. This chapter is an exploration of the eugenic underpinning of the high culture of the period, as well as an assessment of Sackville-West as an author at the time she met Woolf.

In her poem of the Second World War, *The Garden*, Sackville-West presents herself as fiercely patriotic.

> So do I say of England: I do love her.
> She is my shape, her shape my very shape.
> Her present is my grief; her past, my past.
>
> . . . .
>
> I must make
> Impracticable beauty for my England.[1]

Under pressure of war, not only Sackville-West's nationalism but also her instinctive conservatism became even more blatant. Urban bombing, of course, only sharpened her sense

---

[1] V. Sackville-West, *The Garden* (London, 1946), pp. 32-3.

of the countryside as an upper-class refuge for women, a little
removed from the devastations of a violent military masculinity, and from the misery of thousands of city dwellers. She
was furious about the Beveridge Report.

I think it sounds dreadful. The proletariat being encouraged to
breed like rabbits because each new little rabbit means 8/– a
week—as though there weren't too many of them already and not
enough work to go round, with 2,000,000 unemployed before the
war—and everyone being given everything for nothing, a complete
discouragement to thrift or effort. (Sackville-West to Nicolson, 2 Dec.
1942)

Her political opinions differed sharply from those of Harold
Nicolson, who welcomed the report. Sackville-West was only
slightly apologetic: 'I fear Mar [Sackville-West] is an instinctive
Tory' (Sackville-West to Nicolson, 3 Dec. 1942). But the truth
was that her politics were indeed instinctive, embedded in
her sense of herself as a scion of the English aristocracy.
Sackville-West and Woolf shared the feeling that culture was
the prerogative of the upper-middle and upper classes. Woolf,
moving in more socialist circles, had some misgivings about
the relations between class and culture; but Sackville-West had
none at all. Towards the end of the war she wrote: 'I hate
democracy. I hate *la populace*. I wish education had never been
introduced' (Sackville-West to Nicolson, 7 Feb. 1945). This
appalling and dangerous hatred lay behind her decision to
write, in the early 1920s, two novels about exactly that class
that she so disliked.

V. Sackville-West's first published novel, *Heritage* (1919),
turns on the word 'eugenics', coined by Sir Francis Galton. (I
shall return to this later.) Malory, the narrator of the novel,
describes his own theory that inconstant people should only
marry each other, as 'a new kind of eugenics, a sort of moral
eugenics' (p. 10). This opening gambit of his draws together
some of the most significant social issues of the war and post-
war years: heredity, deviancy, and sexuality. The turn of the
century had seen the publication of several studies of sexual
pathology and sexuality: Krafft-Ebing, Havelock Ellis, Freud,

and Edward Carpenter, for example.[2] All these writers and clinicians depended on story-telling—case histories—for the development of their theories. Identities suspended in narrative are the stuff of sexology at the turn of the century,[3] and these narratives, autobiographical and biographical, tend to be, like *Orlando*, stories of 'freaks': homosexuals, neurotics, psychotics. The emphasis in Krafft-Ebing's title on 'sexual pathology' says it all. It is sexual 'abnormality' that is being delineated in these texts; and normative sexual identities are deduced from them, like the 'sunny side' of pathology: what pathology is not.

Now that sexual health was, perhaps for the first time, being visibly defined, handbooks were produced to encourage (heterosexual) lovers to practise 'healthy', enjoyable sex: heterosexual vaginal intercourse. (Now, of course, under pressure from AIDS, we are being encouraged to find 'healthy' heterosexual pleasure elsewhere.) Marie Stopes, inspired by the work of the sexologists and the Eugenics Society, published *Married Love: A New Contribution to the Solution of Sex Difficulties* in 1918, encouraging couples to have intercourse for the sake of their physical and spiritual well-being.

The visible secretions and the most subtle essences which pass during union between man and woman, affect the lives of each and are essentially vital to each other. As I see them, the man and the woman are each organs, part of the other ... There is a *physiological* as well as a spiritual truth in the words 'they twain shall be one flesh'.[4]

This yoking of sexual pleasure to a biological and spiritual imperative, while allaying (as well as feeding) anxiety about

[2] See Richard von Krafft-Ebing, *Psychopathia Sexualis*, (New York, 1925); Havelock Ellis, *Studies in the Psychology of Sex*, 2nd edn., 6 vols. (Philadelphia, 1923–4); the work and practice of Sigmund Freud; and Edward Carpenter, *The Intermediate Sex: A Study of Some Transitional Types of Men and Women* (London, 1909). Lillian Faderman, *Surpassing the Love of Men: Romantic Friendship and Love between Women from the Renaissance to the Present* (New York, 1981), offers an account of these years.

[3] Stephen Heath, *The Sexual Fix* (London, 1982), discusses some of these matters more fully.

[4] Marie Stopes, *Married Love: A New Contribution to the Solution of Sex Difficulties* (London, 1918), 151.

the spread of perversion, also fuelled another fear. If sexual pleasure was to be found only in the reproductive act, then what would happen to reproduction? Who would have children, and how often?

Mrs E. B. Mayne, one of Marie Stopes's birth control campaigners, sent her a letter on 12 February 1920:

> I find the women on the whole suspicious . . . I judge they are a good deal bothered by Mothers' Welcome people, health visitors, Social Welfare workers and I am regarded in most cases as yet another intruder come to tell them how to wash the 'bayby' . . . The words on the cover 'How to have healthy children' frequently raise trouble so I lay stress on 'How to avoid weakening pregnancies'.[5]

Mrs Mayne had been going round the East End of London distributing a pamphlet on contraception to working-class women, and the unease expressed in her letter is confirmed by the figures: on that day, out of twenty women visited, only five took the leaflet. On 26 February, one asked angrily, in Mrs Mayne's rendering: ''ow they'd keep the nation goin' if the poor didn't 'ave children, as the rich wouldn't.'[6] This was the concern of the eugenicists, Malthusians, and Stopesians alike. In Manchester, in 1899, three out of five men applying to enlist had been rejected as physically unfit. In 1908, the Report of the Royal Commission on the Care and Control of the Feeble-Minded had noted the high fertility of its subjects; and in the 1911 census, it was demonstrated that unskilled labourers were reproducing themselves four times as fast as doctors or clergymen. It was statistics such as these that struck fear into the hearts of the middle and upper classes—people like Sackville-West and Woolf—and made them uncomfortably aware that they might soon be a dying minority.[7] Sir Francis

---

[5] Quoted in Ruth Hall, *Marie Stopes: A Biography* (London, 1977), 174.

[6] Ibid.

[7] For discussions of the social context of eugenics, from which the information here is taken see Carl J. Bajema (ed.), *Eugenics Then and Now* (Strondberg, Pa., 1976); C. P. Blacker, *Eugenics: Galton and After* (London, 1952); Jill Conway, 'Stereotypes of Femininity in a Theory of Sexual Evolution', in Martha Vicinus (ed.), *Suffer and be Still: Women in the Victorian Age* (Bloomington, Ind., 1972), 140–54; Greta Jones, *Social Darwinism and English Thought: The Interaction between Biological and Social Theory* (Brighton, 1980); and G. R. Searle, *Eugenics and Politics in England, 1900–1914* (Leyden, 1976).

Galton, a Victorian biologist, had first coined the word 'eugenics' in his *Inquiries into Human Faculty and its Development* (1883), and defined it as 'the science of improving stock'.[8] In 1907, following the Report on the Care and Control of the Feeble-Minded, Galtonian science came into its own. The Eugenics Education Society, a male-dominated enclave that had broken away from the female-dominated Moral Education League, was founded in November 1907, and 'eugenics' quickly became a party-political buzz-word. The membership of the EES was highly renowned both socially and intellectually, and their educational projects were to be very successful in publicizing the aims of eugenics and in insisting on its importance for public policy and planning. Even Sidney Webb and the Fabians were anxious to demonstrate their eugenic sympathies.

Eugenics was fundamentally concerned with issues of sexual reproduction. Charles Darwin, Galton's cousin, had first impressed the Victorians with the significance of prolificacy for survival:

In looking at Nature, it is most necessary to keep the foregoing considerations always in mind—never to forget that every single organic being around us may be said to be striving to the utmost to increase in numbers; that each lives by a struggle at some period of its life; that heavy destruction inevitably falls either on the young or old, during each generation or at recurrent intervals. Lighten any check, mitigate the destruction ever so little, and the number of the species will almost instantaneously increase to any amount.[9]

Anxieties about the rise of socialism and the declining birth rate among the middle classes fed a deep-seated fear of the poorer classes and the threat of their domination. The eugenicists never forgot that 'there is no exception to the rule that every organic being naturally increases at so high a rate, that if not destroyed, the earth would soon be covered by the progeny of a single pair'.[10] Yet eugenicists could not stomach explicit allusion to sexual intercourse. It was many years

[8] Francis Galton, *Inquiries into Human Faculty and Its Development* (London, 1883), 25.
[9] Charles Darwin, *The Origin of Species by Means of Natural Selection: On the Preservation of Favoured Races in the Struggle for Life* (Harmondsworth, 1985), 119.
[10] Ibid. 117.

before the movement could be persuaded wholeheartedly to
support birth control, despite the fact that the Dutch cap was
pioneered as the 'Pro-Race' cap.[11] On the whole the EES
preferred to discuss the institutionalization of the sexual drive.
'Positive' eugenics sought to promote marriage between 'fit'
partners and to hope that children would follow (hence some
of the anxiety about birth control); and 'negative' eugenics
sometimes went as far as advocating segregation or steriliza-
tion of the 'unfit' (who included alcoholics, epileptics, paupers,
tuberculars, criminals, gamblers, the deaf, and sexual inverts).
But the Society was squeamish about direct and explicit intervention in the sexual act. It remained for Marie Stopes to
bring about a marriage of eugenic theory and contraceptive
techniques, and to offer a vocabulary for talking about intimate sexual matters which, unlike the work of academic sexologists, was available to, and directed at, the general public,
and elicited a massive response and floods of letters to her in
the early 1920s.[12]

Unlike the case histories of Krafft-Ebing or Ellis, which are
closed narratives intended to illustrate particular points, the
letters to Marie Stopes are open-ended, unresolved. Many of
them were requests for help, like letters to agony aunts today.
Sexual difficulties had only recently become the subject of
public discussion and dispute. This shift was strongly resisted:
'it is really impossible to find words strong enough to
condemn any suggestion of employing the imagination in
sexual matters', writes W. N. Willis in a fury in 1920.[13] The
sexual imagination seemed to have entered the domain of
public affairs (Willis's use of the word 'employment' is not an
accident), and in particular of public health.

Malory's moral eugenics is thus a phrase characteristic of its
time. Sackville-West's *Heritage* shares with eugenics a profound
fear of the insistence of sexual desire. Havelock Ellis had
offered a description of it as 'an inborn organic impulse,

---

[11] For accounts of the early birth control movement in Britain see Hall, *Marie
Stopes*; and Marie Stopes, *Contraception: Its Theory, History and Practice* (London,
1923).
[12] These have been published in Ruth Hall (ed.), *Dear Dr. Stopes: Sex in the 1920s*
(Harmondsworth, 1978).
[13] From W. N. Willis, *Wedded Love or Married Misery*, quoted in Hall, *Marie Stopes*,
183.

reaching full development about the time of puberty'; or as 'an inherited aptitude the performance of which normally demands for its full satisfaction the presence of a person of the opposite sex'.[14] But this version of the sexual instinct as innate and basically heterosexual contradicts the idea of sexuality as an unstable personal narrative (or narratives), that was just emerging, from the work of Freud, for example. By the early twentieth century, the sexual was seen to be concerned with reproduction of itself as well as of the species. New questions were being asked. How is it that generation after generation feels desire? Is desire inherited, learned, caught like a disease? Fear of homosexual contagion induces the heroine's aunt, in Sylvia Thompson's popular novel *Third Act in Venice* (1936), to ask her comic lesbian friend, Clytie Jones, not to lean on her niece's pillow, as it might be 'dangerous'.[15] The romantic attachments between older and younger girls in schools began to be mistrusted and studied.[16] It was suspected that it might be possible to *learn* different versions of desire —that it wasn't an instinct with a fixed form at all. This of course is exactly the worry that lies behind measures like Section 28 today.

Fear of racial degeneration through the learning of different kinds of 'perversion' was linked to an anxious curiosity about the origin and transmission of 'degenerate' forms of sexual desire. Bizarre theories of heredity began to be bandied around. One of Stopes's correspondents (a doctor) maintained that she had passed on some of her characteristics to the child of her lesbian ex-lover. The child had inherited her:

Way of holding a teacup. Marked courtesy in speaking to persons of inferior social position such as servants. Complete absence of physical fear. Holding one's breath when kissing. Manner of caressing the hair of anyone one loves . . . How they reached the boy passes my comprehension except on the assumption that hero-worship of me had impressed a subconscious memory of them on the brain cells of

[14] Both quotations are from Havelock Ellis, *Studies in the Psychology of Sex*, iii. 309.

[15] Sylvia Thompson, *Third Act in Venice* (London, 1936), 180–1.

[16] See Obici and Marchesini, 'The School-Friendships of Girls', 1898, appendix B, in Ellis, *Studies in the Psychology of Sex*, ii.

his mother and that she had somehow passed on that memory to his brain cells.[17]

Academic scientists shared the doctor's concern. Havelock Ellis wrote details of heredity in all his case histories. The Victorian passion for freaks fuelled Edwardian preoccupations with heredity: C. P. Blacker, writing in 1952 about the history of the eugenics movement, commented:

Endow a wild fly with an aesthetic sense comparable to ours, and give him a glimpse of the experimental flies in the geneticists' bottles. He would be shocked and horrified. The fly's reaction would be the same as that of a human being if he could collect together and survey the assortment of people who are of special interest to geneticists.[18]

The 'freakish' nature of *Orlando* could thus be allied to the distasteful curiosity about mutation and 'sports' that lay behind the eugenic project—including, as we shall see, Sackville-West's *Heritage* and *The Dragon in Shallow Waters*. Woolf wanted to control Sackville-West: to mark her out as different, and to mark her out as *hers*. The eugenic obsession with anomaly demonstrated a desperate anxiety to 'fix' sexual and racial hierarchies: it was fundamentally conservative. Sackville-West's novels attempt to romanticize that tight reactionary grip.

In *Heritage* and *The Dragon in Shallow Waters*, Sackville-West was writing of lives of which she had no first-hand knowledge, and much of the romanticism and fatalism of the novels comes from her distance from, and ignorance about, her subject. Sackville-West's novels were not aimed at a working-class audience: she wanted them to be literature rather than popular fiction. Her early books seem to have been read mainly by a coterie of intellectuals and middle brows, but her popularity as a novelist greatly increased with the publication of *The Edwardians*, which was a best seller.

Sackville-West's early novels were not typical of the popular novel of their day. Authors like Sylvia Thompson, F. M. Mayor, E. M. Delafield, and E. M. Hull, concentrated on descriptions of upper- or middle-class life; but Sackville-West's *Heritage*

[17] Hall, *Dear Dr. Stopes*, 102.   [18] Blacker, *Eugenics*, 247.

and *The Dragon in Shallow Waters* were set in working-class communities.

Heritage was well received. One reviewer wrote: 'we wish all first novels were like Miss Sackville-West's, for we should have fewer qualms about the future of the novel.'[19] It is a story of agricultural life and instinctive, destructive sexual feelings. The male narrator, on holiday in Italy, meets a man called Malory, who proceeds to tell his life story. Malory had, at one time, worked as a farm hand in the Weald of Kent. There he met Ruth, the farmer's daughter, and her gypsy-like cousin, Rawdon Westmacott. 'The man's blood was crazy for her' (p. 21), but Ruth treated him with contempt and perversity; yet 'we always come together again' (p. 49), she said despairingly. On Malory's advice, Ruth's father finally forbade Westmacott the house, but, shortly before Ruth's wedding to the young thatcher, Dymock, Malory came upon Ruth and Westmacott in the stable, and that night she and Westmacott eloped and later married.

This is as far as Malory's story goes. Soon after telling it, he disappears. The war has broken out, and the young narrator, struck by curiosity, and discharged from hospital but indefinitely unfit for service, himself takes a job at the Pennistans' farm. After the war, Westmacott returns and his abusive marriage is resumed. At one point, Ruth leaves him and comes to her parents, but he follows her and brings her home.

After an interval of ten years, the narrator receives a long letter from Malory. Home from the war, he has been to Kent to stay on the farm, but, unable to remain in the proximity of Ruth and her husband, he went to Ephesus to assist an archaeologist, MacPherson, with some excavations. He corresponded desultorily with Ruth and, after MacPherson's death, returned to England. In London, Ruth came to see him and took him back with her, telling him that she has driven Westmacott away: he developed a pathological fear of what he perceived as her violence and infidelity, and finally left. At the time of the letter, Ruth and Malory are happily married.

This strange, double-layered narrative unfolds in a heavily

---

[19] *Nation*, 14 June 1919.

deterministic universe. War, sexual attraction, and heredity together produce a menacing claustrophobia which is realized in Malory's theory of the psychology of rural life.

I have a great love for the country people; they are to me like the oaks of the land, enduring and indigenous, beautiful with the beauty of strong, deep-rooted things, without intention of change ... I love the unconsciousness of them, as they move unheeding, bent only on the practical business of their craft. (p. 10)

Elsewhere, the narrator describes Malory as 'the type of the theorist' (p. 9), and the novel's attitudes towards sexuality and class are informed by Malory's distance from (theorizing of) the community that he watches and finally joins. Malory is a wanderer, an intellectual, temperamentally inconstant. He goes to Kent because 'at one period of my life I had a fancy that I would try my hand at farming' (p. 10). He is involved in the farming community not as an integrated member of its labour force, but because of his passion for Ruth (which, unspoken and even unrecognized as it is for the greater part of the novel, plays no part in the social configurations of the group). It is not exactly that the farm does not need him, but that he could at once be anyone (the narrator later takes his place untrained), and only himself (he is the man that Ruth loves). In his marginality he resembles the gypsies that he and Ruth come upon during one of their Sunday walks. Sackville-West alludes here to the thread that runs through Victorian fiction (notably *The Mill on the Floss*) and into *The Virgin and the Gypsy* of the gypsy community as an image of diaspora and of sexual promiscuity: the underside of civilization. But Malory is carefully distinguished from the gypsies, since his apparent marginalization within the community allows his perspective to dominate in the novel. He observes the gypsies with some unease:

I heard a scream and an outburst of laughter from a neighbouring caravan, and, looking round, I saw Rawdon Westmacott jump to the ground in pursuit of a young gipsy woman, whom he caught in his arms and kissed.
   I looked hastily at Ruth; she had seen the thing happen. (p. 45)

The incident causes a crisis in relations between Ruth, Westmacott, and Malory, in which the refinement of Malory's desire is set alongside the savagery of Westmacott's: 'to my astonishment she yielded suddenly, flexible and abandoned, and he kissed her regardless of my presence; kissed her ferociously, and pushed her from him' (p. 48).

Malory's astonishment is the key to the novel's eugenic underpinning. Watching Ruth decide to elope with Westmacott, he muses: 'they were of the same blood, and I and Leslie Dymock were of a different breed' (p. 78). Ruth, trying to explain to Malory the state of things between herself and Westmacott, gives, in Malory's words, 'that great uneasy heave of the uneducated when confronted with the explanation of a problem beyond the scope of their vocabulary' (p. 49). She says that: 'he cringes to me, and then I bully him; or else he bullies me, and then I cringe to him. But quarrel as we may, we always come together again' (p. 49). The premisses of eugenics are pondered: what exactly is the fit union? Malory recognizes the fitness of Ruth and Westmacott for each other: 'I knew that elemental forces were loose like monstrous bats in the shed which contained us' (p. 80); and yet he, and later the narrator, are intensely concerned to bring about unions that have an emotional, rather than a racial, logic. The extraordinary sexual charge that exists between Ruth and Westmacott brings with it violence, drunkenness, and abuse; yet in their 'moments of reconciliation she found consolation in the renewal of their curiously satisfying communion. I don't pretend to understand this,' says Malory (p. 179).

The obsession with heredity that broods over the novel produces an analysis of sexual attraction in which class and race are equally significant. Malory's outsider's gaze organizes the narrative for us. As far as he is concerned, Ruth and Westmacott are of 'the same blood' not only because they come from the same family, but also because they are of the same class. Malory's shock and incomprehension at the power of the sexual charge between them (and his fascination with it) is a dramatization of the paranoia about working-class sexuality which brought the eugenics movement into being. Francis Galton, father of eugenics, is cited in *Heritage*:

You remember Francis Galton and the waltzing mice, how he took the common mouse and the waltzing mouse, and mated them, and how among their progeny there was a common mouse, a black and white mouse, and a mouse that waltzed; and how in subsequent generations the common brown mouse predominated, but every now and then there came a mouse that waltzed and waltzed, restless and tormented, until in the endless pursuit of its tail it died, dazed, blinded, perplexed, by the relentless fate that had it in its grip. Well, I had my mice in a cage, and Concha, the dancer, the waltzing mouse, sat mumbling by the fire. (p. 36)

Concha is Ruth's Spanish great-grandmother, now a very old woman, and a constant silent presence in the house, sitting over the fire roasting her chestnuts. In her youth, she was a Spanish dancer who met and married Oliver Pennistan, a young English soldier. (Sackville-West is of course writing about her own grandmother, Pepita, here.) The point of the passage is to invoke eugenic theory as an explanation of the way in which an apparently commonplace race can occasionally produce a freak: a wild, passionate creature whose energy is uselessly and destructively spent on itself. This (inauthentic, as far as I can gather) mention of Galton draws a strand of eugenic assumptions into the fabric of the book, indicating a body of knowledge with reference to which its plot and characters were conceived. Is Ruth also, like her great-grandmother, a waltzing mouse? 'Which would prove the stronger, her life-long training, or the flash of her latent blood?' (*H*, 108). That 'southern blood', 'ancient blood', 'tribal blood' (*H*, 78) can flare up in any generation as a reversion, like Galton's waltzing mouse. When it does, it produces a profound incongruity, an unfitness of individual to environment, that violently disrupts social structures (Ruth and Westmacott secretly elope on the eve of her wedding). Malory poses the question of Ruth's nature in terms of the drama of her anomalous heredity, her 'latent blood': 'what am I to believe? that she is cursed with a dual nature, the one coarse and unbridled, the other delicate, conventional, practical, motherly, refined?' (p. 180). The *Nation*'s reviewer objects to this genealogical analysis of desire. Surely, he says, the dualism of Ruth's nature is 'really as much a product of complex nature as of heredity'.[20] But theories of heredity are precisely explanations of the complexities of human nature. They attempt to fix and explain the vagaries of feeling and action, and, in the case of eugenics, to use that explanation to suppress social and sexual elements of which the dominant classes are mistrustful.

It is not only eugenic ideology that determines Sackville-West's early novels. She also trades, as we shall see, on the sexualization of a power differential between men and women: an inequality which was the cornerstone of Darwinian theory. For the account of sexual selection given in *The Descent of Man* (1871) is basically a theory of gender difference. The difference between male and female, vital to sexual reproduction, is the cornerstone of evolutionary theory, although its centrality is not usually acknowledged. Variation between the sexes is a precondition for evolution. If the original hermaphrodite that Darwin imagined had never been superseded (and Darwin found the actual mechanics of the beginnings of gender as impossible to describe as the beginnings of life itself), it would simply have continued to reproduce itself. There would have been no variation, therefore no species, therefore no evolution. A clearer understanding of the chromosomal basis for sexual difference after the publication of Mendel's work filled some writers with an anxious fear of a reversion to that original hermaphroditic universe of Darwin's. Edward Carpenter wrote in 1909 of the apparent increase in the numbers of androgynous beings— usually sexual inverts:

We do *not* know, in fact, what possible evolutions are to come, or what new forms, of permanent place and value, are being already slowly differentiated from the surrounding mass of humanity ... at the present time certain new types of humankind may be emerging, which will have an important part to play in the societies of the future.[21]

Carpenter wrote in support of members of the 'intermediate sex'; he felt they had a specific social and educational role to

---

[20] *Nation*, 14 June 1919.   [21] Carpenter, *The Intermediate Sex*, 11.

play as 'reconcilers and interpreters of the two sexes to each other'.[22] As inversion became apparently scientifically intelligible, so it became more respectable. Havelock Ellis added the following paragraph to his 1897 edition of *Sexual Inversion* when it was reissued as volume 2 of *Studies in the Psychology of Sex* in 1924:

In the opinion of the latest physiologists of sex, such as Castle, Heape, and Marshall, each sex contains the latent character of the other or recessive sex .... A homosexual tendency may thus be regarded as simply the psychical manifestation of special characters of the recessive sex, susceptible of being evolved under changed circumstances, such as may occur near puberty, and associated with changed metabolism.[23]

Mendelian theory was selectively absorbed to produce a biological version of Freud's theory of an original and basic bisexuality which was modified at various stages during childhood and adolescence into normative forms of heterosexuality. Ellis's biological explanation of congenital inversion supported social and cultural defences of homosexuality, like Edward Carpenter's. Lesbians such as Radclyffe Hall could ask for tolerance in the name of biochemical malfunction.[24]

At the same time heterosexuality was being vigorously and anxiously defended. Darwin's belief in the inescapability of heterosexual relations was invoked over and over again. Darwin eclipsed conflict between the sexes by simply ignoring his evidence. His theory of the struggle for existence located aggression between *species*, rather than between *sexes*, and his description of courtship procedures concentrated on fights between members of the same sex, rather than of different ones:

The sexual struggle is of two kinds; in the one it is between individuals of the same sex, generally the males, in order to drive away or kill their rivals, the females remaining passive whilst in the other, the struggle is likewise between individuals of the same sex, in order to excite or charm those of the opposite sex, generally the

---

[22] Carpenter, *The Intermediate Sex*, 14.   [23] Ellis, *Studies*, ii. 79–80.
[24] See the closing pages of Radclyffe Hall, *The Well of Loneliness* (London, 1982; 1st edn. 1928).

females, which no longer remain passive, but select the more agree-
able partners.[25]

The shift from passive to active females is important, and I
shall return to it. For the moment I wish to stress that the
drive towards the opposite sex is assumed to be stable, and
reinforced by radical conflicts occurring *within* each sex. This
is in spite of the following evidence:

As the male has to find the female, he requires organs of sense and
locomotion . . . When the male has found the female, he sometimes
absolutely requires prehensile organs to hold her; thus Dr. Wallace
informs me that the males of certain moths cannot unite with the
females if their tarsi or feet are broken.[26]

A female who flees the male; a female who must be held to
prevent her escaping from the sexual act: male–female violence is crucial to sexual selection.

Darwin's evidence of conflict between the sexes was not too
much of a threat to the maintenance of heterosexuality. In the
lower species, males were specifically equipped, because of
sexual selection, to immobilize females for as long as they
needed to ensure sexual reproduction, and women, as Darwin
recognized, were often forced into marriage for economic and
social reasons. But Havelock Ellis's fears were aroused when
his own scientific and cultural explanations of homosexuality
were reinforced by the new political movement that was
emerging at the turn of the century. Suffragism was often held
responsible for an apparent increase in the number of female
homosexuals. Havelock Ellis commented that women's newly
visible thirst for knowledge extended to the sexual sphere,
and that, because of continued segregation of the sexes, 'a
tendency develops for women to carry this independence still
further and to find love where they find work'.[27] Women
might engage in sexual as well as professional partnerships
with one another.

Ellis thought that the strains of expanded commercial
enterprise had increased nervousness and effeminacy in men
and provided the heredity for a whole new generation of

[25] Charles Darwin, *The Descent of Man and Selection in Relation to Sex* (London,
1901), 939.
[26] Ibid. 322–3.   [27] Ellis, *Studies*, iii. 262.

inverts. It was important now to defend heterosexuality and to explain the violence that Darwin had been able simply to ignore. Hence Havelock Ellis undertook his research on love and pain, and concluded that pain, far from intensifying heterosexual conflict, was sometimes actually a stimulant to desire: 'under certain abnormal circumstances pain, more especially the mental representation of pain, acts as a power-ful sexual stimulant.'[28] Furthermore, worried at the prospect of the suffragettes apparently *choosing* to find love where they found work, he sought to deny, via a complicated analysis of Darwin, any voluntary dimension to female desire. He located a contradiction in Darwin's account of courtship, and quoted him: in one place, 'the lower animals have a sense of beauty, powers of discrimination and taste on the part of the female'; and in another 'males endeavour to charm or excite their mates by love notes.'[29] This is the active–passive split that we noticed earlier: in one scenario, the females choose; in the other, they are chosen. That contradiction opened up a dangerous debate over the relative power wielded by each sex. Ellis conducted the debate in terms of a possible aesthetic faculty in animals.

According to the first theory, the female admires beauty, consciously or unconsciously, and selects the most beautiful partner; according to the second theory, there is no aesthetic question involved, but the female is unconsciously influenced by the most powerful or complex organic stimulus to which she is subjected. There can be no question that it is the second, and not the first, of these two views which we are justified in accepting.[30]

Ellis *appears* to object to the first alternative on the grounds that it was an unjustified anthropomorphism. But his argu-ment is *actually* conducted in terms of active and passive desire: the female 'selects', she is 'subjected'. His endorse-ment of the second view, that the female is affected by an organic stimulus of which she is unaware, validated an account of female desire as manipulable by the male, and quite involuntary on the part of the female. This removed any possibility of sexual choice, Ellis's bugbear, from women; and

---

[28] Ellis, *Studies*, iii. 171.   [29] Ibid. 22 and 23.   [30] Ibid. 24.

implied that her sexual feelings were very intense and at the same time quite outside her control.

Paradoxically, this account of sexual desire could sometimes be invoked to validate women's right to sexual pleasure: it threw responsibility for female 'frigidity' back onto male ineptitude. Harold Nicolson, desperately trying to understand Sackville-West's feelings while she was away with Trefusis in late 1918, followed the advice of Sackville-West's mother and read Van der Velde's *Married Love*. It encouraged him to take the blame for the failure of their sexual relationship:

I can't write to you what the book has taught me. But I know that you must have suffered terribly—& that only a splendid character like yours could have kept from hating me. Dearest—it is one of the noblest things you have done—I can't find other words. But it makes me love you in a different way again—a sort of spiritual adoration & gratitude. And then there are other new aspects which aren't spiritual at all but which are going to make our future life something glorious & real! (Nicolson to Sackville-West, 1 Dec. 1918)

The longed-for revolution never actually occurred, but it is clear from this letter that Nicolson was beginning to understand his sexuality in terms of responsibility and activity: it was up to him to secure Sackville-West's pleasure and his own.

The publication both of Van der Velde's book, and of Marie Stopes's *Married Love*, demonstrated that the era of Victorian prudery was passing, at least in the publishing industry. Appalling loss of life during the First World War meant that reproduction had once again become a matter of urgency. Lydia, in E. M. Delafield's *The Heel of Achilles* (1921), is profoundly shocked by her community's support of hasty marriages before the departure of young men to the front. Her prospective son-in-law puts it in eugenic terms: 'But it's every man's duty now, in my opinion, to fix himself up, and the duty of every healthy young woman to help carry on the race. I didn't put it that way to your daughter,' Mr. Valentine admitted, 'but I guess there wasn't any need for arguments. She and I understand one another, Mrs. Damerel.'[31] It was important suddenly to acknowledge and act on sexual desire. The human race

---

[31] E. M. Delafield, *The Heel of Achilles* (London, 1921), 267.

now seemed to face an even worse threat than degeneration: extinction.

Such sexual frankness inevitably spawned a series of middle-brow and popular novels that dealt explicitly with it, and often with what could be loosely termed sadism. I shall turn now to Sackville-West's 1921 novel, *The Dragon in Shallow Waters*, and analyse the way in which, in this text, the discourses of eugenics, of freakishness, and of sexual sadomasochism are all invoked to produce one of Sackville-West's most compromising novels.

The Dragon in Shallow Waters opens with a description of a soap factory: 'An immense gallery, five hundred feet long, occupied the upper floor of the main factory building. Looking down the gallery, a perspective of iron guides spanned the roof, gaunt skeletons of architecture, uncompromising, inexorably utilitarian, inflexible, remorseless' (p. 1). Glendinning tells us that Sackville-West researched the novel by visiting Lord Leverhulme's factory.[32] Sackville-West's emotional and political investment in the object of her research is clear in this and other passages. Behind the desire to document lies a delicious feeling of romantic horror. The evil-smelling, bubbling vats of liquid soap seem to the narrator like the lakes of hell, and those who work with them are described as 'a sinister race, to whom affliction seemed naturally drawn' (p. 5). At once Sackville-West shows us how she projects 'affliction' and 'sinister' qualities onto the working class; in this way, of course, denying them in herself, and implicitly setting herself up as a paragon of the sane and unafflicted (not how she always felt).

The novel is about two brothers who live next to each other and are looked after by the wife of one of them, Nan. The brothers are both disabled, one blind, the other deaf and mute: 'they were indeed a sinister race to whom affliction seemed naturally drawn. Nature cursed them from the hour of their birth with physical deficiencies and spiritual savagery' (p. 5). The novel grows out of Sackville-West's, and the eugenicists' fear of deviations from the (middle-class) norm: a

---

[32] See Victoria Glendinning, *Vita: The Life of V. Sackville-West* (New York, 1983), 113.

fear that is inflected at once by fantasies of the perfect body, and fantasies of the unthreatened dominance of the middle and upper classes. The assumption that physical deformity necessarily involves moral degeneracy shapes the cathartic climax of the book in which one brother is murdered by the other. Silas, the blind brother, addresses Nan and her lover, Linnet Morgan: 'you are the builders, and we are the destroyers; we are the cursed, and you are the blessed. You and your like must build your security upon the ruins of us and our like; it's the natural law' (p. 169).

Nan is trapped by her marriage to Gregory, the deaf brother. The first woman we meet in the novel is Silas's wife, murdered by Silas, who lies in their bed, 'a mass of almost unidentifiable disfigurement' (p. 6). Nan's life is also spiritually and sexually disfiguring, yet some grim, claustrophobic necessity prevents her from leaving. Her suggestion to the brothers that they should move is met with derision:

The old mournfulness, the old anguish, closed down upon them again. They were like haunted people, who could not help themselves. They seemed haunted by the past,—which contained indeed the death of Hannah, a death so rough and dingy,—by the present, and by the overcharged future. But their dread was not to be defined; it was of the nature of a mystic sentence, presaged from a long way off. (pp. 114–15)

Their imprisonment in their community is symbolized by the soap factory which towers over the town, and in which all the town's inhabitants work. Sackville-West distinguishes between a family of labourers, forced to stay together because they cannot survive apart, and a family, like that at Knole, which is held there by shared emotional and financial investment in an ancestral home. In Sackville-West's fictional (fantasy) world, there could be no real meeting-place for rich and poor. Silas enters into a secret friendship with the wife of one of the factory's directors:

And although they maintained the disguise afforded by her tone of slight condescension, and by his of conventional respect, underneath this disguise fermented the perpetual and manifold contest, of class against class, of the rough against the fastidious, of the man against the woman. (p. 143)

The three conflicts are parallel: working class, rough, male against upper class, fastidious, female. 'He changed; he towered; he dwarfed her; all her superiority went in a flash' (p. 183). Silas's presence is always menacing, partly because of his disability: 'his quietness, and the knowledge that he could not see her, disconcerted her' (p. 73). Christine's fear is of his class as well as of his gender and his blindness. She is prey to the same paranoia that impelled the eugenics movement. Silas seems the embodiment of the revolutionary threat: desperate, and with little to lose. Nan experiences a similar paranoia within her marriage: her deaf—'degenerate'—husband watches hawk-like every move she makes, creating an atmosphere of danger and suspicion.

The novel pivots on a scene of attempted rape.

[Nan] woke with a cry, to find Gregory's [her husband's] face near hers as he knelt on the floor. It was very fortunate that he could not hear the cry, which, at first merely startled, changed to horror as she recognised him. His sardonic smile and her widened eyes were terribly close; their two faces, by reason of their nearness, seemed large to one another. She pushed with both hands against his chest, struggling silently; only half awake, she had not the wisdom not to struggle; now, she knew only his distastefulness. (p. 208)

Luckily, they are interrupted by the cry of the factory supervisor from outside the bedroom window. It is as though the novel is haunted by a violation that never quite occurs: 'she had never known anything like the wild, fainting rapture of this half-surrender' (p. 204). The novel closes with a description of a brawl between the brothers which could easily be mistaken for a rape. Silas and Gregory are in a gallery of the soap factory. 'Gregory leapt suddenly upon him, and in an instant their limbs were locked' (p. 240). The brothers' fight is the most unequivocal and consenting form of physical contact the novel has known. It demonstrates a racial and sexual order that sets the brothers apart because of their physical handicaps. Within this order there is no possible heterosexual relation apart from rape. The fight between the brothers is like an act of lovemaking:

So they remained, arrested, stirred only by that almost imperceptible rocking, until doubt might have arisen whether they so held one another grasped with deadly intent, or, as the likeness between them more palpably emerged, in a brotherly welding against some danger imminent and extraneous. (pp. 240–1)

The imminent danger is of their final degeneration. Throughout the novel Silas becomes more and more abased as more and more people realize his cowardice, and his murder of his own brother (he throws Gregory into a vat of boiling soap) represents his ultimate disintegration, prey to a disturbance from within that reflects his subversive action within his own community: 'I disapprove of your methods, because they stir up trouble amongst the men' (pp. 19–20), says the factory supervisor to Silas. The brothers have always been presented as conspiratorial. There is an unsettling understanding between them. Nan has 'the alienating sensation that her husband understood his brother better than she did, although he could hear no word' (p. 23). Their downfall at the end is Sackville-West's symbolic annihilation of the working class, assumed to be incapable of ensuring even its own survival. *The Dragon in Shallow Waters* is a novel of eugenic wish-fulfilment: the brothers, deformed as they are, are unable either to reproduce themselves, or to support one another in the battle to survive. This is a eugenic Utopia, the kind of society Galton and others were trying to bring about. And this was the kind of vision with which Sackville-West was living, only a year before she met Virginia Woolf.

The other side of Sackville-West's dislike of the working class was a fascination—albeit at times sheepish, and even downright rebellious—with her own aristocratic history. In the next chapter I shall look at the ways in which both Woolf and Sackville-West used autobiographical narratives to explore not only their own identities, but also those of other women in an attempt to establish and develop intimacies.

CHAPTER 3

'Maternal Explanation':
Autobiography and Gender

BOTH Woolf and Sackville-West, imaginative and introspect-
ive, were constantly concerned with explanation. As we have
seen, Vita Sackville-West relied in her early novels on eugenic
theory to 'explain' class difference. But in her and Woolf's
autobiographical writing, explanation of the self and of others
required the forging of new narratives, rather than the adaptation of old ones. Sackville-West's interest in the intersection of
public policy and theories of heredity was also an anxiety
about who she was herself. What did heredity mean in her
own life? Her family history had already been under pressure
during the trial which established her father's right to Knole
(see Appendix A). In this chapter I shall show how, as their
emotional and sexual circumstances changed, Woolf and
Sackville-West continually rewrote their life stories, trying out
new 'explanations', modifying their stories in response to
those offered by each other and by other women, and, most
significantly, continually redeploying the 'maternal explanation' of Sackville-West's poem.

> Can you, who made my flesh and made
> A poet's complicated mind,
> For such pale haunted moonlit woods
> Maternal explanation find?[1]

Autobiography has only fairly recently been subjected to
theoretical attention.[2] Even in the years since Shumaker's
pioneering history of the form (1954), and Gusdorf's article

---

[1] V. Sackville-West, 'To my Mother', unpublished poem, Sissinghurst.

[2] See e.g. James Olney, 'Autobiography and the Cultural Moment: A Thematic,
Historical and Bibliographical Introduction', in James Olney (ed.), *Autobiography:
Essays Theoretical and Critical* (Princeton, NJ, 1980), 3–27; and Stephen A. Shapiro,
'The Dark Continent of Literature: Autobiography', *Comparative Literature Studies*,
5 (1968), 421–54.

setting out the problems and issues involved (1956), the terms of the debate have shifted from the status of the written text to the nature of the writer's relationship with it.[3] Rodolphe Gasché, for example, in an issue of *Modern Language Notes* devoted to the topic 'Autobiography and the Problem of the Subject', chooses to concentrate on 'aspects of autobiography in which the metaphysics of the subject is evident'.[4] This concern with the subject, in the wake of Lacanian theory, is characteristic of recent discussions of autobiography. How can narrative, with its movement towards closure and completion, represent a subjectivity whose construction is by definition never complete? Jacqueline Rose has explored this dilemma in her 1991 study of images of Sylvia Plath.[5] Reacting to a critic's readings of a transcendent female self emerging from Plath's late poems, Rose comments that such readings depend on 'a specific, unitary conception of language as tending, like the subjectivity it embodies, towards the ultimate fulfilment of itself'.[6] In fact, as Rose points out, following psychoanalytic theory, 'there is no such thing as an ego on its own, since the ego exists, comes into being, only as difference from itself'.[7] The writing of autobiography is then a dramatization of the self's difference from itself. The last thing that we would look for in an autobiographical narrative is an emerging, unitary self. The complexity of the relationship between life-writing and a life, its engagement with conciliation and aggression, is just as marked when the life written is one's own as when it is someone else's (as in the case of *Orlando*, for example).

Many modern theories of autobiography, although acutely aware of the unconscious, tend to ignore gender. Paul Jay in 1984 offered a Freudian and Lacanian interpretation of the genre citing almost exclusively Freud's metapsychological papers, which conceptualize the subject as ungendered.[8] This

---

[3] Wayne Shumaker, *English Autobiography: Its Emergence, Materials, and Form* (Berkeley, Calif., 1954); Georges Gusdorf, 'Conditions and Limits of Autobiography', 1956, trans. James Olney, repr. in James Olney (ed.), *Autobiography: Essays Theoretical and Critical* (Princeton, NJ, 1980).

[4] Rodolphe Gasché, 'Introduction', *Modern Language Notes*, 93 (1978), 573.

[5] See Jacqueline Rose, *The Haunting of Sylvia Plath* (London, 1991).

[6] Ibid. 144.   [7] Ibid. 146.

[8] Paul Jay, *Being in the Text: Self-Representation from Wordsworth to Roland Barthes* (Ithaca, NY, 1984).

enabled Jay neatly to sidestep the question of women. Yet theories of the subject have a particular urgency for women. For Freud himself, father of the 'master-narrative' of the development of subjectivity, the construction of the female subject was enormously problematic: 'the riddle of the nature of femininity', as he remarked.[9] The path to a relatively stable normative femininity is, in Freudian terms, extremely slippery: 'she slips—along the line of a symbolic equation, one might say—from the penis to a baby.'[10] In fact, as Rachel Bowlby has pointed out, Freud's account of what the 'place'—the 'nature'—of femininity might be is so contradictory that femininity ends up as a kind of psychical accident, intent on repudiating itself.[11] In this drama of repudiation and recovery, other people, either in their actuality or in the internalized images of them in the psyche, play a crucial role—as Freud himself stressed when he placed the origins of subjectivity in the Oedipal situation. The mother and father are endlessly implicated in the relationship between the conscious and the unconscious, through the processes of introjection—whatever they might be—that accompany the subject's entry into the symbolic, and social life.[12] As Woolf herself wrote: 'If we cannot analyse these invisible presences, we know very little of the subject of the memoir; and again how futile life-writing becomes. I see myself as a fish in a stream; deflected; held in place; but cannot describe the stream' (SP, 93). 'Invisible presences' are there in every account that we give of our selves; there too, in every explanation that we try to find.

Woolf and Sackville-West each wrote more than one version of her autobiography. Woolf's autobiographical work, unpub-

---

[9] Sigmund Freud, *Standard Edition of the Complete Psychological Works*, xxii. 'Femininity', in *New Introductory Lectures on Psychoanalysis*, ed. and trans. James Strachey (24 vols.; London, 1966–74), 113. More recently, there has been a considerable amount of work on women's autobiography, for example Estelle C. Jelinek (ed.), *Women's Autobiography: Essays in Criticism* (Bloomington, Ind., 1980); Shari Benstock (ed.), *The Private Self: Theory and Practice of Women's Autobiographical Writing* (London, 1988); and Domna C. Stanton (ed.), *The Female Autograph* (New York, 1985).

[10] Sigmund Freud, *Standard Edition of the Complete Psychological Works*, xix. 'The Dissolution of the Oedipus Complex', pp. 178–9.

[11] See Rachel Bowlby, 'Still Crazy after all these Years', in Teresa Brennan (ed.), *Between Feminism and Psychoanalysis* (London, 1989), 40–59.

[12] See Freud, 'The Dissolution of the Oedipus Complex'.

lished during her lifetime, was collected and published in
1976 by Jeanne Schulkind under the title *Moments of Being*.
The volume contains five separate pieces. The first two,
'Reminiscences' and 'A Sketch of the Past', were written over
thirty years apart (1907 and 1939–40), but contain reworkings
of much of the same material. 'Reminiscences' is addressed
to Julian Bell, Vanessa Bell's first child, and is ostensibly a biography of his mother; in fact the reader is constantly aware of
Woolf's central consciousness as she tells the story of her own
and her sister's lives.[13] Both pieces ('Reminiscences' and 'A
Sketch of the Past') were shown only to a few intimates. The
last three pieces in the volume are selections Virginia Woolf
read to the Memoir Club, which was formed in March 1920.
'Old Bloomsbury' met periodically to dine, read memoirs, and
talk. It was a close-knit and intimate circle. '22 Hyde Park
Gate' was written between March 1920 and May 1921; 'Old
Bloomsbury' in late 1921 or early 1922; and 'Am I a Snob?'
around 1936.

Sackville-West's work is similarly diverse. In 1920 she wrote
an account of her life (a 'confession, autobiography, whatever
I may call it' (*PM*, 10)), culminating in a description of her
elopement with Violet Trefusis and her eventual return to her
husband. When the piece was finished, Sackville-West locked
it in a bag and hid it. It was discovered and published after her
death by her son, Nigel Nicolson, who gave the volume its
title of *Portrait of a Marriage*. In 1937, Sackville-West herself
published a very different version of her family history and her
early years: *Pepita*, a biography of her Spanish, flamenco-
dancer grandmother, and of her flamboyant and unusual
mother. But, as Alison Hennegan comments, 'what appears to
be a straightforward joint biography of her grandmother and
mother becomes the means whereby Vita explores and makes
sense for herself of those warring elements in her own past
and temperament which most exercised and perplexed her'.[14]
Her account of her matriliny is also an exploration of her own
character and her own past, and, for Alison Hennegan, 'a gift

---

[13] For detailed studies of the sisters' relationship see Jane Dunn, *A Very Close
Conspiracy: Vanessa Bell and Virginia Woolf* (London, 1990); and Mary Ann Caws,
Women of Bloomsbury: Virginia, Vanessa and Carrington (London, 1990).

[14] Alison Hennegan, 'Introduction', in *Pepita* (repr. London, 1986), p. vi.

to herself of the mother she almost had . . . an extended love-letter to the woman she wanted her mother to be'.[15] A gift, a love-letter, a fantasy. It is striking how close the terms used to discuss *Pepita* and *Orlando* seem to be.

In composing the story of 'the mother she almost had', Sackville-West was drawing on the accumulated resentment and desire of a lifetime, blending fantasy and aggression to commemorate the mother who was now irrevocably lost in death. Sackville-West thought of *Pepita* as an expression of love: 'I hope that my love of her has been implicit in all the foregoing pages of this book', she wrote at the end (p. 282). *Orlando* (1928) too was born of love, as we have seen, but of the same kind of vexed, ambivalent feeling that could not let the beloved go, and certainly wished to control whatever she had left behind. It is significant also that one of the aspects of Sackville-West's love for Woolf that was most valued by Woolf was its maternal quality: Sackville-West 'lavished' on her 'the maternal protection which, for some reason, is what I have always most wished from everyone' (*D*, iii. 52, 21 Dec. 1925).

Both *Pepita* and *Orlando* were, in their different ways, texts about the loss, and the recovery, of maternal care. Sackville-West's text is quite specifically a fantasy of resurrection:

Pepita, my grandmother,—it is difficult for me, your grandchild, to think of you as a grandmother, for you seem to me so eternally young,—come back to me. I wish I had known you in the flesh. My mother, who was only nine when you died, told me so many stories about you that she made you into a living person for me from my childhood upwards. (*P*, 33)

The recovery of Pepita is also a recovery of her mother's own story-telling: the remembering of a narrative in which mother hands down to daughter the story of the 'strange career which after many vicissitudes made you the mother of my mother' (*P*, 32). It is motherhood itself, maternal genealogy, which is being handed down through the generations. As we shall see, the gift of maternity was not one that was always either welcome or uncontested.

The image of the mother has a specific intensity for women.

---

[15] Alison Hennegan, 'Introduction', in *Pepita* (repr. London, 1986), p. viii.

It is largely in dialogue with her mother's (always the prototype for any female caretaker of children) version of womanhood that a girl learns her femininity. Mothers are of course important to their little boys as well, but the importance is different: little boys will not become women. Nancy Chodorow and Dorothy Dinnerstein suggest some of the effects that this difference has. For a boy, the path to heterosexuality is 'relatively continuous'.[16] A heterosexual man is destined to form sexual relationships with people of the same gender as the person who originally satisfied his emotional needs. This means that he can repress his attachment to his mother and feel fairly confident of replacing it. Repression also aids his developing masculinity. In terms of his gender, it is not desirable that he identify with a feminine subject position. As he grows up, he becomes more and more different from his mother.

For a girl, however, each stage of female sexual development confirms her closeness to her mother, as her body changes into a woman's. 'A girl retains her preoedipal tie to her mother (an intense tie involved with issues of primary identification, primary love, dependence, and separation) and builds oedipal attachments to both her mother and her father upon it'.[17] As Freud had already suggested, the relationship with the mother continues to be crucial, and to demand endless negotiation, for the daughter in a way that is not symmetrical with the son's less ambiguous relationship to the mother. For the girl, the promise of a 'perfect' identification —of growing up actually to *be* the mother—provokes intense anxiety, as well as a deep pleasure. The difficulty of the achievement of a functional self causes acute, and often contradictory, reactions.

We would expect, then, to find the mother playing a pivotal role in women's autobiography, concerned as it is with issues of female development and the construction of the self. This is indeed the case. Many women autobiographers show themselves to be preoccupied, sometimes to the point of obsession,

---

[16] Nancy Chodorow, *The Reproduction of Mothering: Psychoanalysis and the Sociology of Gender* (Berkeley, Calif., 1978), 192; and see also Dorothy Dinnerstein, *The Rocking of the Cradle and the Ruling of the World* (London, 1978).

[17] Chodorow, *The Reproduction of Mothering*, 192–3.

with their mothers. Sackville-West writes in the grip of a fascinated ambivalence:

No photograph or portrait ever showed her as she was, for no photograph or portrait could indicate the changes of her expression or the extraordinary sweetness of her smile. If ever the phrase 'turn one's heart to water' meant anything, it meant when my mother looked at you and smiled. (*P*, 161)

Virginia Woolf, whose mother died when Woolf was thirteen, admits a similar force:

Until I was in the forties . . . the presence of my mother obsessed me. I could hear her voice, see her, imagine what she would do or say as I went about my day's doings. (SP, 93)

Sackville-West's lover, Violet Trefusis, closes her autobiography with:

In losing my mother, I lost everything. She was my youth. I was her old age.
  What has happened to me since is but a postscriptum. It really doesn't count.[18]

None of these women show the same kind of passionate tenderness for any other figure in their lives. There is violence and contempt—often indifference—in Sackville-West's feeling for Trefusis, as it is described in *Portrait of a Marriage*, and none of the extraordinary idealization found in the picture of Lady Sackville quoted above. Virginia Woolf was not obsessed, as she was with her mother, with her father or sister after their deaths; Violet Trefusis describes her aged mother's death-bed in terms of romantic tragedy, but says almost nothing about her husband's, who died of tuberculosis at the age of twenty-nine. It seems that for these women, the relationship with the mother is the site of a peculiar passion, a peculiar intensity, a peculiar fear. For the woman writing herself, and the process of her individuation, the image of the mother—the object of her primary identification—takes on a unique and ambivalent importance.

  The intensity of the mother–daughter relationship was interpreted by some women in the 1920s as a quasi-sexual feel-

---

[18] Violet Trefusis, *Don't Look Round* (London, 1952), 232.

ing. Perhaps, after Havelock Ellis and Freud, sexual terms were the only ones in which such powerful emotions could be expressed in a period which, by the time Woolf and the others were writing autobiography, was heavily invested in the promotion of heterosexual sex. Marie Stopes's *Married Love* (1918) was typical in its suggestion that coital sex between men and women was crucial not only to physical, but also to spiritual health.[19] Vera Brittain, in her biography of her friend Winifred Holtby, comments that many of their acquaintances assumed they were sexually involved because of the depth and stability of their intimacy.[20] Only the insistence of genital pleasure, it was thought, could explain such a commitment.

Of course the suggestion of sexuality in connection with a daughter's love was a much more delicate proposition. Composer and writer Ethel Smyth, writing to Virginia Woolf early in their friendship, explains:

I was telling my brother (a great pal who adored my dead sister) that the most violent feeling I am conscious of is . . . for my mother. She died 38 years ago & I never can think of her without a stab of real passion; amusement, tenderness, pity, admiration are in it & pain that I cant tell her how I love her (but I think she knows) Now you can imagine how much sexual feeling has to do with such an emotion for one's mother!![21]

As this letter shows, the birth of a new intimacy (in this case, with Virginia Woolf) provokes a reiteration of maternal images, a retelling of the daughter's story. Smyth takes her feeling for her mother as the touchstone for subsequent passions, although the uniqueness of that original relation, sexual only in the broadest sense of the word, is signalled by the half-flippant, half-scandalized final sentence of the passage cited, with the self-consciousness of its double exclamation mark. Compare Sackville-West's use of quotation marks in the passage already cited: 'if ever the phrase "turn one's heart to water" meant anything'. The enormity of her feelings for her

[19] Marie Stopes, *Married Love: A New Contribution to the Solution of Sex Difficulties* (London, 1918).

[20] Vera Brittain, *Testament of Friendship: The Story of Winifred Holtby* (London, 1980), 117–18.

[21] Smyth to Woolf, 2 May 1930 (Berg Collection, New York Public Library).

mother is qualified by her suggestion that they are some-how only hypothetical: '*if*' it meant anything. The obsessive passion for the mother can be acknowledged only obliquely and defensively, as though it were the story or the words of another.

Sackville-West, Woolf, Trefusis, and Smyth were all women who acknowledged and acted on lesbian desires. Their feelings for each other seem often to provide the narrative context within which the conjunction of filial and lesbian love can be explored. As they got to know one another, and exchanged narratives of their histories, of their past and present feelings and identities, tales and images of their mothers became more and more insistent, appearing to provide a para-digm upon which their relationships with each other were built.

Smyth's love for Woolf drew her into narrative.

One of the deepest attachments of my life (for Lady Ponsonby) began by the way she handled the sealing-wax & red ink on her writing table . . . to meet you and find that I care as much about you, am as incapable of imagining the world without you as I was in 1892 when I first met Lady P—a woman old enough to be my mother & felt in one hour that I loved her . . . then & for ever (as the event proved) . . . well, that to me is a shatteringly conclusive proof that love, for me, lies in the region of one's imagination.[22]

Part of the process of Smyth's love for Woolf is the constant retelling of her own story, comparing past and present feelings. Woolf encouraged her, demanding letters and diar-ies—'I evolve you and your life and your friends and your whole tremendous intricacy backwards, from letters and diar-ies' (*L*, iv. 214, 15 Sept. 1930). Woolf even, uncharacteristically, responded in kind: 'I can assure you that I dont romanticise quite so freely about myself as a rule—It was only that you pressed some nerve, and then up started in profusion the usual chaos of pictures of myself' (*L*, iv. 188, 16 July 1930).

As well as indulging in conversational autobiography with Smyth, Woolf sent her, in 1932, a copy of an old memoir she had written for the Memoir Club in the early 1920s, and

[22] Smyth to Woolf, 2 May 1930 (Berg Collection, New York Public Library).

in April 1939 she began to write 'A Sketch of the Past'.[23] A month after her last addition to the 'Sketch', Woolf was relieved and happy to find that Smyth too was writing yet another autobiographical volume. Woolf felt that their own relationship, and perhaps her own recent experiment in auto-biography, was at least partly responsible for Smyth's enthusi-asm: 'I'm awfully proud—thats not the right phrase—that you've started again on the autobiography, partly owing to me. I was thinking the other night that there's never been a womans autobiography' (L, vi. 453, 24 Dec. 1940). Writing autobiography was a mutual endeavour, to which each in-spired and encouraged the other. In the last decade of her life, after the friendship with Sackville-West had faded, Woolf once again found the activity of writing central to her relation-ship with a woman.

Where Woolf and Smyth exchanged autobiographies in pursuit of intimacy, as a way of exploring each other's differ-ence, for Virginia Woolf and Vanessa Bell (as for most siblings) autobiography was, as well as an acknowledgement of difference, also an exposure of mutuality. Woolf's 'Reminis-cences', while it has been regarded as a piece of autobio-graphy (and edited as such), is actually cast as a biography of Vanessa Bell. Autobiography and the biography of a sister's early life, in the case of these women who had already shared so much in childhood, were generically almost indistinguish-able. Woolf conceived To the Lighthouse as autobiographical fiction. On 14 May 1925, she wrote in her diary:

This is going to be fairly short: to have father's character done complete in it; & mothers; & St Ives; & childhood; & all the usual things I try to put in—life, death & c. But the centre is father's character, sitting in a boat, reciting We perished, each alone, while he crushes a dying mackerel. (D, iii. 18)

Vanessa Bell's response is famous:

I suppose I'm the only person in the world who can have those feelings, at any rate to such an extent . . . it seemed to me that in the

[23] Ethel Smyth was an inveterate autobiographer. As well as several collections of autobiographical essays, she published four volumes of serial autobiography: *Impressions that Remained*, 2 vols. (London, 1919); *As Time Went On* (London, 1936); and *What Happened Next* (London, 1940).

first part of the book you have given a portrait of mother which is more like her to me than anything I could ever have conceived of as possible. It is almost painful to have her so raised from the dead. You have made one feel the extraordinary beauty of her character, which must be the most difficult thing in the world to do. It was like meeting her again with oneself grown up and on equal terms and it seems to me the most extraordinary feat of creation.[24]

Bell found in Woolf's novel the world of her own putative autobiography. Ethel Smyth commented on *To the Lighthouse*: 'how could one explain how much it meant to me i.e. what is behind one of the best bits of literature you ever pulled off—the dedication of that book to yr. sister.'[25] In fact Smyth's memory was playing her false. It was *Night and Day* (1919) that was dedicated to Vanessa Bell. *To the Lighthouse* has no dedication. But Smyth's alertness picked up on the deep resonance of *To the Lighthouse* in the sisters' feelings for each other. She knew from experience the extraordinary intimacy of print.

To the Lighthouse was not the only occasion on which Woolf used biographical narratives to repair someone else's loss. Sackville-West agreed with Nicolson when he suggested that *Orlando* was 'really a unique consolation' (Nicolson to Sackville-West, 13 Oct. 1928) for the loss of Knole when Sackville-West's father died, and the estate passed to a cousin. But it was to Vanessa Bell that Woolf gave the gift not only of a resurrected mother, but of a resurrected lover also. Bell wrote to Woolf after reading Woolf's biography of Bell's old lover, Roger Fry: 'since Julian died I havent been able to think of Roger—now you have brought him back to me—Although I cannot help crying I cant thank you enough.'[26] The intensity of her involvement was so acute that she could hardly write. She had been given back both the past and the present.

Such transactions with the past have been seen as vital to women's existence. As Adrienne Rich says, 're-vision—the act of looking back, of seeing with fresh eyes, of entering an old text from a new critical direction—is for women more than a

---

[24] Vanessa Bell to Virginia Woolf, 11 May 1927, repr. in an appendix to *L*, iii. 572. [25] Smyth to Woolf, 2 May 1930 (Berg).
[26] Bell to Woolf, 13 Mar. 1940 (Berg).

chapter in cultural history: it is an act of survival.'[27] Women
have turned to autobiography with a sense of urgency. Patricia
Spacks points out, and we shall see this confirmed in the case
of Vita Sackville-West, that the autobiographical text can be
a place not only of re-vision, but of self-justification, myth-
making, fantasy.[28] 'What is striking in the work of virtually
all women writing about themselves, in the present and in the
past, is the degree to which writing is itself a solution to their
most pressing problems.'[29] A pessimistic reading of this
conclusion might see in it an indication of the extreme
limitation of women's sphere of action: all they can do
when things go wrong is to write them down. But another,
more complex—and perhaps even more pessimistic—reading
would see that it is the individual's past itself which is the
problem, even the obsession. It is her identity, as constituted
by her history, which needs continual reassessment and
renegotiation.

Sackville-West's *Pepita* is a striking example of the kind of
myth-making, solution-seeking, that Spacks describes. Sackville-
West interpreted conflict in her own nature as a struggle
between 'masculine' and 'feminine', between English and
Spanish. In *Pepita* she sought to understand herself through
her portraits of her grandmother and mother. But Ethel
Smyth, who knew Lady Sackville, was critical of parts of the
book. 'I suppose it is a fault that she so obviously suppresses
truth in Part II—Her mother was frankly an evil woman.'[30]
Woolf agreed. 'My only criticism, a personal deficiency I
expect, is that I cannot altogether sympathise with your
mother. There's something antagonistic in her. But no doubt
my relations with her queer the pitch' (Woolf to Sackville-
West, *L*, vi. 175, 1 Oct. 1937). (Lady Sackville had not been
slow to take against Woolf, accusing her of 'stealing' Sackville-
West.) Smyth continued:

What a portrait V. has unconsciously drawn of herself—loving,
amoral, able to endure this tragic & dreadful, this cheap detestable

---

[27] Adrienne Rich, 'When We Dead Awaken: Writing as Re-Vision', in *On Lies,
Secrets and Silences: Selected Prose 1966–1978* (New York, 1979), 35.
[28] Patricia Meyer Spacks, 'Reflecting Women', *Yale Review*, 63 (1973), 26–42.
[29] Ibid. 34.   [30] Smyth to Woolf, 5 Nov. 1937 (Berg).

evil woman & to love her, remembering how the gracious qualities draped her in her youth & hid the rest. I think the weak part of the book is this tampering with the truth as regards her mother.[31]

Again biography and autobiography occupy the same narrative space: Smyth read *Pepita* more as Sackville-West's story than her mother's. This produces odd contradictions in her response. Sackville-West's ability to be generous to her mother at once enhances the book, by indicating the beauty of her own character; and detracts from it, in its distortion of what Smyth thinks of as the 'truth'. This is of course the central contradiction, the dilemma of autobiographical writing, poised on the interface between inner and outer worlds and throwing into question the status of 'truth' as such. For if Sackville-West did indeed see her mother in this way, in what sense can the portrait be seen as a 'tampering with the truth'? These are real questions in relationships as well as in texts.

Sackville-West herself writes a different 'truth' in *Portrait of a Marriage*:

I liked [Dada] a great deal better than Mother, of whose quick temper I was frightened. I don't even remember thinking her pretty, which she must have been—lovely, even. My impression of her was that I couldn't be rough when she was there, or naughty, and so it was really a great relief when she went away. (p. 11)

Pepita, written after Lady Sackville's death, and written for publication where the other text was not, is much more divided in its acknowledgement of negative feelings.

She was tiresome, of course, and wayward, and capricious, and thoroughly spoilt; but her charm and real inward gaiety enabled her to carry it all off. One forgave her everything when one heard her laugh and saw how frankly she was enjoying herself. As a child can be maddening at one moment and irresistible the next, so could my mother be maddening and irresistible by turns. (p. 201)

In fact, there were long periods—on one occasion, a couple of years—when Sackville-West and her mother simply severed all relations, and both believed their relationship to be finished, other than in name. True, they always re-established contact

---

[31] Smyth to Woolf, 5 Nov. 1937 (Berg).

in the end; but the conflicts between them were far more destructive than the above passage suggests.

Sackville-West's hypothetical reversal of their roles (imagining her mother as a difficult child) was one of the ways in which she sought to control the destructive tendencies of their relationship. She mythologized her mother into a determined and extravagantly beautiful child, and in the process arrogated the maternal role to herself. This dispute over who could claim the role of mother was a crucial one in their relationship, as we shall see. As in the relations of Woolf and Smyth, and Woolf and Bell, autobiographical writing for Sackville-West revolved around the axis of mothering and being mothered. The Trefusis she describes in her unpublished autobiographical manuscript (*Portrait of a Marriage*) is as wilful and as childish, and as in need of protection, as the mother she made for herself in *Pepita*.

Autobiography is inextricably bound up with fantasy. This much is clear from Sackville-West's metaphorical shifting of the maternal role between her mother and herself. (Whether or not this occurred in actuality, what is significant here is the way in which the relationship between Lady Sackville and the 'maddening child' is introduced as speculation, as analogy, rather than as fact.) But autobiography's seductiveness derives as much from the openness of its form, as from the opportunities it offers for fantastic self-projection and denial. As one critic has put it:

Form is really a multiplicity of formal options in the simplest autobiography: options of selection and exclusion, interpretive refocus or rearrangement, conflations of historical and expository arrangement, development rhythms in narrative and situational rhythms in the autobiographer's sense of movement towards his end [*sic*].[32]

The 'his' is unfortunate, since 'options' are particularly congenial, in fact, to women, the multidimensionality of whose social roles demands a similar flexibility in the form they choose to represent themselves.[33] Woolf was juggling

[32] Francis R. Hart, 'Notes for an Anatomy of Modern Autobiography', *New Literary History*, 1 (1970), 502.

[33] See Jelinek, *Women's Autobiography*, 17; and Elizabeth W. Bruss, *Autobiographical Acts: The Changing Situation of a Literary Genre* (Baltimore, Md., 1976), 164, for discussions of this issue.

identities as writer, wife, lesbian, and sister; Sackville-West was writer, daughter, lesbian, and wife. Negotiating the shifts between these roles could at times seem impossible. Sackville-West describes in *Portrait of a Marriage* how, in spite of a fierce desire to be 'uninterruptedly together' (p. 131), she could not bear to have Trefusis to stay in her conjugal home (Harold Nicolson, significantly, was prepared to condone it).

She, feeling the place to be an enemy, would turn yet more fierce, yet more restless, while I stood bewildered and uncertain between the personification of my two lives. When I passed from one to the other, keeping them separate and apart, I could just keep the thing within my control; but when they met, coincided, and were simultaneous, I found them impossible to reconcile. (*PM*, 131)

Writing could hold her separate lives in suspension, could ponder the links between them, and their incompatibilities, without provoking a direct confrontation between them. It was writing and solitude that kept Sackville-West sane, that allowed her to retreat and remake what she often referred to in poems as the 'patchwork' of her life.[34] I shall explore this further in the next chapter.

Autobiography, as well as holding various fantastic and formal options in play, could have a studied informality about it which meant that it could be picked up and put down at will by the writer. In this way, writing could become a playful, everyday activity. Virginia Woolf opens 'A Sketch of the Past' with:

There are several difficulties. In the first place, the enormous number of things I can remember; in the second, the number of different ways in which memoirs can be written. As a great memoir reader, I know many different ways. But if I begin to go through them and to analyse them and their merits and faults, the mornings —I cannot take more than two or three at most—will be gone. So without stopping to choose my way, in the sure and certain knowledge that it will find itself— or if not it will not matter—I begin: the first memory. (p. 74)

---

[34] See, for instance, the 'diary poem' of 16 May 1933, quoted in Victoria Glendinning, *Vita: The Life of V. Sackville-West* (New York, 1983), 280.

Woolf simply plunges in, without planning her work; and if a form does not emerge, 'it will not matter'. For her, autobiography begins with her own beginning—the first memory, the foundation of consciousness and of the subjective past (I will discuss the implications of this more fully in Chapter 5). Woolf, unlike most autobiographers, draws attention to previous autobiographical texts; but ironically, their variety means that she does not have to take them into account. There are so many different ways of writing memoirs that adding one more will scarcely matter.

Woolf sees her autobiography as an interruption, taking time off from writing her biography of Roger Fry. This bears out Paul de Man's comment on the problem of an aesthetics of autobiography: 'compared to tragedy, or epic, or lyric poetry, autobiography always looks slightly disreputable and self-indulgent in a way that may be symptomatic of its incompatibility with the monumental dignity of aesthetic values.'[35] Autobiography can be, in the phrase used by Woolf of *Orlando*, a 'writers holiday' (*D*, iii. 177, 18 Mar. 1928). For women, less used than men to professional routines, it is peculiarly undaunting. As Julia Swindells says, working women's autobiographies are not read because 'the experience of working women, our lives, our writing, remains categorised in culture as amateur'.[36] Perhaps for women wanting to write their life stories that stigma of the amateur was a relief rather than an indignity.

The formal irregularity of autobiography (it can include reverie, cited diary entries, cited published writings, narrative, dialogue) allows it to draw attention to the dispersed conditions under which it was written. St Theresa of Avila, the subject of one of Sackville-West's own biographies, complains in her autobiography of interruptions: 'I can never settle down to what I write but have to do a little at a time.'[37] St Thérèse of Lisieux, another of Sackville-West's subjects, is plagued by visiting nuns in the convent where she lives and

---

[35] Paul de Man, 'Autobiography as De-Facement', *Modern Language Notes*, 94 (1979), 919.

[36] Julia Swindells, *Victorian Writing and Working Women* (Cambridge, 1985), 204.

[37] *The Life of St. Teresa of Avila*, 1562–5, trans. E. Allison Peers (London, 1979), 86.

writes: 'I don't know if I have been able to write ten lines with-out being disturbed.'[38] Virginia Woolf constantly comes back to 'A Sketch of the Past', and the episodic nature of the writing gives the text a developmental rhythm of its own. 'I write the date, because I think that I have discovered a pos-sible form for these notes. That is, to make them include the present—at least enough of the present to serve as platform to stand upon' (SP, 86). The dating of the passage serves as commemoration and stresses the interrupted nature of the piece so that the narratives of the past and of the present unfold simultaneously. Sackville-West does the same thing in her text published as *Portrait of a Marriage*: 'I start writing, having spent no consideration upon this task. Shall I ever complete it? and under what circumstances?, begun as it is, in the margin between a wood and a ripe cornfield, with the faint shadows of grasses and ears of corn falling across my page' (pp. 9–10). Sackville-West's tale of passion and betrayal is situated in a rural present which offers the illusion of emotion recollected in tranquillity. But the illusion—the fiction—breaks down again and again as the emotions of the past metamorphose into those of the present: 'I now hate [Denys Trefusis, Violet's husband] more than I have ever hated anyone in this life, or am likely to; and there is no injury I would not do him with the utmost pleasure' (*PM*, 109). In Woolf's narrative, memory depends on a stable peace in the present: 'the past only comes back when the present runs so smoothly that it is like the sliding surface of a deep river' (SP, 114). For Sackville-West, on the other hand, memory and autobiography are an alibi for the mapping of present feelings and their aetiology in the past. The text that became *Portrait of a Marriage* was written in an attempt at self-location, and at retrenchment, a calling of energies to account: 'I would not give it *her*—perilous touchstone!, who even in these first score of lines should teach me where truth lies. I *do* know where it lies, but have no strength to grasp it; here am I already in the middle of my infirmities' (p. 9). Her writing was an effort to negotiate the unstable boundary between truth and fantasy;

---

[38] *Story of a Soul: The Autobiography of St. Thérèse of Lisieux*, trans. John Clarke, 2nd edn. (Washington, DC, 1976), 228.

an attempt to understand and confirm the self in relationship, and the self after loss.

The question of who could and could not see this 'truth' that was proving so elusive, was central to Sackville-West's autobiographical project as a whole. The relation of the truth–fantasy axis to the published/unpublished status of the manuscripts is crucial, as Jacqueline Rose has so convincingly demonstrated in the context of Sylvia Plath's work.[39] In Sackville-West's case, she herself engineered the division between the 'truth' of her lesbianism (a story that was locked away as soon as it had been written), and the 'fantasy' of her bewitching mother (written to be published in *Pepita*). A feeling of self-division was central to Sackville-West's sense of who she was: English and Spanish, masculine and feminine, tame and wild. Across those divisions she came and went, and to them, in her autobiographies, she added the complication of the secret confession, crossing the boundaries between the public and the private in a way that is structural to many accounts of lesbian and gay identity.[40] For Sackville-West's lesbianism was exactly the 'open secret' of which Eve Kosofsky Sedgwick and others speak.[41] Her affair with Violet Trefusis had been the cause of widespread scandal; and yet Sackville-West persisted in concealing the evidence of it—her own 'confession'—as if it would otherwise be 'found out'. Yet the question of her relationship with her mother, in a way more difficult and certainly of greater duration, is posed with some courage in *Pepita*, despite its cavils and its defences. Culturally, of course, rows with one's mother are more acceptable than rows with one's lesbian lover; and Sackville-West's decision to make public the one story rather than the other bears out Eve Kosofsky Sedgwick's point about the centrality of the concept of the closet to Western understandings of sexuality and identity.[42] Even though the 'truth' of Sackville-West's lesbianism was widely known, it could only be written as a 'secret'; and, as we shall see in the next chapter, she did not use the word 'lesbian' in print until 1961.

[39] J. Rose, *Sylvia Plath*, 65–105.
[40] See, e.g. Eve Kosofsky Sedgwick, *The Epistemology of the Closet* (Hemel Hempstead, 1991).
[41] See D. A. Miller, *The Novel and the Police* (Berkeley, Calif., 1988).
[42] Sedgwick, *Epistemology of the Closet*, 67–90.

Sackville-West raises the question of access at the opening of *Portrait of a Marriage*:

Having written it down I shall be able to trust no one to read it; there is only one person in whom I have such utter confidence that I would give every line of this confession into his hands, knowing that after wading through this morass—for it is a morass, my life, a bog, a swamp, a deceitful country, with one bright patch in the middle, the patch that is unalterably his—I know that after wading through it all he would emerge holding his estimate of me steadfast. (p. 9)

We do not know whether or not Sackville-West did actually show the piece to Harold Nicolson. Nigel Nicolson assumes that she showed it to no one (*PM*, 3), but also points out that, when she knew she was terminally ill, she did not destroy it, aware that he would find it after her death. He finally came across it in a locked bag in the corner of her little turret room, and, having no key, had to cut the leather round the lock to open it (*PM*, 1). Despite the secrecy which was her 'passion' (*PM*, 18), Sackville-West envisaged readers of her manuscript (*PM*, 107), and saw it as a scientific document that would promote understanding of homosexuality in years to come (*PM*, 107–8).

When *Portrait of a Marriage* was finally published, it was carefully edited. Nigel Nicolson, deeply attached to the memory of his father, broke up Sackville-West's text with at least as much again of his own interpretation of his mother's history. His justification for this was the pursuit of justice: 'to present the autobiography unexplained and without its sequel would do my parents less than justice, for it was written in the eighth year of a marriage which lasted forty-nine' (p. 4). After the crisis described by Sackville-West, Nicolson points out, his parents' marriage developed and stabilized into a union of the greatest depth and intimacy. He had questions of loyalty to think about. 'My parents' love for each other survived all further threats to it, and made out of a non-marriage a marriage which succeeded beyond their dreams' (p. 5).

However, the text that Nicolson published, in the form in which he published it, is differently accented from the one that Sackville-West wrote. He guides the reader's attention away from Sackville-West's affair with Trefusis, and on to her marriage, which, in her own text, seems simply a prelude to the climactic involvement with Trefusis. *Portrait of a Marriage* might equally have been titled *Portrait of Two Women*, and it appears that this was how Sackville-West thought of the manuscript:

I am not writing this for fun, but for several reasons which I will explain. (1) As I started by saying, because I want to tell the *entire* truth. (2) Because I know of no truthful record of such a connection—one that is written, I mean, with no desire to appeal to a vicious taste in any possible readers; and (3) because I hold the conviction that as centuries go on . . . the psychology of people like myself will be a matter of interest. (*PM*, 107)

Again the question of the relationship of 'truth' to fantasy is raised: the 'entire truth' is offered this time as the opposite of fantasy, assumed actually to *prevent* 'viciousness' (an interesting choice of word, given the 'vice' about which the manuscript speaks) in its readers. Nigel Nicolson's editing is in line with his mother's intentions. He sought to put the record straight, to emphasize not the 'vicious' but the moral, decent side of the story, its apparently happy ending.

Woolf's autobiographical work is less clearly divided. The boundary that she negotiates is less obviously that of public and private in relation to the manuscript itself (none of her autobiographical essays were written for publication, although some, as we saw, were delivered as lectures). Rather, the transition with which she is primarily concerned is that from the private world of the child (or childish role) to the public world of the mother (or maternal role). The moment Woolf singles out as the pivot of her emotional history is the death of her mother when Woolf was only thirteen. It was this event which precipitated Woolf from the fantasy world of childish pleasure into the adult world where responsibilities must be shouldered, and there is no longer a protective maternal presence. Julia Stephen, Woolf's mother, before her death guarantees a spatial order that allows irresponsibility and merriment. Her mother, Julia Stephen, is the axis around which the domestic wheel revolves:

And of course she was central. I suspect the word 'central' gets closest to the general feeling I had of living so completely in her atmosphere that one never got far enough away from her to see her as a person. . . . She was the whole thing; Talland House was full of her; Hyde Park Gate was full of her. (SP, 96)

Julia Stephen is not experienced as a person. She is rather the principle of organization and saturation of the family's practical and emotional life. After her death, there is no more irresponsibility: 'the shrouded, cautious, dulled life took the place of all the chatter and laughter of the summer. There were no more parties; no more young men and women laughing' (SP, 110). Rather, Vanessa and Virginia are bound into the domestic structure as the maternal function, as part of their inheritance of femininity. Their mother leaves them 'a legacy of dependence on [their father's] side which became a terrible imposition after her death' (SP, 133). So their lives after her death sustain the illusion of a maternal presence, but one that they must now supply, forfeiting their identities as daughters. Woolf's mother dead is not absent: 'she was one of the invisible presences who after all play so important a part in every life' (SP, 93). But the radical discontinuity of family life that is brought about by her death and masked by a series of figures—Stella, Vanessa—who try to take her place, is sharply expressed in an image of the splitting of domestic space. 'The division in our life was curious. Downstairs there was pure convention: upstairs pure intellect. But there was no connection between them' (SP, 158). Julia Stephen's death removes the centre from the family; her absence causes it to collapse into disconnection and disorder. That rupture was experienced most vividly in Woolf's serious breakdown in response to her mother's death.

It is against the overpowering image of the mother, and of her body, that Woolf and Sackville-West finally find themselves establishing their femininity, at least textually. The implications of this are various. In Woolf's case, her mother's and her sister Stella's early deaths tend always to draw femininity back into the past; tend to establish it as something that is past. The enterprise of autobiography then becomes the recovery of that femininity so prized by Woolf, and apparently so out of her reach: (Sackville-West is 'what I have never been, a real woman' (D, iii. 52, 21 Dec. 1925)). Julia Stephen was for

Woolf an image of the perfect woman, of supreme beauty and femininity. In writing her mother's story and her own, in autobiography—biography, Woolf sought somehow to fuse the two, to reclaim her mother's image as a part of her own fantasy world and the stable ground of her own identity and identifications. But that recovery is rendered impossible by the mother's own past, inaccessible to her daughter, and discountenancing her activity of repossession. Always haunting the daughter's aspirations to her mother's sex and sexuality is the knowledge of a sexual union that produced her, that she can never hope to grasp: that establishes her mother's sexuality in excess of her own. Femininity, for Woolf, was inaccessible, both because her mother, who seemed to guard its secret (in her extraordinary beauty, for example), was dead; but also because her womanliness seemed so far beyond anything Woolf herself could hope to achieve.

This pitting of her mother's sexuality against her own is obvious in an unpublished autobiographical fragment.

So the bedroom, the bedroom on the first floor with the double bed was the sexual centre . . It was not a large room; the bedroom, looking onto the street; but how soaked its walls must be, if walls take pictures & hoard up what passes; for there in that bed we four children were begotten; there we were born; & there first mother died, & then father died, with a picture of mother hanging in front of him.[43]

The union of Woolf's parents is seamless. It progresses effortlessly through sexual congress, to childbirth, to a double death. Maternal sexuality is central to the story of reproduction that the room has to tell, and despite the fact that they were born there, the children have no place in this room. Leslie Stephen dies facing a picture of his wife, her image mirroring and complementing his, so that their marriage is a completed narrative, the story of a double death. By contrast Woolf's own adolescent room is perceived as riven, conflicted:

Which should I describe first—the living side or the sleeping side? They could be described separately yet they were always running

[43] Virginia Woolf, unpublished autobiographical fragment, 'The tea table was the centre of Victorian family life', probably written Oct. 1940 (Berg). There are no page numbers in the manuscript and all further quotations in this paragraph are from this text.

together. And how they fought each other: how often I was in rage & in ecstasy; & torn between all the different forces that entered that room, whether one calls them the living side or the sleeping side.

For her the bed—associated only with sleep—is out of harmony with the rest of the room, the intellectual side, where she reads and writes; and the only mirror in the room, which might have confirmed her identity, is a destabilizing intrusion: 'to encourage my vanity—for I dressed badly— George gave me the *swinging* glass I still have' (*my emphasis*). George's gift is peculiarly disturbing, for George himself, as we learn in another autobiographical piece, was in the habit of entering Virginia's room for sexual purposes—George, not her full brother, but her mother's son.[44] His mirror reminds Woolf that what sexual experience she does have is incestuous and confuses, rather than clarifies, her sexual identity and her role in the family. Woolf cannot find a centre for herself and her sexuality, and always mocking her attempts is the image of the true sexual centre of the house, the double bedroom where her mother and father reflect each other even in death.

The bedroom and maternal sexuality are important symbols also in the vexed relationship between Sackville-West and her mother. One of the most serious of their many crises arose over a locked door. It occurred at the birth of Sackville-West's elder son, Ben, in 1914. Lady Sackville's account of the episode in her diary runs as follows (Olive is Olive Rubens, Lord Sackville's mistress, at that time living with her husband at Knole).

At 3 ocl. in the night I sat outside poor Vita's room, in the Ball Room side; she was in the first pains till 4.30 . . . Olive and I were in the Ball Room at 4.45 and we heard him cry & we met Harold who was running & shouted: Mikki 3! He asked Olive to be extra godmother; I asked him if since last night (and I asked again tonight) if Vita had sent me any messages; I asked the same of Dr. S. and of the nice nurse Mrs. Evans but they had to admit that altho she had thought of Olive as extra godmother, she had never expressed any wish to see me, or asked for me. It is quite heartbreaking to me to realise all this.[45]

---

[44] See '22 Hyde Park Gate', in *Moments of Being*, 180.
[45] Diary of Lady Sackville, 6 Aug. 1914 (Lilly Library, Bloomington, Ind.).

The image of Sackville-West's mother locked out of the room in which Sackville-West's own transformation into a mother is occurring, echoes the image in Woolf's essay of a dispute between herself and her mother over whose room is the true 'sexual centre'. From now on Sackville-West too will be a mother, and a paranoid fear of substitution begins to affect Lady Sackville with peculiar force. She absents herself from Knole the day after Ben's birth, unable to see her own identity as mother doubled, and further threatened by the idea that Sackville-West in the pain of childbirth denied her own mother and acknowledged her false mother, her father's mistress who was already usurping Lady Sackville's role as chatelaine of Knole.

Lady Sackville's response (although we must deduce this from other letters—her own diary is abruptly silent at the end of August 1914 until July 1915) is to try to erase Sackville-West's motherhood by naming Sackville-West's son. Nicolson and Sackville-West had chosen the name Benedict; Lady Sackville favoured Lionel. Rosamund Grosvenor, Sackville-West's childhood friend, wrote to her from Knole on 26 September 1914 that Lady Sackville would not relent at all. She was trying to re-establish herself as sole mother. 'She says "If she prefers the name Benedict to her mother's love she is welcome to it." The awful thing is that she should be able to make it turn for ever upon one word, so to speak.'[46] Sackville-West felt herself undermined as a parent, denied her identity:

I have not refused this to you out of any petulant egoism, but out of a real mothers longing to call her own baby what pleases her. You say this is the only favour you have asked, but I answer that he is the only thing in life which is absolutely mine—mine through the pangs of hell—& that it is more than bitter for me to be called ungrateful because I cling to the name I have chosen for him. Why you yourself say that you had called me Vita before I was born so you can't pretend now not to realise how much the chosen name of one's little baby means.[47]

In her anxiety, Sackville-West appeals to exactly the fact that is causing all the trouble: that she and Lady Sackville must now

[46] Rosamund Grosvenor to Vita Sackville-West, n.d. (Lilly).
[47] Vita Sackville-West to Lady Sackville, n.d. (Lilly).

share the privileged maternal position. But somehow there seems to be not quite enough maternity to go round.

So Sackville-West and her mother, repeatedly in conflict, battle over femininity: who has it, and who has got it right. Behind that obsession with the mother in women's auto-biographical writing, which we noted originally, is a lengthy history of gender formation. The attempted resurrection of maternal figures in autobiography represents a woman's desire to claim her own sex, to possess and remodel the original maternal femininity against which she continually fights for self-definition.

For Sackville-West, the development of her gender is a process of exchange between herself and her mother: her identity as a woman is grounded in their struggle to control each other's lives. Under pressure—Ben's birth, for example —exchange explodes into war. Reciprocity is disputed as each woman accuses the other of taking more than she is entitled to, of seeking to deprive the other of a vital component in her gender: the right to name children, for example, or the possession of jewels (Lady Sackville was convinced that Sackville-West had stolen her emeralds).[48] The dark side of Sackville-West's and Woolf's elegiac autobiography—mourning the loss of the mother's femininity after her death—is a vindictive perception by Lady Sackville at least of Sackville-West's femininity as something that has been taken from Lady Sackville by force, and which she tries to defend even to the point of denying the maternal bond (Lady Sackville threatens to sever relations with her daughter). The control over the images of their mothers which both Sackville-West and Woolf achieve by representing their mothers in their own texts, is the central skirmish in a war whose battles can be read everywhere in Sackville-West's life, and whose griefs can be seen tragically inscribed throughout Woolf's.

[48] See Lady Sackville's notes in her diary for the week of 14 May 1928 (Lilly).

CHAPTER 4

'A Private Matter':
V. Sackville-West's Later Novels

THE years following the end of Sackville-West's relationship with Trefusis were a time of adjustment and consolidation. Having caused great scandal by her elopement, Sackville-West returned to Nicolson and, with him, devoted much energy to the stemming of the publicity she had created. Like her autobiographical writing, her life would now be a continual negotiation of the relationship between pleasure, privacy, and openness. This chapter will explore the way this nexus is represented in some of her later, more popular novels.

The following quotation from *All Passion Spent* (1931) suggests the direction in which her life was moving. 'Pleasure to her was entirely a private matter, a secret joke, intense, redolent, but as easily bruised as the petals of a gardenia' (p. 268). Many things had encouraged her to think of pleasure as something vulnerable, something to be hidden away and protected. The damage her flamboyantly public involvement with Trefusis had inflicted on Nicolson, and on her marriage, meant that from then on, her lesbian relationships, and her one extra-marital affair with a man, would be conducted with much greater gentleness and discretion. The turmoil with Trefusis forced Sackville-West to renegotiate the terms of her marriage, but left her with an even greater reliance on it and on Harold Nicolson's support. It continued to operate as a contract, a set of conventions. 'Please don't fall too much in love with Mr. Jebb', wrote Sackville-West to Nicolson on 6 November 1925. 'I don't mind who you sleep with, so long as I may keep your heart! I really don't mind anything, so long as I may have you for my own ultimately.' Emotional loyalty, rather than sexual fidelity, was the rule by which they were now playing the marital game.

The delicacy and fragility of this new set of conventions meant, however, that the contract had to be constantly reinvoked and confirmed. As Nigel Nicolson has noted (*PM*, 191), epistolary rituals replaced the ceremonies of the marriage-bed. Continual reiteration of their love for each other, and the terms on which they were together, fills the daily letters which were, in Nigel Nicolson's words, the 'warp and woof of their marriage' (*PM*, 191). The exchange of texts in the pursuit of intimacy was a way of life for Sackville-West: the pivot of her relationships both with women and with men. The Nicolson–Sackville-West letters repeatedly restate their faith in each other and in their marriage. 'There are 2 Vitas (1) V. when she's there (2) V. when she's not there. No. 1 is much the nicest, but No. 2 is *you* just the same, a constant undertone to my life, a warm comforting presence' (Nicolson to Sackville-West, 22 July 1926). Sackville-West, for her part, reaffirmed marriage as a sacrament: 'it is, in a way, as though everything I did were consecrated to you: everything I write, everything I plant' (Sackville-West to Nicolson, 23 July 1926). She did not, significantly, add 'everything I love'.

The complex structure of their marriage required constant maintenance and attention. As well as frequently reassuring one another of their love, they also developed a strong sense of tact and respect for the other's privacy. This meant protecting each other from unwanted revelations. After the episode with Trefusis, neither Sackville-West nor Nicolson ever went into detail (at least in their letters, which are otherwise remarkably frank and specific) about their current sexual involvements. Sackville-West's remarks to Nicolson, quoted in the Introduction, about her erotic encounters with Woolf, were exceptional: she made them in response to his unease not about their own relationship, but about Woolf's precarious mental balance. Otherwise Sackville-West's passionate lesbian identity is almost always absent from the letters. She protected that intensity as jealously, and as obsessively, as she guarded the intricacies of her marriage.

Her sexuality, as I showed in the Introduction, was made up of multiple and apparently contradictory roles which were at one level continuous (Nicolson and she knew exactly the kind of life the other was leading). But at another level she and Nicolson rigorously compartmentalized their various sexual encounters. Nicolson did not need or want to know all the

ins and outs of her turbulent affair with Mary Campbell: that
was Sackville-West's private obsession. Sackville-West came to
perceive her sexuality as a series of different territories, each
needing defence against the others. Conventions, like the
ones she established for her marriage, were designed to stave
off conflict and chaos, to control her multiple energies, and
to produce a coherent and functional identity for herself. In
her later novels, those published during and after the affair
with Trefusis, those who reject established rules are severely
punished. In her own life, marriage as an institution, with a
set of agreed conventions, was central to her identity. She and
Nicolson kept the promises they had made to each other,
seeing them not as restrictions but as sources of comfort and
safety that allowed each of them to experience the excitement
of extra-marital sex without their security ever being really
threatened by it. It is Sackville-West's fictional expression of
this attitude to traditional institutions that I shall explore
in this chapter. In her life and her work she managed to
reconcile the conservative and the disruptive through various
strategies of evasion and concealment. At the same time she
was bold and energetic in her expression of what she felt and
thought—in the passionate avowals of her lesbian encounters,
for example, and the blatant eugenic commitment of her
early novels. This combination of disguise and declaration was
made possible by a strict sense of boundary, already apparent
in her careful dividing-up of her autobiographical work into
hidden and published texts, and echoed in one of her
heroines' sense of the past: '[She] could even pick out a
particular field and wander around it again in spirit, though
seeing it all the while as it were from a height, fallen into its
proper place, with the exact pattern drawn round it by the
hedge, and the next field into which the gap in the hedge
would lead' (APS, 141). The image of the patchwork of the
landscape appears also in some of Sackville-West's poems
about her own divided identity:

> Days I enjoy are days when nothing happens,
> When I have no engagements written on my block,
> When no one comes to disturb my inward peace,
> When no one comes to take me away from myself
> And turn me into a patchwork, a jig-saw puzzle,

> A broken mirror that once gave a whole reflection,
> Being so contrived that it takes too long a time
> To get myself back to myself when they have gone.[1]

The price of maintaining multiple identities was a feeling of self-dispersal, so that writing and solitude sometimes seemed the only situations in which Sackville-West could gather herself into a unity. Solitude, as we shall see, is as obsessive a motif in her later fiction as form and boundary.

There is a strange paradox about the development of Sackville-West's writing career. As we saw in Chapter 1, her early novels are grounded in eugenic theory and the work of Francis Galton in particular. In the late 1930s and 1940s, in her response to the Beveridge Report, for example, she gave vent to enormous resentment of the working class in her diaries and her letters. In her fiction, however, she seems to have become increasingly circumspect. The change parallels her changing attitude to her marriage and her sexuality. As she grew used to discretion in her dealings with Nicolson, so she became more doubtful and tentative in her political statements in her novels. Some of this reticence was part of a pattern which would culminate, during the 1930s, in her almost complete withdrawal to Sissinghurst and her growing interest in mysticism and religion. Sackville-West, having courted publicity in her late twenties during the relationship with Trefusis, avoided it more and more as she approached and passed 40. This retreat, and its connection with her friendship with her sister-in-law, and her biographies of female saints, will be explored more fully in the next chapter. Its foundations were being laid, however, during the 1920s and early 1930s, and the change is apparent in the contrast between the content and style of her early novels, and of those that marked the middle, and the most successful, phase of her writing career. There was, however, another influence working on her during those years, whose presence is evident in the later group of novels. That influence was, of course, Virginia Woolf.

Some of Woolf's influence is fairly general. The sometimes

---

[1] Quoted in Victoria Glendinning, *Vita: The Life of V. Sackville-West* (New York, 1983), 280.

clumsy prose of Sackville-West's early texts has given way to a
mellifluous fluency that repeatedly echoes Woolf's characteristic inflections and rhythms. Take, for example, this passage
about marriage from *All Passion Spent*: 'Oh, what a pother, she
thought, women make about marriage! and yet who can blame
them, she added, when one recollects that marriage—
and its consequences—is the only thing that women have to
make a pother about in the whole of their lives?' (p. 159).
Sackville-West's indirect free style owes much to Woolf's
experiments in *To the Lighthouse*. She wrote to Woolf that she
was 'dazzled and bewitched' by it: 'how did you do it? how did
you walk along that razor-edge without falling?'[2] Later in her
own writing she too would venture onto the razor-edge of
indirect narration, weaving in and out of characters' minds
with a deftness that sometimes matches that of her mentor.
She would even, possibly unconsciously, parody some of
Woolf's most famous episodes: I shall discuss later her
recasting of the scene in *To the Lighthouse* in which Mr Ramsay
seeks reassurance from his wife, for example. Just as the
excitement and the ambivalence of her feelings for Sackville-
West flooded some of Woolf's texts, particularly *Orlando*, so
the unique tone of Woolf's prose resonates through much of
Sackville-West's later work. Woolf and Sackville-West did not
write collaboratively, but they wrote, at least, in parallel.

It may be, too, that some of the solemnity of Sackville-West's
early prose had succumbed to Woolf's mocking tongue. Her
naïve and reactionary consciousness of class difference had
encountered a mind which would write tartly of the pomp and
ceremony with which Sackville-West's family were so closely
involved:

Still the tradition, or belief, lingers among us that to express worth
of any kind, whether intellectual or moral, by wearing pieces of
metal, or ribbon, coloured hoods or gowns, is a barbarity which
deserves the ridicule which we bestow upon the rites of savages. A
woman who advertised her motherhood by a tuft of horsehair on the
left shoulder would scarcely, you will agree, be a venerable object.[3]

---

[2] *The Letters of Vita Sackville-West to Virginia Woolf*, ed. Louise A. DeSalvo and
Mitchell A. Leaska (London, 1985), 196, 12 May 1927.

[3] Virginia Woolf, *Three Guineas*, (Oxford, 1992; 1st edn. 1938), 179–80.

Sackville-West had already produced her own version of this towards the end of *The Edwardians*, when Sebastian attends the coronation in full ducal regalia:

After his sly and deprecatory smile of acknowledgement he rapidly continued his descent of the stairs, unaware of the billowing of his crimson robes behind him or of the corresponding emotion in the breast of his dependents. What a fool he must look—that was his only thought, so far as he had a thought about himself at all. (p. 332)

Sackville-West, it seems, shared Woolf's sense of the absurdity of many of the conventions of the English upper classes, but it seems only to have increased her fascination with the dilemmas of an anachronistic aristocracy. (This fascination with aristocratic life was a strong factor in Woolf's response to Sackville-West herself, as we shall see in Chapter 6.) Sackville-West's presentation of Sebastian and his mother as 'ordinary people', with emotional difficulties like the rest of us, was the staple of a conservative press then as now. Sackville-West managed, in her prose, to neutralize the revolutionary implications of her critique of upper-class life mores, as, in her life, she domesticated her lesbianism. Her encounter with the sharper, if still conflicted, Woolf meant the assimilation of a socialist feminist perspective into her fiction in a way which still preserved the appeal of her writing to the snobbish and nostalgic element in her reading public. Much of her later fiction seems to draw back from the consequences of its own satire. In the same way, after Trefusis, she never allowed her lesbianism to undermine her belief in, and her endorsement of, marriage as an institution. This control, political, emotional, and sexual, was accomplished by allowing different, sometimes subversive narratives to develop beneath, and in tension with, the 'surface' narrative of the plot. So in her life the private narratives of her lesbian loves flourished in the protective shade of the public narratives of her marriage.

This kind of protective concealment is apparent in the first published text to grow out of Sackville-West's relationship with another woman, *Challenge*, published in the USA in 1924. Sackville-West wrote it while in France with Violet Trefusis, and, according to Nigel Nicolson, Trefusis made considerable contributions to the novel, 'suggesting extra touches to the drama and her own portrait, and adding from time to time huge chunks of her own invention' (*PM*, 151). The novel developed from and paralleled its own writers' situation, rather in the manner of *Orlando*. Nigel Nicolson notes that: 'While Vita was writing it, she was living her life on two levels, the actual and the fictional, and as her love for Violet intensified, so did that between Julian and Eve in the novel, with incidents, conversations and letters lifted into the book from reality' (*PM*, 151). Much of the erratic and declarative style of *Challenge's* prose is Trefusis's rather than Sackville-West's, but nowhere in the text that was finally published is Trefusis acknowledged. Trefusis was insistently and desperately, even dangerously present in Sackville-West's life at the time *Challenge* was written, and integral to the process of its writing, but her presence and her contributions are written out of the published text completely. The dangerous voice of Trefusis's lesbian passion is contained and domesticated by Sackville-West's incorporation of its characteristic intonations into a novel about heterosexual love.

This displacement of the homosexual into the heterosexual is the novel's central evasion. The book was conceived explicitly as a text about Sackville-West and Trefusis. Julian, the name of the hero of *Challenge*, was the name by which Trefusis addressed Sackville-West in their intimate exchanges. Trefusis wrote to Sackville-West about *Challenge*: 'the description of Julian I thought most adequate. You say it's not like you! It *is* you, word for word, trait for trait.'[4] In the same letter Trefusis suggested various descriptions of Julian which would have turned the novel into an erotic exchange, along the lines of *Orlando*: 'how resentfully [Eve, the novel's heroine and Julian's lover] probed those heavy-lidded eyes, green in repose, black in anger, ever smouldering with some fettered impulse.'[5] Sackville-West and Trefusis used the novel to express their feelings for each other, to flirt and to cajole. In *Orlando* this mutuality was lost, as Woolf relentlessly excluded Sackville-West from the production of the text. But in *Challenge*

---

[4] *Violet to Vita: The Letters of Violet Trefusis to Vita Sackville-West, 1910–21*, ed. Mitchell A. Leaska and John Phillips (London, 1989), 79, 5 June 1918.
[5] Ibid.

disguised lesbian exchanges—the 'open secret'—take place before our eyes.

The transformation of Vita and Violet into Julian and Eve may seem to us now to be an evasion. But to the respective parents of Sackville-West and Trefusis, it was nowhere near evasive enough. Harold Nicolson and Sackville-West's mother tried to persuade Sackville-West to withdraw the novel after they had read the proofs. Nicolson later changed his mind and supported Sackville-West (we have already seen in the Introduction how ambivalent he felt about homosexual texts). Sackville-West's liaison with Trefusis was a public scandal on such a scale that Nicolson was convinced that the altered gender of the main character would make no difference to the way in which people would read the novel. In the end Sackville-West agreed and, nervous as always of unambiguous statements about her lesbianism, withdrew the book—not yet bound but already in page proof—in March 1920. She also asked that American publication be postponed. *Challenge* eventually came out in New York in 1924, and caused some inspired guesswork about the reason for its withdrawal from the UK. American critics seem not to have known the true story. The novel was finally published in England by Collins in 1974.

Many characteristic motifs of Sackville-West's later prose appear already in this early text. A young English aristocrat, Julian Davenant, leads a revolution among a group of Greek islanders, who want independence from the mainland state of Herakleion. Meanwhile he has also started a passionate love-affair with his cousin Eve, who comes with him to the island but then, jealous of his commitment to politics, betrays him to the politicians in Herakleion who capture him and take him back to Herakleion. Eve, appalled at the hatred that Julian now feels for her, commits suicide by walking into the sea. The island, often a central metaphor in Sackville-West's fiction, and a crucial image for lesbian writing after Sappho, is literally central to *Challenge*; and Sackville-West's concern with the ethics and the romance of political leadership is also apparent, ten years before *The Edwardians*.

It is on the island, away from their families and their every-day lives, and amidst the violent struggle for national liberation, that the love of Eve and Julian is consummated. The islands represent seclusion and glamour:

There was something symbolical in their detachment from the mainland—in their clean remoteness, their isolation; all the difference between the unfettered ideal and the tethered reality. An island! land that had slipped the leash of continents, forsworn solidarity, cut adrift from security and prudence! (*C*, 60)

The lovers' withdrawal to the island, like that of Sackville-West and Trefusis to France, symbolizes a rejection of rules and traditional sexual institutions (Julian's punishment of Eve is an offer to marry her). At the same time it is a retreat, a carving out of an enclosed space for a sexual and political rebellion which will, in the end, easily be contained by the superior forces of the mainland. Julian stresses that his military action will be defensive only: 'let us swear that our only guilt of aggression shall be to preserve our coasts inviolate' (*C*, 69). The islands are an area of sexual and political energy which ask simply to be left alone.

Within the enchanted space, where 'the indignities of hypocrisy were indeed remote' (*C*, 204), however, there are certain continuities with the reactionary force of the mainland. Sackville-West's understanding of sexual rebellion was in some ways still determined by the institution which it appeared to reject. Eve and Julian have strong and conventional ideas about men's and women's roles. '[Julian] found himself inwardly approving her standpoint, that man, in order to be worthy of woman, must fight, or be prepared to fight, and to enjoy the fighting' (*C*, 186). This equation of masculinity with aggression, and the idealization of that aggression, was one to which Sackville-West and Trefusis also subscribed in their own relationship. Trefusis wrote to Sackville-West in April 1920, just after the withdrawal of *Challenge* from the publishers:

You get like that when you are with—[Harold]. All that is feminine in you mounts to the surface—All that isn't remains in abeyance. Most scandalously, I prefer *all that isn't*! To put it brutally, a masculine interior beneath a feminine exterior. . . . Your eyes were like a primeval forest, dark with some crouching, nameless menace.[6]

---

[6] *Violet to Vita: The Letters of Violet Trefusis to Vita Sackville-West, 1910–21*, ed. Mitchell A. Leaska and John Phillips (London, 1989), 207, n.d. [Apr. 1920].

Like so many of their contemporaries (Radclyffe Hall and
Una Troubridge, for example), Sackville-West and Trefusis
conceived their lesbianism in terms that were heterosexual in
origin. As we have seen, Sackville-West sometimes dressed as
a man when they were together (*PM*, 111–12). Their retreat
into sexual rebellion preserved links with the conventions of
heterosexuality: the island of lesbianism had a bridge into
traditional notions of gender difference.

Eve and Julian's relationship is tabooed as Sackville-West
and Trefusis's had been, but in a slightly different way. Unwill-
ing to write explicitly about lesbianism, Sackville-West made
Eve and Julian cousins, so that Julian, on occasion, feels guilty
of incest. 'He banished violently the recollection of her in that
brief moment when in his anger he had lifted her out of her
bed and had carried her across the room in his arms. He
banished it with a shudder and a revulsion, as he might have
banished a suggestion of incest' (*C*, 116–17). Eve and Julian's
involvement is shot through with the same flashes of guilt
as Sackville-West's own relationship with Trefusis: guilt and
self-hatred about her own lesbianism as well as about hurting
Nicolson. She wrote of meeting him at Victoria shortly before
her planned elopement: 'the recollection of him goes through
me like a stab even now' (*PM*, 118). Nicolson noted her tendency to self-loathing: 'one of your old letters says "I hate
myself more than I can say"—& yet you go on doing hateful
things' (Nicolson to Sackville-West, 7 June 1919). It was
in an attempt to contain this compulsion to destroy that
Sackville-West developed her strategy of secrecy and self-
containment: a strategy that was continuous with the geo-
graphical isolation of her sexual pleasure with Trefusis, and
of that of Eve and Julian.

For most of *Challenge*, Eve and the islands are almost
interchangeable. The islands are: 'as innocent and fragile as a
lovely woman asleep, veiled by the haze of sunshine as the
sleeper's limbs by a garment of lawn. Julian gazed till his eyes
and his heart swam in the tenderness of passionate and
protective ownership' (p. 77). Later, he will have almost the
same feelings about Eve: 'she summoned in him, uncivilised
and wholly primitive, a passion of tyranny and a passion of
possessive protection' (p. 163). The vocabulary of ownership

shifts almost imperceptibly into images of rape and robbery. As Julian becomes master of Aphros, so he becomes master of Eve:

He shut his eyes for a second as he realised that she could be, if he chose, his own possession, she the elusive and unattainable; he might claim the redemption of all her infinite promise; might discover her in the role for which she was so obviously created; might violate the sanctuary and tear the veils from the wealth of treasure hitherto denied to all; might exact for himself the first secrets of her unplundered passion. (pp. 188–9)

Eve, once remote and elusive like the islands out at sea, is now close at hand and vulnerable; and like the islands she is inviolate and secret. Julian conquers both at once, 'not with secret weapons, but with the manhood of his body' (p. 204).

But the identification of Eve with the islands is precarious. Eve acquiesces in Julian's symbolic equation for a time, because she realizes that otherwise she will lose him; but in the end she feels engulfed by the islands whose essence she is supposed to represent. Both Eve and the islands are actually led into servitude, and finally destroyed, by Julian's democratic rhetoric. By turning against the islands, and betraying military secrets to the Greeks, Eve disrupts the symmetry of Julian's feelings for the islands, and for her. When Julian is no longer the leader of a political rebellion, he loses all sense of himself as a sexual rebel, and his love for Eve disappears. Outside the island setting they cannot survive as lovers: 'we had to do only with love—love and rebellion! And both have failed me. Now, instead of love, we must have marriage; and instead of rebellion, law. I shall help on authority, instead of opposing it' (p. 243). Julian's domination over Eve and over the islands is seen not as a form of authority, but as a dangerous and passionate sexual initiative which is by nature opposed to any form of control. As soon as it comes into conflict with legitimate forms of authority, it dies.

Intervening between *Challenge* and the best-selling novels of the 1930s was Sackville-West's most acclaimed piece of writing, and one which demonstrated her return to the traditional life of country landowner and wife. This text was her long poem

The Land, which won the Hawthornden Prize in 1926. Where the love of Eve and Julian seemed to grow out of its exotic Mediterranean setting, the values celebrated in *The Land* are all to do with Englishness, and with historical and agricultural continuity. Louise DeSalvo has commented that there are very few women in *The Land.*[7] The poem celebrates the safety of England, and the serenity of its community of male labourers. Women, and their dangerous sexuality, would have destabilized this careful plotting of an English rural tradition. Sackville-West, in retreat from the scandal of her lesbian affair, is concerned now to emphasize her aristocratic roots in the history and landscape of England. As in *Challenge,* issues of political and economic power are obfuscated. Sackville-West writes about a working population of which she was, in fact, the employer rather than a member. The attitudes she celebrates are those of the ideal employee rather than of the agricultural labourer whose Union was about to participate in the General Strike of 1926. *Challenge,* too, had confused celebration and exploitation. Sackville-West's fantasy that the island peasants, all in the employ of Julian's family, would call on him to lead their revolution, was at best politically naïve; and at worse an impassioned romanticization of an unjust hierarchy.

In spite of its preoccupation with 'the mild continuous epic of the soil' (p. 3), *The Land* does contain two sections devoted to women. Both are conceived as interludes and the first is explicitly presented as such, printed in italics and separated by blank space from the main text.

The second episode about women, on which I shall concentrate here, occurs near the end of the poem, in the final section, 'Autumn'. It describes how women, in legend, have used woods as a refuge from heterosexual pursuit: Apollo and Daphne, for example. This mythic connection persists in a kind of unconscious kinship: 'And women still have memories of woods, / Older than any personal memories' (p. 95). There is a sexual aptness in this connection (p. 96):

---

[7] Louise A. DeSalvo, 'Every Woman is an Island: Vita Sackville-West, the Image of the City, and the Pastoral Idyll', in Susan Merrill Squier (ed.), *Women Writers and the City: Essays in Feminist Literary Criticism* (Knoxville, Tenn., 1984), 101.

> Of such a tall and airy world are they,
> Women and woods, with shadowed aisles profound
> That none explore.

The secrecy that linked Eve and the islands also links the female body and the paths through the wood. The 'shadowed aisles profound' are the enticing entrances to the woman herself, as well as to the secrets of the woods. The passage signals the prohibition in Sackville-West's published texts of the explicit exploration of lesbian desire and its 'unexplored' contours. It was a prohibition laid down in the name of conformity and discretion. But, as we shall see, she found many ways, even in this passage, to bypass it and to speak the conditions of her own desire in spite of this largely self-imposed constraint. Sackville-West's careful concealment of her lesbian activities had for her a certain erotic logic.

As Louise DeSalvo notes, the woods are hardly a safe retreat for women.[8] In *The Land*, the lines following those quoted above present woods—and women—as enclosed and dangerous spaces (pp. 96–7):

> There is a kinship: down the open ride
> She strays, eternal nymph, and glances swift
> Into the ambushed depths on either side;
> Now fears the shadows, now the rift,
> Now fears the silence, now the rustling leaf
> That like a footfall with a nearing stride
> Startles the stronghold of her unbelief.
> Woods are her enemies, yet once she went
> Fleeing before a god, and, all but spent,
> Slipped from his arms, herself become a tree.
> She has forgotten; wood's an enemy;
> She has no knowledge of the woodland tracks,
> Only a knowledge of her jeopardy.
> And with lost steps, neglectful of her pride,
> Stumbles towards the music of the axe.
> There, brown old sylvan god, the woodsman plies
> His craft and drives his wedge,
> Spitting to ease the rub of tool on hands,
> And she arrested at the clearing's edge

---

[8] Ibid.

Awakened stands,
With panic terror fading from her eyes.

DeSalvo interprets this passage as an indication that the 'sylvan retreat', safe for men, is uncomfortable and dangerous for women, who are disenfranchised from even the land in which they live—as Woolf would confirm in *Three Guineas*.[9] But this reading, while obviously valid, ignores much of the passage's complexity, particularly in the light of Sackville-West's previous history with Trefusis and the imagery she had used to describe it in *Challenge*. DeSalvo notes that it was in foreign cities—Paris, Monte Carlo—that Sackville-West felt able to express her lesbianism openly.[10] She suggests that the woods of England are implicitly contrasted with the exotic anonymity of urban environments as places that are hostile to women's sexuality. But, remembering the tradition of lesbian pastoral I outlined in the Introduction, this passage from *The Land* can also be read as an exploration of the dangers and the compulsive beauty of the lesbian body which threatens the untroubled continuity of English feudal lineage.

Sackville-West's marriage to Harold Nicolson was mediated through their joint commitment to the creation of gardens, first at Long Barn, and then, after 1930, in Sissinghurst Castle. Gardens were the expression of their love, an example of their two temperaments working together in harmony: Nigel Nicolson calls the garden at Sissinghurst 'a portrait of their marriage. Harold made the design, Vita did the planting' (*PM*, 220). Gardening, though, even in their imaginative and inspired version of it, is a domestication of natural space, a taming of the wilderness. But woods in *The Land* are wild and female, places of fear and excitement which the woman enters willingly and leaves in panic. The forest of *The Land* is contrasted, I would argue, not with European urban environments, but with the ordered landscape of horticultural and agricultural endeavour, with exactly that landscape which Sackville-West, at this stage, associated with her marriage and her heterosexual self. The woman who enters the woods—

---

[9] Louise A. DeSalvo, 'Every Woman is an Island: Vita Sackville-West, the Image of the City, and the Pastoral Idyll', in Susan Merrill Squier (ed.), *Women Writers and the City: Essays in Feminist Literary Criticism* (Knoxville, Tenn., 1984), 102; and Woolf, *Three Guineas*, 311–13.

[10] DeSalvo, 'Every Woman is an Island', 98.

already explicitly likened to the damp intricacies of the female body—enters in full knowledge of a 'kinship'. This 'kinship' could be the knowledge that woods have, in the past, sheltered her sisters when threatened with rape; but it could also be the kinship of entering another body—another space—which she recognizes as her own. Read this way, the passage is an encoded description of a lesbian sexual encounter.

Various other features of the passage confirm this reading. For Sackville-West, still reassembling and consolidating her domestic life after the agony of the affair with Trefusis, lesbian pleasure meant danger; it meant pain and fear. The nymph's nervous glance at the 'rift'—what rift? in a wood?—needs no further comment. The passage also seems to work in parallel with Freudian and Kleinian interpretations of the relationship of lesbianism to the pre-Oedipal, as I suggested in the Introduction. The woman can no longer remember the time when she was at home in the sylvan, or the female, space. Such memories have been repressed as ruthlessly as the memory of the pre-Oedipal desire for the mother. Now the experience of female sexuality is a dangerous trip into the unknown. She risks getting lost, being engulfed by this wood whose nature is ambiguous: 'Birches, frail whispering company, are these? / Or lovely women rooted into trees?' (*La*, p. 96). This passage in *The Land* prefigures Sackville-West's attempts in *Pepita* to disentangle herself and her mother. She fears, like Eve in *Challenge*, that she will be engulfed by the threatening pleasure of a retreat into a world of women.

It is significant that it is, in the end, a woodsman who symbolizes safety to the terrified nymph. She emerges stumbling from the wood of lesbian pleasure and danger, to be confronted with a symbol of the ordered male world of rural tradition. The woodsman is cutting down the trees that have given her so much pain, containing and isolating the dangerous space from which she has just escaped. In the same way Sackville-West emerged from the torment of her passion for Trefusis to throw herself into a commitment to the domestic and horticultural environment. Nicolson was willing for her to act on her lesbian feelings, as long as they never again overstepped the boundaries of what could be contained by a heterosexual existence. Again, as in *All Passion Spent* (quoted near the beginning of this chapter), the imagery is territorial:

the wood is clearly demarcated from the clearing, and the clearing is distinct from the larger world of the surrounding rural community.

In 1928, two years after the publication of *The Land* and in the middle of the writing of *Orlando*, Sackville-West's father died. This meant that Knole, the childhood home for which her mother had fought (during the 1910 lawsuit), and the symbol of her feudal connection with the land, passed into the ownership of an uncle with whom she was not on very good terms, and whose wife she disliked. She felt as though a lifeline had been severed: 'I feel as though a knife had been plunged into my heart the day Dada died, and as though it had cut its way slowly round ever since, until a great chunk of flesh had been cut out, and had now fallen bleeding to the ground' (Sackville-West to Nicolson, 10 Oct. 1928). The loss of Knole seemed like a violation of her identity, the severance of her relationship to the feudal past that was once again, after Trefusis, central to her life and work. She saw the Edwardian setting of her solitary childhood passing away: 'Although I approve whole-heartedly of Charlie's activities,—such as altering the ball-room window, and removing those bloody plaster casts from the Cartoon Gallery (which I never could get Dada to do,)—I absurdly mind *anything* being altered' (Sackville-West to Nicolson, 10 Oct. 1928). To her the innovations at Knole were about far more than the adaptation of a living space. They meant a turning away from a way of life, from a history, and from an ideology.

This mixture of nostalgia and the desire for change—a conflict between the conservative and the progressive sides of her nature—shapes the narrative of her most popular novel, *The Edwardians* (1930). Woolf, who published it at the Hogarth Press, noted that it had a 'gigantic sale' ((*D*, iii. 306, 16 June 1930), verging on 20,000 in the first two weeks. Even today, when the market for novels has greatly expanded, it would be considered a best seller. Sackville-West told Woolf she was writing it for the money: 'I'm going to write it this summer and make my fortune. Such a joke it will be, and I hope everybody will be seriously annoyed.'[11] She knew quite

[11]   *The Letters of Vita Sackville-West to Virginia Woolf*, 327, 21 Feb. 1929.

well what passions she was playing on in her public: 'I feel that for snobbish reasons alone it ought to be highly popular!'[12] But at the same time she admitted that she was not as emotionally or intellectually detached from it as she claimed: 'the novel is about the Edwardians,—a fascinating subject, if only I can do it justice.'[13] Woolf didn't think much of it, and teased Sackville-West with the hope that she might be going to write a companion to *Orlando*: 'is your new novel to be all about Potto [Sackville-West's name for Woolf]? He thinks so. He is willing to help you in anyway [*sic*] he can' (*L*, iv. 28, 23 Feb. 1929). Years later Sackville-West would jokingly claim that there was a lesbian subtext:

Lady Roehampton is Lady Westmoreland,—a lovely sumptuous creature who came to Knole when I was eight, and who first set my feet along the wrong path, I fancy, but who died, herself, relatively young, of drugs and a plethora of lovers. (No, it wasn't Lady Westmoreland who set my feet along the wrong path, now I come to think of it, but the Queen of Romania who appeared in my schoolroom one day.)[14]

After *Orlando*, Woolf and Sackville-West were accustomed to the encoding of unconventional relationships within apparently conventional texts.

In *The Edwardians*, however, lesbian intensity has been displaced into an account of a male homoerotic relationship, which, like the love of Julian and Eve in *Challenge*, takes place in secret and is part of a wider rebellion against tradition and marriage. Sebastian, the hero, is the heir to the Chevron estate, at present owned by his mother Lucy. His attitude towards the anachronistic splendour in which they live is divided, and he is only prevented from leaving on a trip with explorer Anquetil by the fact that the night before the invitation is offered, he has started a love-affair with his mother's friend Lady Roehampton. That affair ends when Lady Roehampton's husband finds out about it, and Sebastian becomes involved first with a doctor's wife, then with the gamekeeper's daughter, and finally with a painter, before giving in to family pressure and courting the aristocratic, but

[12] Ibid. 334, 6 May 1929.   [13] Ibid.   [14] Ibid. 381, 18 Aug. 1933.

plain, Alice O. The novel ends with Sebastian on the way back from the coronation, dressed in his ducal robes, catching sight of Anquetil in the street and agreeing to go away with him.

Terry Castle has noted that much lesbian fiction seeks to displace earlier texts, rewriting them to liberate hitherto unforeseen energies—like the relationship between Minna and Sophia in Sylvia Townsend Warner's *Summer Will Show* (1936), for example.[15] Sackville-West's choice of names for her hero and his sister, Viola, is surely indicative of such a desire in relation to *Twelfth Night*. Sebastian and Viola in *The Edwardians* are united in discontent with their mother's way of life. But Sackville-West's Viola is a very different creature from the Shakespearian Viola who must obey her master, and only ever speak her love obliquely. Sackville-West's Viola, unlike her brother, is uncompromising in her critique of the society in which she grew up. Her voice rings clear and true through the political and emotional obfuscations of the other characters, and the novel closes with her flaunting convention by living alone in London.

The complexities of gender, and the multiple possibilities for the release of sexual energy in *Twelfth Night*, should alert us to a similar ambiguity in *The Edwardians*, despite its apparently heterosexual narrative. As Lisa Jardine and others have pointed out, the use of boy actors rather than actresses on the Elizabethan stage produced a homosexual subtext to heterosexual plays.[16] The action of *Twelfth Night* includes the wooing of one woman by another. Apparently stable plots threatened to dissolve and multiply when such issues were taken into account. Such instability is written into *The Edwardians*.

The novel's most daring moment is a pursuit of Sebastian by Anquetil across the roofs of Chevron (clearly modelled on the Knole Sackville-West had so recently left). Anquetil, who has been thoroughly confused by his own reaction to Chevron, is relieved that Sebastian has led him far above the trivial rituals of his mother's house party. 'But ardently, ardently, he wished Viola away' (p. 84). The trip is an experi-

---

[15] Terry Castle, 'Sylvia Townsend Warner and the Counterplot of Lesbian Fiction', *Textual Practice*, 4 (1990), 230–1.

[16] Lisa Jardine, *Still Harping on Daughters: Women and Drama in the Age of Shakespeare* (Brighton, 1983).

ment in masculinity. 'Never once did Sebastian look back to see if his companion still followed him, but climbed and leapt and ran as one possessed by genius, or as one that puts another man to the test, mischievous, unmerciful, and mocking' (p. 84). Basically this is an erotic pursuit, dangerous and exciting. Rather than be overtaken, Sebastian leaps into 'the black pit of the courtyard below' (p. 85), and is caught, at the last moment, by Anquetil. They then hold the following conversation:

'You have had your fun with me, my young friend; now I think it's my turn. You look very foolish, let me tell you, lying there spread-eagle on the tiles of your ancestral home. Pride has had a fall—very nearly a nasty fall. But you seem quite calm. I see that the patrician can face death with dignity—even a ludicrous death. I congratulate you.'

'Well, you are a queer sort of fellow, to be sure,' said Sebastian.

'Do I seem queer to you? I assure you, you seem equally queer to me. There are several things I have been wanting to say to you. Shall we talk?'

'Like this?' said Sebastian.

'No, not like this,' said Anquetil, and pulled Sebastian up so that they sat facing one another. (p. 86)

The hold that Anquetil has over Sebastian is literalized as they hang together over the abyss of the courtyard. The roof to which they cling is the bastion of freedom and independence; the darkness into which they may fall is that of convention and hypocrisy. Anquetil tells Sebastian: 'Look, you're hanging over a big drop. Down there, you die; but up here, beside me, you breathe and live. Which is it to be?' (p. 93). But the drop is also the void of sexual danger. The risk of speaking honestly is physical: saying what they mean exposes them to the risk of death or serious injury. Sebastian would be liberated from tradition by accepting Anquetil's invitation; but it is clear also that for Sebastian being with Anquetil means willingly risking everything, even his life.

Sackville-West's remarkable use of the word 'queer' does nothing to neutralize the situation. The first recorded use in the *OED* of 'queer' to mean 'homosexual' is in 1932 in a text by Auden, himself gay and therefore privy, as was Sackville-West herself, to the vocabulary of a homosexual subculture. For a word to appear in print, it must have been in frequent conversational use for some time. It seems therefore highly likely that Sackville-West knew of the connotations of the word when she used it in this highly provocative context in 1930; and possible also that she thought its subversive resonances would be picked up only by the initiated. We know that she regretted the banning of *The Well of Loneliness* in 1928: 'it is not in the least interesting apart from the candour with which it treats its subject; but at least it is perfectly serious and sincere . . . Of course I simply *itch* to try the same thing myself', she wrote to Harold Nicolson on 8 August 1928. Anquetil's invitation ('Come away with me' (*E,* 93)) is an attempted seduction as well as an effort to raise Sebastian's political consciousness. It is crucial that Sebastian refuses simply because he has just taken a lover. As soon as he confesses this, the interview with Anquetil comes to an end.

The world of *The Edwardians* is a bad island: an island of social and sexual anachronism. Its self-enclosed, narcissistic nature is emphasized by the failure of Lady Roehampton's mirror to break when she flings it to the floor in despair at her enforced separation from Sebastian (p. 174). Endlessly reproducing itself (Sebastian's mother wants him to marry Lady Roehampton's daughter), the world of Chevron refuses to establish productive relations with the rest of society, and the visit of a doctor and his wife to Chevron is a humiliating failure. Sackville-West is clear that social islands of this kind are doomed, like the island of Eve and Julian's love; Sebastian's only hope is to escape. At the end of the novel, in his ducal carriage, he is physically imprisoned: 'Sebastian frantically sought the door-handle before he remembered it was not there' (p. 346). Only an act of violence—he 'banged on the tiny window at the back with such violence that he broke it' (p. 346)—can liberate him, and let Anquetil in. They agree to what is basically an elopement, desexualized by Anquetil's announcement that he plans to marry Sebastian's sister in three years' time. He may be going to become her husband; but it is with her brother that he has his most intense relationship.

The unlikeliness of the plot, particularly for Sackville-West, who was perfectly capable of writing very convincing realist fiction, should alert us to some kind of hidden agenda. Terry Castle's observation that lesbian fiction is implausible could equally well apply to writing about male homosexuality:

Precisely because it is motivated by a yearning for that which is, in a cultural sense, unplausible—the subversion of male homosocial desire —lesbian fiction characteristically exhibits, even as it masquerades as 'realistic' in surface detail, a strongly fantastical, allegorical or utopian tendency.[17]

The fact that *The Edwardians*, like *Orlando*, is highly coded and implicit brings it in line with other of Sackville-West's texts, in which disruptive energies are domesticated and stabilized for the sake of narrative and sexual coherence, and respectability. The banning of *The Well of Loneliness* because of one euphemistic sentence ('and that night they were not divided'[18]) showed how careful authors had to be.

The novel that Sackville-West moved on to write is much more cautious in its raising of the possibility of subversive madness. But it is the novel in which her closeness to Virginia Woolf is stylistically most apparent. Motifs derived directly from Woolf's work—*To the Lighthouse* and *Orlando*—found their way into *All Passion Spent* (1931). Lady Slane's 'there were many selves' (*APS*, 174) echoes *Orlando*'s 'these selves of which we are built up' (*O*, 294); Lady Slane's 'fish of memory on a long line' recalls 'the sudden conglomeration of an idea at the end of one's line' of *A Room of One's Own* (1929)[19]; and the central theme of *All Passion Spent*, the retreat of Lady Slane into a house of her own after her husband's death, realizes the basic idea of *A Room of One's Own*.

The novel is concerned with the last years of Lady Slane's life. Her husband has just died when the novel opens, and Lady Slane, who has been meek and submissive all her life, shocks her children by announcing that she is going to live alone in a house she saw in Hampstead thirty years earlier. During her time there, she thinks over her past life and tries to reassess her life, also renewing a friendship with a man

---

[17] Castle, 'Sylvia Townsend Warner', 229.
[18] Radclyffe Hall, *The Well of Loneliness* (London, 1982; 1st edn. 1928), 316.
[19] Virginia Woolf, *A Room of One's Own* (Oxford, 1992; 1st edn. 1929), 6.

she met once as a young woman in India. When he dies, he leaves her his large fortune which, to her children's horror, she gives away. Just before her death, she has an emotional meeting with her great-granddaughter who, unlike her great-grandmother before her, has broken off her engagement in order to pursue a career as a musician.

All Passion Spent is Sackville-West's most feminist novel. Louise DeSalvo calls it an 'outgrowth' of *A Room of One's Own*,[20] for it describes the stifling of a woman's creativity—Lady Slane has always secretly wanted to paint—by her duties as wife and mother. As a study of marriage and maternity it was clearly conceived with Woolf's *To the Lighthouse* (1927) in mind. Lady Slane, like Mrs Ramsay, is concerned to weigh up what she has lost and gained through her marriage. Both characters are in a state of chronic emotional ambivalence. They take pleasure in reassuring their husbands.

When, mooning, he strayed up to her and drooped over her chair, saying nothing, but waiting (as she knew) for some soft protection to come from her and fold itself around him like a cloak, yet it must all be done without a word directly spoken; she must restore his belief that the obstructiveness of his Government or the opposition of his rivals was due to their short-sightedness or envy, and to no deficiency within himself, yet must not allow him to know that she guessed at his mood of self-mistrust or the whole fabric of her comfort would be undone. And when she had accomplished this feat, this reconstruction of extreme delicacy and extreme solidity—when he left her, to go back strengthened to his business—then, with her hands lying limp, symbol of her exhaustion, and a sweet emptiness within her, as though her self had drained away to flow into the veins of another person—then, sinking, drowning, she wondered whether she had not secretly touched the heights of rapture. (*APS*, 173–4)

Lady Slane's state of mind—her perception of her husband's need, her sympathetic responsiveness, and her feeling of exhausted ecstasy at having successfully accomplished her emotional task—closely echoes Mrs Ramsay's when her husband comes to her seeking reassurance.

Immediately, Mrs Ramsay seemed to fold herself together, one petal closed in another, and the whole fabric fell in exhaustion upon itself,

[20] Louise A. DeSalvo, 'Lighting the Cave: The Relationship between Vita Sackville-West and Virginia Woolf', *Signs*, 8 (1982), 211.

so that she had only strength enough to move her finger, in exquisite abandonment to exhaustion, across the page of Grimm's fairy
story, while there throbbed through her, like the pulse in a spring
which has expanded to its full width and now gently ceases to beat,
the rapture of successful creation. (*TTL*, 54)

Both passages share imagery of a fragile emotional edifice, of
a quasi-post-coital exhaustion and emptiness, and of a climactic feeling of 'rapture'. But, typically of Sackville-West, much
of the abrasive feminism of Woolf's prior text is lost in the
later reconstruction. Where Woolf uses the point of view of
Mrs Ramsay's little son, James, to suggest that the male
demand is sterile and aggressive—'the arid scimitar of his
father, the egotistical man, plunged and smote, demanding
sympathy' (*TTL*, 53)—Sackville-West excludes the son and
removes much of the passage's (and *To the Lighthouse*'s) hostility towards men. Lady Slane's experience is on the whole
fruitful: the surface of Woolf's prose, on the other hand, is
contracted by exactly that 'spasm of pain' to which she had so
strongly objected in the work of Charlotte Brontë.[21] Once
again in Sackville-West's text a socially disruptive energy,
women's dissatisfaction, is domesticated and contained within
acceptable limits, as was her lesbianism in her life. Lady Slane
is not as angry as Mrs Ramsay; she accepts the limits which
marriage has placed on her life; and her mood throughout
the book is one simply of wistful speculation about how it
is that such things can happen. The fatalism that allowed
Sackville-West to yield to her passion for Trefusis, on the
grounds that the two of them were somehow 'destined' to be
together, meant that she could represent Lady Slane as pass-
ively wistful, rather than angrily resentful. Even her engagement takes place because of a misunderstanding which she
never quite has the courage to put right.

Sackville-West's account of this misunderstanding, though,
shows her awareness that women, if they are not careful,
do not speak but rather are spoken for—exactly Woolf's
realization, when in the British Library, she discovers that
more books have been written about women by men, than by
women themselves.[22] When Lord Slane proposes, Lady Slane

---

[21] Woolf, *A Room of One's Own*, 95.   [22] Ibid. 33–5.

looks at him in shock with 'the glance of a startled faun.
Instantly interpreting that glance according to his desire, Mr.
Holland had clasped her in his arms and had kissed her with
ardour but with restraint upon the lips' (*APS*, 144). In *All
Passion Spent*, women have decisions taken for them; they find
it hard to say what they mean. Edith, Lady Slane's daughter,
is plagued by a Freudian fear of uttering obscenities: 'Edith
could have told them that all her life she had been trying to
say what she meant, and had never yet succeeded. Only too
often, she said something precisely the opposite of what she
wanted to say. Her terror was that she should one day use
an indecent word by mistake' (p. 21). Woolf's young woman
writer is also shown coming up against the constraints of
convention: 'the consciousness of what men will say of a
woman who speaks the truth about her passions had roused
her from her artist's state of unconsciousness. She could
write no more.'[23] In order to be sure of speaking their own
truths, women must speak only to themselves, in the silence
of solitude, in the serenity of private recollection, in the
safety of woman's intimacy. So Lady Slane, wondering 'what,
precisely, had been herself?' (p. 145), retreats to the peace
of Hampstead with only a maid for company. Even her
grandchildren are barred from the house.

   All Passion Spent, then, describes the establishment of female
solitude. By the time it was written, Sackville-West was with-
drawing emotionally from Woolf, but the attitudes that shape
All Passion Spent show how deeply she had absorbed Woolf's
opinions, her politics, and even her prose style. Compare,
for example, these passages from *All Passion Spent* and *Orlando*:

Lady Slane, then, looked down at her hands as though Genoux [the
maid] had for the first time drawn attention to them. For one's
hands are the parts of one's body that one suddenly sees with the
maximum of detachment; they are suddenly far off; and one
observes their marvellous articulations, and miraculous response to
the transmission of instantaneous messages, as though they belonged
to another person, or to another piece of machinery; one observes
even the oval of their nails, the pores of their skin, the wrinkles of

---

[23] Virginia Woolf, 'Professions for Women', in *Virginia Woolf: Women and
Writing*, ed. Michèle Barrett (London, 1979), 62.

their phalanges and knuckles, their smoothness or rugosities, with an estimating and interested eye; they have been one's servants, and yet one has not investigated their personality; a personality which, cheiromancy assures us, is so much bound up with our own. One sees them also, as the case may be, loaded with rings or rough with work. (*APS*, 74–5)

Such was his shyness that he saw no more of her than her ringed hands in water; but it was enough. It was a memorable hand; a thin hand with long fingers always curling as if round orb or sceptre; a nervous, crabbed, sickly hand; a commanding hand too; a hand that had only to raise itself for a head to fall; a hand, he guessed, attached to an old body that smelt like a cupboard in which furs are kept in camphor; which body was yet caparisoned in all sorts of brocades and gems; and held itself very upright though perhaps in pain from sciatica; and never flinched though strung together by a thousand fears; and the Queen's eyes were light yellow. (*O*, 21–2)

Sackville-West's prolonged lyric meditation on Lady Slane's hand—presented from Lady Slane's point of view as the passage from *Orlando* is presented from Orlando's—draws on *Orlando*'s rhapsodic prose, but, again characteristically, with less daring. Woolf's fantastic licence, her yielding to an intoxication with language which produces the lyric improbability of 'strung together with a thousand fears', is transformed, in Sackville-West's prose, into a rather cautious literal-mindedness. It was the same caution, born, ironically, of a sexual boldness which Woolf never even approached, which led Sackville-West to censor the feminist anger from her own version of the encounter between the Ramsays in *To the Lighthouse*. Reckless in some areas of her life, Sackville-West was careful to toe a stricter line than Woolf in others. Her sexual and social conservatism are directly linked to her passionate lesbianism: the one guarantees the other.

There is more than a reference to *Orlando* in the passage quoted above. Lady Slane is contemplating her hands because she is about to give away her jewellery. She is quite clear about what her many adornments are: 'tokens of affection, certainly, but no less tokens of the embellishments proper to the hands of Lord Slane's wife' (*APS*, 73–4). Giving them away is thus to relinquish her uxorial identity, to free herself from the needs and expectations not only of a husband now dead, but also from the expectations of a society which assumes she is merely Lord Slane's widow. There was, though, for Sackville-West, a deeper and more painful resonance. It was in 1928 that her own mother had accused her of stealing the family jewels:

What about my 4 big brilliants which [Vita] wrote might be 'paste', It looks as if the brilliants had been changed with paste & the emeralds of the leaves Tiara ditto. And 4 beautiful brilliants are missing from my necklace. What is one to think, my God! with such dishonourable lying people, that *liar* [Vita] who became executrix through such a deliberate lie, backed by both Pembertons [the family solicitors].[24]

For Lady Slane's daughters and daughters-in-law, desperate for the jewels she hands over to them, their mother's necklaces and earrings are an implicit humiliation.

Becoming they were not, to Mabel's faded little face, for Mabel who had once been pretty had now faded, according to the penalty of fair people, so that her skin appeared to be darker than her hair, and her hair without lustre, the colour of dust. The pearls, which had once dripped their sheen among the laces and softness of Lady Slane, now hung in a dispirited way round Mabel's scraggy neck. (*APS*, 77–8)

The jewels, symbols of adult femininity, fail in their task where Mabel is concerned, bringing out not the brilliance of an achieved beauty and sexual maturity, but the dreariness of a woman who has never quite found her own identity or voice. Mabel's husband rarely says anything to her except 'Be quiet', and Mabel rarely succeeds in 'getting beyond her four or five opening words' (*APS*, 35). Mabel, silenced and downtrodden, has no self to express; and she is too ill-defined to accept the self her mother-in-law is offering her. Sackville-West, struggling as we have seen with her mother's demands and her accusations, is gently suggesting that femininity is simply not in the mother's gift: that the daughter must come to find and express her own version of their shared womanhood. This is, of course, the message of Woolf's book about her parents, *To the Lighthouse*. Lily finds herself only by refusing the gifts—of

---

[24] Lady Sackville's diary, notes for the week of 14 May 1928. See my 'Fakes and Femininity: Vita Sackville-West and her Mother', in Isobel Armstrong (ed.), *New Feminist Discourses* (London, 1992), for a more detailed analysis of these exchanges.

William Bankes, for example—that Mrs Ramsay is keen to give
her.

But *All Passion Spent* does close on a gift between women,
and on an affirmation of women's intimacy: appropriately, in
this novel which draws more closely than any of Sackville-
West's others on her involvement with Virginia Woolf. At the
close of the novel, Lady Slane receives a visit from her great-
granddaughter, who shares her name, Deborah. As Deborah
talks about her ambitions to be a musician, and her broken
engagement, Lady Slane can no longer distinguish her own
identity from that of the younger woman. 'Was it an echo that
she heard? or had some miracle wiped out the years? were the
years being played over again, with a difference?' (*APS*, 281).
Deborah's actions correct those of her great-grandmother
without criticizing them; the parallel narratives confirm the
identity of each woman without degenerating into rivalry
or hostility. It is the dictum of *A Room of One's Own*, 'we
think back through our mothers if we are women', realized
in action.[25] The forging of complementary narratives was
just what Woolf and Sackville-West were preoccupied with
throughout their intimacy, and throughout their lives.

Louise DeSalvo has written on the novel that followed *All
Passion Spent*, *Family History* (1932), as a lesbian text.[26] Evelyn
Jarrold, emotionally entangled with her niece Ruth when the
novel opens, ends up dying of an illness contracted as a result
of an affair with a man her niece is also in love with. Because
DeSalvo has already written about *Family History*, I shall not
spend too much time on it here, beyond suggesting that, in
terms of Sackville-West's development as a novelist and a
married lesbian, other themes in the novel are as important
as the emotional intensity between Ruth and Evelyn. The two
are undoubtedly excited by each other—'Ruth was always
strangely elated when she had been with Evelyn' (*FH*, 32)
—but to suggest, as DeSalvo does, that if Evelyn had loved
Ruth, she would have had a happier life, seems to me a distortion of what is, in fact, a less daring novel than many that
Sackville-West wrote.[27] Evelyn's attitude to Ruth is callous: 'it

---

[25] Woolf, *A Room of One's Own*, 99.
[26] DeSalvo, 'Lighting the Cave', 207–8.   [27] Ibid. 208.

was rather unfair, she thought, to play with the girl like this, but she must needs have all the Jarrolds at her feet, though she despised herself for it' (*FH*, 31). Evelyn is only emotionally vulnerable in relation to her male lover, Miles Vane-Merrick; and their idyll is broken, significantly, when Miles invites friends to join them at his home in the country. Evelyn accuses him of seeming 'not to care that those other people should rob us of what is so precious to me if not to you?' (*FH*, 208). She has been carefully holding different areas of her life apart: the arrival of Miles's friends will destroy the precarious compartmentalizing of her life without which she cannot survive. But *Family History*, coming at the end of the highly productive period in which Sackville-West published a novel a year, feels tired. It merely restates the issues she had been exploring with so much energy in previous books.

It was not until her final novel, *No Signposts in the Sea* (1961), that Sackville-West would actually run the risk of naming her sexual choices for the first time. By the time it was published she was nearly seventy, although still as emotionally and perhaps as sexually intense as she had been in her youth. In 1957, she and Nicolson had gone on one of the winter cruises which were to become a regular feature of their lives until Sackville-West's death in 1962. The experience of being adrift for months on what was essentially an island had resonances for Sackville-West beyond those of exotic adventure, and on their last cruise of all, in early 1962, her friend Edie Lamont accompanied them. The habits of a lifetime were weakening their hold; the emotional territories that had been so carefully kept apart were blurring together now, towards the end of their lives. Now it was ill health rather than sexual intensities that Sackville-West kept from Nicolson: when she had a haemorrhage on the train as they were leaving London, she told Lamont rather than her husband.

This emotional relaxation was reflected in her writing. Having strictly refrained all her life from referring to lesbianism in print, her last novel would, finally, make reference to it. The novel is the diary of Edmund, who knows he is dying and decides to spend his last months on a cruise with a woman with whom he is secretly in love. He realizes that his feelings are returned just before he breaks off the diary and is found dead the next morning. Sackville-West's themes are still there: isolation (Edmund is separated from Laura not only by his love for her, but also by the knowledge of his illness), the negotiation of sexual feeling (Edmund and Laura talk constantly about love and marriage), and the danger of secluded and uncontrollable relationships. But the mood of the book is far from the melodrama of *Challenge* nearly forty years before. It is meditative and reflective, and most of its events—like those in Woolf's novels—occur in the characters' heads: it is an emotional rather than a visible drama.

Laura and Edmund discuss the conditions necessary for a successful marriage. 'Mutual respect. Independence, as I have said, both as regards friends and movement. Separate bed-rooms—no bedroom squalor . . . Separate sitting-rooms if the house is large enough. Separate finances' (*SS*, 87). This image of dispersal, of a relentless holding-apart, was of course drawn straight from the model Sackville-West and Nicolson had themselves negotiated and maintained. But Laura, who suggests this model, apparently contradicts herself some pages later.

One is weak, Edmund. I have come to believe that even the strongest, the most self-sufficient, need one other person in their lives from whom nothing is concealed, neither the most important things nor the most trivial. Someone with whom at the end of the day one can sit over the fire and talk or be silent as the fancy moves one. (*SS*, 135)

The conventions for a successful marriage seem here to depend on a fantasy of absolute intimacy: sharing a fire and perhaps even a bedroom. But Laura is not thinking of her husband, nor even of another man.

I had that kind of relationship with the friend I was telling you about. And yet I don't know. Perhaps a relationship between two women must always be incomplete—unless, I suppose, they have Lesbian inclinations which I don't happen to share. Then, or so I have been given to understand, the concord may approach perfection. (*SS*, 135)

It is to make room for this perfect union that marriage must hold itself apart. The gratuitousness of Laura's reference to lesbianism—this is simply a conversation, which does little to move on the plot (such as it is)—suggests that Sackville-West was at last making a statement about herself and her own experiences. Marriage was necessary to structure her identity and to guarantee a safe space in which she could risk passionate, but discreet, lesbian affairs. In the same way her books, formally unadventurous, were the vehicle for concealed exploration of emotional and sexual ambiguities. It was *because* much of her life and writing was conventional that she was able to abandon convention within certain well-defined limits. These were limits that she and Nicolson set and maintained together for their mutual benefit. Without her marriage, and without her cautious, almost pedantic observance of literary and social proprieties, she would never have allowed herself to risk so much.

CHAPTER 5

'The Girl beside me':
V. Sackville-West and the Mystics

THE best-selling novels of the early 1930s established Vita
Sackville-West as one of the better-known novelists of her
time. But it was not only to novels that she turned as the 1930s
wore on and Europe watched with trepidation the tightening
hold of Fascism on its peoples. Sackville-West's response to the
political tensions of the time was to draw back into her own
concerns. She and Nicolson bought Sissinghurst Castle as a
ruin in 1930, and on 16 October 1930, Vita Sackville-West
spent her first night at Sissinghurst. She slept alone, in the
tower where, in future, she would establish her writing room.
This retreat to Sissinghurst, a withdrawal from London and
social life, symbolized a tendency towards introversion that
was linked to her growing preoccupation with religion and
mysticism. She wrote to Virginia Woolf in April 1926:

And as I get older (I had a birthday only the other day,) I find I get
more and more disagreeably solitary, in fact I foresee the day when I
shall have gone so far into myself that there will no longer be
anything to be seen of me at all. Will you, please, remember to pull
away the coverings from time to time? or I shall get quite lost.[1]

But by the time she began to shut herself away in her beloved
tower, Virginia Woolf no longer had the power—maybe not
even the desire—to pull away the covers. Their friendship was
changing; Woolf involved herself more and more with Ethel
Smyth, and Sackville-West grew more and more absorbed in
the creation of her garden. In 1931, the Hogarth Press
brought out her poem, *Sissinghurst*, dedicated to 'V.W.' and
describing the strange underwater world in which she was now
moving:

[1] *The Letters of Vita Sackville-West to Virginia Woolf*, ed. Louise DeSalvo and
Mitchell A. Leaska (London, 1985), 118–19, 8 Apr. 1926.

> I've sunk into an image, water-drowned,
> Where stirs no wind and penetrates no sound,
> Illusive, fragile to a touch, remote,
> Foundered within the well of years as deep
> As in the waters of a stagnant moat.[2]

From now on, Sackville-West's writing would be increasingly pervaded by a longing for silence, for immersion, for seclusion, and the underwater world of *Sissinghurst* was a farewell to Woolf using one of the images of which Woolf was especially fond.

In the summer of 1933, Sackville-West had a visitor. Gwen St. Aubyn, Harold Nicolson's younger sister, had been in a serious car accident, and came to convalesce at Sissinghurst. The two women, previously distant from one another, gradually became closer. Each was looking for some kind of spiritual solution to the problems of their lives, and Sackville-West accompanied her sister-in-law to her reception into the Roman Catholic Church in February 1935. But institutional worship filled Sackville-West with doubt, and during the following years she combined the obsessive solitude of her writing with an equally lonely religious search, turning to the texts and lives of female mystics in an attempt to find a private faith. In her biographies of female saints (*Saint Joan of Arc*, 1936, and *The Eagle and the Dove: A Study in Contrasts, St. Teresa of Avila, St. Thérèse of Lisieux*, 1943), she was, as she had in *Pepita*, re-creating the stories of other women in an attempt to shape her own. This exploration of female mysticism was undertaken under the inspiration of her closeness to her sister-in-law. This chapter will trace a tradition of mystic companionships between women, and suggest an alternative reading of the image of the female mystic to that proposed by French psychoanalyst Jacques Lacan.

In the early decades of the twentieth century, there was a general renewal of interest in mysticism and mystic states of mind. Although one of the strongest elements in that revival was an openness to Eastern mysticism—the popularity of Rabindranath Tagore, for example—the dominant tradition in England was Judaeo-Christian and patriarchal. All the

---

[2] V. Sackville-West, *Sissinghurst* (London, 1931), no page numbers.

mystics discussed here, including Sackville-West, situated themselves, however problematically, within that tradition; thus my remarks on mystic philosophy apply only to the Judaeo-Christian culture. The mystic experience itself, within that culture, is by definition inexpressible. It is described in terms of a heightened consciousness, a feeling of the harmony of the world, a sense of oneness or union with godhead: Evelyn Underhill's *Mysticism* scrupulously documents all the variants.[3] But, in her biographies, Sackville-West is less concerned with the nature of the mystic consciousness, than with the conditions of its growth and its effects on daily life. The emphasis of her life-writing is on the everyday: how the women lived, what they did, and how they integrated their mysticism into a routine. Thus she pays great attention to Joan's military strategy, to the details of Teresa's initial resistance to convent life, and to St. Thérèse of Lisieux's fight to join the Carmelites. Sackville-West's interest is in adaptation, which she takes to be the crux not only of her own autobiography, as we have seen, but also of the lives of others. Lacan suggests that the essence of female mysticism is a movement beyond the possibility of meaning and the everyday. 'There is a *jouissance*, since we are dealing with *jouissance*, a *jouissance* of the body which is, if the expression be allowed, *beyond the phallus*.'[4] To go beyond the phallus is to go beyond language and the law, to be excluded, as Lacan says, 'by the nature of things which is the nature of words'.[5] But for Sackville-West and her contemporaries, mystic feelings, far from exceeding the everyday, are (sometimes vexatiously) simply part of it. Moreover, where for Lacan mystic feeling is quintessentially feminine (even when the mystic is male), for the women I shall consider in this chapter, mysticism seems to trouble, rather than to guarantee, gender. Sackville-West used her religious sense to develop her sense of her own sexuality and her gender: to experiment and to affirm.

This was not a direction in which most mystic philosophies

---

[3] See Evelyn Underhill, *Mysticism: A Study in the Nature and Development of Man's Spiritual Consciousness* (London, 1911).

[4] Jacques Lacan, 'God and the *Jouissance* of Woman. A Love Letter', trans. Jacqueline Rose in Juliet Mitchell and Jacqueline Rose (ed.), *Feminine Sexuality: Jacques Lacan and the Ecole Freudienne* (London, 1982), 145.   [5] Ibid. 144.

of the early twentieth century were going. All the same, Sackville-West's work was part of a more general trend of research on the history and practice of mysticism. May Sinclair, in her philosophical book *A Defence of Idealism* (1917), comments that although belief in the supernatural is dying out, mysticism, 'so far from being near its death in this century . . . seems to be approaching a rather serious revival'.[6] Women were a significant presence in that revival. Evelyn Underhill, for example, published *Mysticism* in 1911, and followed it up with the even more successful *Practical Mysticism* in 1914. She had converted to Christianity in 1906, after a prolonged period of doubt:

For eight or nine years I really believed myself to be an atheist. Philosophy brought me round to an intelligent and irresponsible sort of theism which I enjoyed thoroughly but which did not last long. Gradually the net closed in on me and I was driven nearer and nearer to Christianity, half of me wishing it were true and half of me resisting violently.[7]

Christopher Armstrong suggests that she was one of the main architects of the mystic revival preceding the war. Her prominence naturally drew attention to the peculiar contribution women could make to the wider debate, and throughout the 1930s Underhill led a series of retreats for women only.

The traditions of mysticism were a central concern of the revivalists. For May Sinclair, mysticism almost did not have a history: 'They are so unanimous that, divided as they are by centuries and continents, there is less distance between a Christian mystic of the thirteenth century and a Buddhist mystic of the present day than there is, say, between Mr. Bertrand Russell and Mr. Gilbert Chesterton.'[8] Dean Inge, in *Christian Mysticism*, on the other hand, saw mystics as an anticipatory glimpse of the heights to which humankind would eventually rise; mystic experience was, he maintained, 'a sort of higher instinct, perhaps an anticipation of the evolutionary process'.[9] Sackville-West went even further. She was concerned

---

[6] May Sinclair, *A Defence of Idealism* (London, 1917), 283.
[7] Quoted in Christopher Armstrong, *Evelyn Underhill (1875–1941)* (London, 1975), 31.   [8] Sinclair, *A Defence of Idealism*, 272.
[9] Quoted in Armstrong, *Evelyn Underhill*, 66.

to find a scientific account of mysticism, and consulted the *Proceedings of the Society for Psychical Research* as well as the work of eugenicist Francis Galton, for her biography of Joan of Arc. Galton she found reassuring partly, one may speculate, because of his mapping of mysticism onto his theories of heredity and class with which Sackville-West was already so involved.

Historians and philosophers, in looking to the inner life of men and women, were mimicking the tendencies of the new religious consciousness itself. Dean Inge, in the *TLS* in 1913, notes a large increase in the numbers of Quakers, a phenomenon which was dramatized in Dorothy Richardson's *Pilgrimage* (reviewed by May Sinclair and Virginia Woolf), in which the central character, Miriam Henderson, is deeply attracted to Quakerism.[10] The Quaker faith, with its emphasis on private experiences, and its rejection of a formal creed, mirrored the increasing interest in the individual and his or her psychology. Nor was mysticism's influence on religious institutions only. At the same time that the Society for Psychical Research was using scientific experiment to explore occult phenomena, scientific disciplines were beginning to share some of mysticism's assumptions and methods. The work of psychologist Henri Bergson on intuition suggested the possibility of a mode of perception which could transcend the division of subject and object: exactly what mysticism claimed to do. Bergson contrasted intuitive modes of perception with 'intellectual' ones, and suggested that intuition allowed the dynamic flow of energies within and between human minds.[11] I shall discuss Bergson's work more fully later on.

Mysticism in the late nineteenth–early twentieth century was not only, as May Sinclair suggested, the gradual merging of Eastern and Western philosophies (although she had little patience with theosophy); it was also part of a growing fashion for the occult, for telepathy, and for hypnosis.[12] The

[10] See ibid. 156.

[11] See Henri Bergson, *Creative Evolution*, trans. Arthur Mitchell (London, 1911), p. xi.

[12] For accounts of May Sinclair's mystic philosophy see T. E. M. Boll, *Miss May Sinclair, Novelist, a Biographical and Critical Introduction* (Rutherford, NJ, 1973); Rebecca Neff, 'New Mysticism in the Writing of May Sinclair and T. S. Eliot', *Twentieth-Century Literature*, 26 (1980), 82–100; and H. D. Zegger, *May Sinclair*

respectability and public profile of the Society for Psychical Research was only one aspect of this. Radclyffe Hall and Una Troubridge had presented a joint research paper on their weekly seances with Hall's dead lover, Mabel Batten, which was warmly received by the SPR; but when in 1920 the Society wished to co-opt Hall onto its council, Fox-Pitt, already a council member, objected to her on grounds of morality. Hall sued for slander and won, but the whole affair highlighted the conservative and stuffy atmosphere of a society that was desperately keen to preserve its scientific and social credentials. There was even some dispute over whether it was Hall's life, or her paper, that was immoral![13]

Soon after the furore over Hall and Troubridge (which established at least an anecdotal link between lesbianism and spiritualism), Ouspensky arrived in London to rapturous acclaim. His success demonstrated public interest in what Ouspensky called, in his best-selling *Tertium Organum* (translated in 1923), different levels of consciousness and multiple psychical lives.[14] Increased knowledge of the occult, and of the relation between the mind and body, raised hopes about the cure of disease. Medicine and mysticism grew closer, just as experimental science and research into occult phenomena had done. The dying Katherine Mansfield sought out Ouspensky's teacher Gurdjieff and entered his institute at Fontainebleau, in the hope that he could cure her tuberculosis.[15] William James wrote extensively about the 'mind-cure', in which auto-suggestion is used to improve mental and physical health; and May Sinclair was to dramatize a case of healing via states of mystic consciousness in her story 'The Flaw in the Crystal'.[16]

(Boston, 1976). For more general discussions of spiritualism and the occult in the period see Alex Owen, *The Darkened Room: Women, Power and Spiritualism in Late Victorian England* (London, 1989); and Diana Basham, *The Trial of Woman: Feminism and the Occult Sciences in Victorian Literature and Society* (London, 1991).

[13] For an account of these events see Michael Baker, *Our Three Selves: A Life of Radclyffe Hall* (London, 1985), 123–32.

[14] P. D. Ouspensky, *Tertium Organum: The Third Canon of Thought*, trans. Nicholas Bessaraboff and Claude Bragdon, 2nd edn. (London, 1923), 198–9.

[15] For a more detailed discussion of Katherine Mansfield's mysticism see James Moore, *Gurdjieff and Katherine Mansfield* (London, 1980).

[16] See William James, *The Varieties of Religious Experience* (Harmondsworth, 1982); and May Sinclair, 'The Flaw in the Crystal', 1911, repr. in Sinclair, *Uncanny Stories* (London, 1923), 59–142.

The publicity given by the medical profession to hysteria, and the close resemblance between the symptoms of hysteria and the physical effects of a mystic trance (St Teresa suffered paralysis and so on), ensured that mysticism would be interpreted by some as an indication of disease. The dying Katherine Mansfield's desperate approach to Gurdjieff seemed to confirm the idea that illness, and a belief in mysticism, were somehow connected. The pathology of her illness was the aetiology of her mysticism. May Sinclair, however, defended mysticism against the charge of neurosis: 'the specialist in morbid psychology will tell you that the history of Mysticism is a history of neurosis.' But, she maintains, this is a result of a misguidedly literal reading of mystic texts: 'its criticism rests on the assumption that ends have the same form as origins, which is contrary not only to evolution, but to the psychoanalyst's own pet theory of sublimation.'[17] Sinclair admits that Teresa may have expressed an unsublimated libido in her trances, but 'New Mysticism' (as she calls it) guards against such an event by stressing the integration of body and mind, and the spiritual aspects of earthly life. Sackville-West also is keen to defend Joan of Arc from imputations of neurosis:

Jeanne was neither an ecstatic, nor a mystic, nor in any sense of the word a 'hysterical' person. We can find no signs in her of any exaggeration of feelings or temperament. Neither ecstasy nor despondency affected her unduly. She was neither disproportionately lifted up nor disproportionately cast down. (*JA*, 382)

In fact, as Sackville-West emphasizes, her feelings about the voices that she heard were fairly pragmatic, and apparently far from the incomprehension that Lacan describes: 'they [women] don't know what they are saying.'[18] In Sackville-West's narrative, Joan of Arc is practical, shrewd, and self-knowing, working always to fulfil the demands and predictions of her voices in her everyday life.

Traditionally, mystico-religious crises have been sexual: Augustine, for example. But for Gwen St. Aubyn, and for other religious women of the period, the story was rather different. She was driven to religion by maternal, rather than

---

[17] Both quotations are from Sinclair, *A Defence of Idealism*, 322.
[18] Lacan, 'God and the *Jouissance*', 144.

sexual, anxiety. When St. Aubyn arrived at Sissinghurst, she was simultaneously engaged in spiritual and maternal endeavours, investigating Catholicism, and editing a book of advice to parents (*The Family Book*, 1934). It was her feelings of inadequacy as a mother and educator that drove her to religious enquiry: 'how could I avoid issues? I must know and believe more to teach. I was giving them nothing. I must find out, know and practise the doctrines of the Church of England to which I belonged.'[19] But Vita Sackville-West, on the other hand, who Virginia Woolf noted was rather cold with her sons (*D*, iii. 52, 21 Dec. 1925), experienced spiritual crisis not as a maternal but as a sexual event. Her attitude was more conventionally masculine, implicitly taking Augustine as a model.

> Thus love, bright charlatan, besieged my heart,
> And took my time, and set my sense apart,
> Wasting my days and nights, when other streams
> Were damned by those fair, delusive dreams
> We label love, and then as truth impart.[20]

Her oscillation between masculine and feminine identifications in her spiritual development underlined its link with her gender and her sexuality, also conceived as part masculine, part feminine. (As we saw in the Introduction, the lesbian gaze in her poetry is conceived as a collaboration of male and female.) For Sackville-West, sexual feeling was a shifting between gender positions, and *Solitude* is grounded in the confusion of identity to which that shifting gives rise:

> O God!—and here, as at the altar's bell,
> I, unbeliever, bow in suffering
> Before immortal anguish greatly told,—
> O God! I ask, as with my graveyard knell,
> I ask, beseech, I, unbeliever, bold,
> Beg to enclose my life within the ring
> Of that secure belief, so blindly pure.
>
> There is the crux, the Cross; which, none can tell.
>
> But silence meets me; all my prayer is vain,
> Returned petition lacking signature.[21]

---

[19] St. Aubyn, *Towards a Pattern* (London, 1940), 26.
[20] V. Sackville-West, *Solitude* (London, 1938), p. 28.   [21] Ibid., pp. 50–1.

'The ring of that secure belief' could as easily be the wedding ring, with its apparent guarantee of sexual roles, as the ring of faith. We have seen that Sackville-West depended on the conventions of her marriage to give structure and coherence to her sexual identity; she also longed for institutional rules to organize her sometimes frightening feelings of mystic insight. The poem dramatizes a rejection of 'cheap and easy loves' and a consequent movement into solitude and sexual and spiritual experimentation.

Sackville-West's validation of sexual evasiveness and isolation as a part of her mysticism challenges any easy correlation between neurotic exhibitionism and feminine mysticism. St Teresa, in Sackville-West's *The Eagle and the Dove*, is embarrassed and ashamed about her frequent visions and sudden levitations.

Often she went away to hide herself from view; and sometimes she would not even dare to ask for holy water when devils were present although one knew it to be the sovereign remedy. This shrinking, this desire for secrecy and privacy, is far removed from the exhibitionism of the hysteric determined to be interesting at any cost.[22]

Most depictions of Teresa's ecstasy, including the Bernini statue commented on at such length by French psychoanalyst Jacques Lacan, illustrate the short account in her autobiography of her piercing by the angel's lance.[23] This has been easily interpreted as an image of sexual penetration, and Crashaw's poem, quoted by Sackville-West, mentions 'that final kiss / That seized thy parting soul, and sealed thee His'. In fact, this shaping of Teresa's story, and the emphasis on this one episode, contradicts her own version of events. She makes it clear that her piercing by the lance is a recurring vision: 'it would please the Lord that I should sometimes see the following vision.'[24] Far from being the unique climax of her spiritual pilgrimage, the vision of the angel pulsed through the whole of her journey, and was only one among

---

[22] V. Sackville-West, *The Eagle and the Dove: A Study in Contrasts, St. Theresa of Avila, St. Thérèse of Lisieux* (London, 1943), 29.

[23] The statue by Bernini in Rome, for example, on which Lacan comments at length in his seminar, dramatizes exactly this moment.

[24] St. Teresa of Avila, *The Life of St. Teresa of Avila*, 1562–5, trans. E. Allison Peers (London, 1979), 192.

many such images. St Teresa's reticent and practical life is hardly adequately summarized in this image of an orgasmic swoon. Sackville-West seeks to put the record straight. In her commentary on Crashaw's poem, she stresses 'the other note he was discerning enough to introduce—the reference to her "large draughts of intellectual day".'[25] Teresa's intellectualism, in Sackville-West's words, 'implicitly discountenances the misjudgment that she indulged almost voluptuously in the fits of possession that sometimes came upon her'.[26] Sackville-West's biography determinedly resists conventional expectations, and in doing so begins to redefine the terms of representation of female ecstasy and female mysticism.

Nor was Sackville-West the only lesbian writer to offer a reconsideration of St Teresa in the 1930s and 1940s. On 8 February 1934, Gertrude Stein's opera *Four Saints in Three Acts* opened to rapturous audiences in Hartford, Connecticut, USA. It was intended as an event rather than as a narrative. Stein envisaged it as a 'landscape', of sound and of colour. The music was by Virgil Thomson, the staging by Frederick Ashton, and it had a black cast. After a week the opera transferred to New York, where it continued to enjoy an enormous success.[27]

It is a curiously static and repetitive piece of work. St Teresa is placed on the threshold of her house: 'Saint Therese very nearly half inside and half outside the house and not surrounded.'[28] The public and the private are also invoked: 'Saint Therese. Who settles a private life.'[29] At the same time, 'nobody visits more than they do visit them'.[30] The mystic, unable to express what has happened to her, is sought after exactly because of her silence. Her body can become ambiguous, as the container of her vision, and its ambiguity can be hypnotic:

Saint Therese seated and not standing half and half of it and not half and half of it seated and not standing surrounded and not seated

[25] Sackville-West, *The Eagle and the Dove*, 14.   [26] Ibid.

[27] For an account of this see Janet Hobhouse, *Everybody who was Anybody: A Biography of Gertrude Stein* (New York, 1975), 170–4.

[28] Gertrude Stein, *Four Saints in Three Acts: An Opera to be Sung* (New York, 1934), 23.

[29] Ibid.   [30] Ibid.

and not seated and not standing and not surrounded and not not surrounded not not not seated not seated not seated not surrounded not seated and Saint Ignatius standing standing not seated Saint Therese not standing not standing and Saint Ignatius not standing standing surrounded as if in once yesterday. In place of situations.[31]

The insistence of Stein's prose echoes St Teresa's preoccupation with the bodily status of her visions and voices: 'she was not even sure whether she *heard* the words or not.'[32] Stein, and Sackville-West (following Teresa) are concerned to unsettle assumptions about the physical manifestations of mystic experience: Sackville-West emphasizes Teresa's struggles to resist fainting rather than her participation in it. For Stein, St Teresa, generally taken as the symbol of the most intense ecstasy, is actually half sitting, half standing, confused, alien.

This concern with redefinition is clear also from Sackville-West's choice of Joan of Arc as the subject of her first saint's life. Joan's virginity and the image of her as a prepubescent girl, stressed by Sackville-West, prevent explanation of her experience in terms of excessive sexual excitement. Sackville-West's book opens on the question of portraiture: 'no contemporary portrait of Jeanne d'Arc is known to exist. Possibly none ever existed at all' (*JA*, 1). This is Joan's first act of evasion: not to have been depicted in any way. Evasiveness, the shifting of ground, becomes her characteristic mode during her trial: 'ce n'est pas de votre procès; Am I obliged to tell you that?; passez outre—she objects repeatedly', notes Sackville-West (*JA*, 321). Sackville-West complains about the 'double image' of posthumous representation ('Jeanne pensive and pastoral, or . . . Jeanne embattled and heroic' (*JA*, 2)):

The lover of truth sighs in vain for one plain portrait, unflattering, authentic, crude; . . . a quiet statement of what Jeanne looked like, whether in daily life at her father's house, or in the few strenuous months when by popular acclaim she became known throughout France. (*JA*, 2)

Sackville-West is particularly frustrated by this omission because Joan's personality, in her view, was so undramatic. 'Throughout all her strange experiences she preserved a

---

[31] Ibid. 24.   [32] Sackville-West, *The Eagle and the Dove*, 55.

remarkably constant level. The darker passages of the soul seem never to have affected her life at all' (*JA*, 382). It is Joan's good sense that complicates her mysticism. Sackville-West notes how different Joan of Arc is from her 'fellow-saints', with her level-headed shrewdness and her bad manners:

She never, for instance, used such conventional expressions as 'my heavenly Spouse', or 'my Betrothed', as are common to most women of mystical inclination. I think that possibly she had no need thus to sublimate her earthly desires in this pseudo-sexual fashion, since she found her outlet in her ardent devotion to the Dauphin and to the cause of France. (*JA*, 383)

Joan's sexuality, then, was bound up for Sackville-West, with her feelings of patriotism rather than with her feelings of religious faith. Her mysticism was channelled into fighting for France, rather than into fighting for her own sexuality.

This refusal to live her mysticism as a sexual experience is signalled in her adoption of masculine dress. Her costume made it impossible to produce images of her like the Bernini statue of St Teresa in ecstasy. Her identity as a woman was compromised by her clothes. Sackville-West, herself keen on wearing men's clothing, is peculiarly fascinated by Joan's choice in this matter: 'one wonders what her feelings were, when for the first time she surveyed her cropped head and moved her legs unencumbered by her red skirt' (*JA*, 10). Sackville-West is eager to find a practical explanation for Joan's behaviour, and suggests that 'she ran less danger of rape than if she went about dressed as a woman' (*JA*, 326).

But Joan must have had more reasons than the threat of sexual attack for her choice of clothes. Sackville-West, in spite of her insistence on Joan's common sense, does finally admit to some puzzlement. Joan, in prison, deprived herself of Mass through her refusal to put on women's clothes.

One can understand her adoption of men's clothes as a reasonable and indeed necessary precaution for the preservation of her virginity; it is harder to understand her obstinacy at such a cost. Either it must have turned into a matter of principle by then, mixed up with all the other dictates of her voices, or else a very bitter experience must have convinced her that therein lay her only safety in a world of men. (*JA*, 345)

Joan, protecting herself from rape, is also refusing a sexual identity, as a 'matter of principle'. Her avoidance of a traditionally feminine life involves rejection of any kind of sexual narrative, and her male clothing is another instance of her characteristic evasiveness.

Unlike St Teresa, Joan cannot be represented as all body, because her body is constantly elusive. As Sackville-West tells us, she was repeatedly examined to see if she was a virgin—the coverings constantly pulled away. The examination became something of a spectacle: 'the Duchess of Bedford either came in person or sent other women to investigate the matter. Boisguillaume suggests that Bedford himself witnessed the inspection, hidden in a secret place' (*JA*, 304). But the spectacle of Joan as woman was constantly refused. She seemed to move in a world without body, and refused to be drawn on the physical features of the saints in her visions: 'I do not know. I do not know whether they have any arms or other members' (*JA*, 325). In spite of her earthiness, Joan and her heavenly visitors were somehow not there: not there because not female, and not there because not sexual.

Joan's elusiveness is paralleled in Sackville-West's own fading persona within the biography itself. Woolf was unsure about the book: 'My only criticism is that you've been so damned fair that one feels now and then a kind of wrench towards the middle of the road, not quite enough rush and flight to make Jeanne angular: to make her I mean rise up identical above all these facts' (*L*, vi. 49–50, 29 June 1936). Sackville-West's pseudo-scientific scrupulousness resulted in both her and Joan getting lost. To Ethel Smyth, Woolf wrote that Sackville-West 'sat too firm on the hedge for any picture to emerge' (*L*, vi. 57, 20 July 1936). Sackville-West's strategy as a biographer was a self-effacement which echoed that of her first subject. Both Joan and Sackville-West refused many of the trappings of femininity, and thus disappeared somehow from the sexual map. This tentativeness is exactly counter to Lacan's contention that female mysticism is a form of certainty for the spectator: 'you only have to go and look at Bernini's statue in Rome to understand immediately that she's coming, there is no doubt about it'.[33] Mysticism is the *spectacle*,

---

[33] Lacan, 'God and the *Jouissance*', 147.

rather than the experience, of truth. In Lacan's words, 'it is clear that the essential testimony of the mystics is that they are experiencing it but know nothing about it.'[34] Sackville-West's narrative of Joan of Arc seems to contradict this absolutely. Joan's experience simply *cannot* be seen; and yet her own belief in it is unshakeable. The lesbian context and tradition of women's mysticism gives the lie to Lacan more powerfully than many feminist commentaries on his work have done.

Nor is Sackville-West the only woman to challenge Lacan's paradigm. Woolf too sees her own mystic narrative as a self-conscious negotiation of questions of sexuality and identity. She writes of a private rhapsodic feeling that she experienced when she was a child. 'The most important of all my memories', she says, is of lying in bed in the nursery in her family's house in St. Ives listening to the waves on the nearby beach, and the tapping of the blind in the breeze.

If life has a base that it stands upon, if it is a bowl that one fills and fills and fills—then my soul without a doubt stands upon this memory . . . It is of lying and hearing this splash and seeing this light, and feeling, it is almost impossible that I should be here; of feeling the purest ecstasy I can conceive. (SP, 75)

The scene is associated with her mother, with the innocent safety of childhood, and with some kind of initiation—the beginning of consciousness and of a personal identity: it 'seems to be my first memory' (SP, 74). This memory's counterpart, Woolf's other image of the 'base' of her life, is a picture of her lost Cornish garden.

The apples were on a level with one's head. The gardens gave off a murmur of bees; the apples were red and gold; there were also pink flowers; and grey and silver leaves. The buzz, the croon, the smell, all seemed to press voluptuously against some membrane; not to burst it; but to hum round one such a complete rapture of pleasure that I stopped; smelt; looked. But again I cannot describe that rapture. It was rapture rather than ecstasy. (SP, 77)

Though the terms are erotic (pressure against a membrane) there is no climax: the membrane never bursts, the blind taps but never blows open. The setting is a child's secret space, a

---

[34] Lacan, 'God and the *Jouissance*', 147.

child's secret body. 'I am hardly aware of myself, but only of the sensation. I am only the container of the feeling of ecstasy, of the feeling of rapture' (SP, 78). This unthinking and immediate pleasure—'I stopped, smelt, looked'—is shattered in her autobiography by her brother George, who puts his hand beneath her clothes and starts a feeling of shame and fear—'I must have been ashamed or afraid of my own body' (SP, 79). Woolf's story, perhaps consciously (she had by this time read Sackville-West's biography), recalls Joan's rejection of the sexual, her repeated vaginal examinations, her first vision in the fields—or, in one account quoted by Sackville-West, in the garden—near her home.

The close connection between mystical and autobiographical narratives has sometimes been noted, but rarely been analysed or commented on at length. Both William James in *The Varieties of Religious Experience* (1902) and Evelyn Underhill in *Mysticism* (1911) draw heavily on autobiographical testimony for their evidence. In Underhill's words:

If we want to see what it really means to be 'in love with the Absolute',—how intensely actual to the mystic is the object of his passion, how far removed from the sphere of pious duty, or of philosophic speculation, how concrete, positive and dominant such a passion may be—we must study the literature of autobiography, not that of poetry or exhortation.[35]

James, writing about 'saintliness', maintains that 'if we wish the undiluted ascetic spirit . . . we must go to autobiographies, or other individual documents'.[36] Autobiography is assumed to be a private space in which the mystery of mysticism can be uniquely articulated. William James repeatedly quotes from the manuscript and letter collection of Starbuck (author of *The Psychology of Religion*); Starbuck, in the course of his 'statistical inquiry' into conversion, apparently elicited autobiographical accounts and letters from large numbers of people, and used them—as does James—as the evidence for his research.

When we read this kind of evidence for women, we see how

---

[35] Underhill, *Mysticism*, 104.
[36] James, *The Varieties of Religious Experience*, 304.

misguided is the view that the mystic experience is somehow the climax of the life narrative, in which selfhood is
finally achieved. In much women's autobiography, mysticism
is seen as the beginning of the whole problem, the engen-
dering of subjectivity itself. Women's autobiographical self-
construction often takes as its point of departure a moment
of almost extra-corporeal intensity—Dorothy Richardson's
'bee-memory' in *Pilgrimage*, for example. A mystical experience is located as the initiation of a sense of identity, the
origin to which subsequent developments are always account-
able. The Edenic or rural nature of Woolf's earliest memories
—even her first memory of her mother involves 'red and
purple flowers' (SP, 74)—suggests that this pattern in
women's autobiographies is linked to the lesbian pastoral
evoked in the poetry discussed in the Introduction. Lesbian
poems and autobiographies reach back to a world before
the assumption of heterosexuality, a world in which the
women—and particularly the mother—collude to keep men
out. Woolf comments that 'Nessa and I formed together a very
close conspiracy. In that world of many men, coming and
going, we formed our private nucleus' (SP, 144). And
Sackville-West had only one friend as a child—the same Violet
Keppel who would later return to disrupt her marriage with
such explosive force (*PM*, 26). The pull of autobiography, and
the pull of mysticism, was back towards a time when gender
was in suspension, not yet resolved; but when the attentions
of women were all-encompassing. It is not surprising, then,
to find so many lesbians of this period viewing a shared exploration of religious feelings as an essential bond.[37]

For Sackville-West, whose sexual identity, like Orlando's and
Joan's, seemed to contain both the masculine and the feminine, the lesbian context was particularly powerful. Her affection for Gwen St. Aubyn seemed to allow the expression both
of multiple gender identifications (by this stage Sackville-West
almost never wore a skirt), and of feelings of religious revelation. In 1940, Gwen St. Aubyn published a book called

---

[37] For further discussion of this issue see Joanne Glasgow, 'What's a Nice
Lesbian Like You Doing in the Church of Torquemada? Radclyffe Hall and Other
Catholic Converts', in Karla Jay and Joanne Glasgow (ed.), *Lesbian Texts and
Contexts: Radical Revisions* (New York, 1990), 241–54.

Towards a Pattern. In it she describes her early spiritual history, and her conversion to Catholicism. The text takes the form of a series of letters to an unnamed correspondent, 'dearest'. But the addressee is clearly identifiable: the one person to accompany St. Aubyn to her first confession, an incident to which reference is made in the text, was Sackville-West. The letters chronicle the two women's growing intimacy as well as St. Aubyn's deepening faith, and their friendship provides a grounding for her religious belief. St. Aubyn describes a crucial moment in her history:

> Over a fortnight later I was sitting at my table writing my daily letters.
> The room was quiet and warm.
> I was happy, occupied, and at ease.
> Suddenly the room seemed to fade. I heard your pen scratching as you wrote, then that too ceased to strike my senses.
> Instead I only saw a great white light. I can only use the word Radiant. It was opaque, but shone and dazzled me. It was soundless, heatless, shapeless, motionless, yet vividly a live light.
> The whole impression lasted only a second. It ceased to exist abruptly, almost sharply. The room, and you, were there, and so was I, but I was conscious of an enormous change in me.[38]

Sackville-West's presence, and the scratching of her pen (again writing is crucial to the relationship between the two women), frame St. Aubyn's vision, grounding it in the friendship between the two women while at the same time allowing St. Aubyn spiritual privacy. Later, Sackville-West will be her only confidante, apart from two Catholic friends. It is evident that they offer institutional guidance; and that Sackville-West, at once friend and sister-in-law, functions as a personal, private collaborator in the search for faith: 'strange revealer of myself, dear gentle guide, wild and undisciplined, childish philosopher, "my poet and my friend"', as St. Aubyn says.[39]

Sackville-West herself gave an account of their relationship in a novel published in 1934, and dedicated to Gwen St. Aubyn, *The Dark Island.* The central character, Shirin, marries Venn in order to gain access to the Scottish island on which he lives; but her deepest affinity is with her friend Christina,

---

[38] St. Aubyn, *Towards a Pattern,* 49.   [39] Ibid. 73.

who shortly after Shirin's marriage moves up to live with her and act as her secretary. Virginia Woolf clearly thought she knew what it was about. Writing to Ethel Smyth about *The Dark Island* she says: 'we lunched with them: she never sits at ease; Gwen: like a scissors. Have you read the book "their" book' (*L*, v. 338, 12 Oct. 1934). Earlier, Woolf criticized Sackville-West for 'writing too much in the personal zone'; but then she suspects that 'my knowledge of the real people has queered the pitch for me; and no doubt I'm subcutaneously jealous' (Woolf to Sackville-West, *L*, v. 333, 23 Sept. 1934). Shirin and Christina over the years build up an 'absolute intimacy, trust and confidence . . . partly mystical in its character', and Shirin, secure in her love for Christina, manages to develop a 'private mysticism which now at least enabled her to accept the wounds of life'.[40] In the novel, as in St. Aubyn's autobiography, the relationship between the two women is seen as the source of a mystic consciousness, protecting and enabling the women involved.

If St. Aubyn and Sackville-West were the only women who had ever discovered mysticism in each other's company, lesbian feelings and mystic experiences would have little more than a random connection. But here too Sackville-West and her sister-in-law seem to have been part of a social and cultural tradition that is easily overlooked. Sackville-West is keen to emphasize that Joan of Arc, contrary to her image, was from time to time thrown into intimacy with women: 'this young fighting captain could consort with women in an even more natural freemasonry than she could consort with men' (*JA*, 264). Other women of Sackville-West's time also link the experience of conversion with the influence of one woman on another. Annie Besant, describing her introduction to theosophy in her autobiography, emphasizes the personal magnetism of Helena Blavatsky, the movement's leader. After reading Blavatsky's *The Secret Doctrine*, Besant pays her a visit:

We rose to go, and for a moment the veil lifted, and two brilliant, piercing eyes met mine, and with a yearning throb in the voice: 'Oh, my dear Mrs. Besant, if you would only come among us!' I felt a well-

---

[40] V. Sackville-West, *The Dark Island* (London, 1934), 259, 227.

nigh uncontrollable desire to bend down and kiss her, under the compulsion of that yearning voice, those compelling eyes.[41]

Later Besant, under instruction from Blavatsky, reads a disparaging account of theosophy, accusing its leaders of exaggeration, inaccuracy, and corruption, but Besant laughs and flings the report aside: 'could I put such against the frank, fearless nature that I had caught a glimpse of, against the proud fiery truthfulness that shone at me from the clear, blue eyes, honest and fearless as those of a noble child?'[42] Her reception into the Theosophical Society is dramatized not as the signing of an application form (which was in fact all that was involved) but as a ceremonial self-dedication to Blavatsky: 'I knelt down before her and clasped her hands in mine, looking straight into her eyes . . . Her stern, set face softened, the unwonted gleam of tears sprang to her eyes; then, with a dignity more than regal, she placed her hand upon my head.'[43] Besant's commitment to theosophy is imaged, in the autobiography, as synonymous with her devotion to Blavatsky. The two strands of feeling feed on and strengthen one another.

Besant's life poses very directly the question of sexuality and control over the body (that control that Teresa of Avila, suddenly levitating in the middle of a sentence, felt she had lost). Before she became a theosophist, Annie Besant was already famous, with Charles Bradlaugh, for publishing a banned pamphlet on birth control. Besant felt theosophy to be incompatible with contraception, and in 1896 issued a justification of her change of attitude: 'Theosophists should sound the note of self-restraint within marriage, and the restriction of the marital relation to the perpetuation of the race . . . passing from Materialism to Theosophy, I must pass from neo-Malthusianism to what will be called asceticism.'[44] Besant's theosophy strengthened her belief in evolution and the gradual development of a superior race. Indeed theosophy must have seemed an ideal version of mysticism for

---

[41] Annie Besant, *An Autobiography* (London, 1893), 341.

[42] Ibid. 343.   [43] Ibid. 344.

[44] Annie Besant, 'Theosophy and the Law of Population', 1896, repr. in S. Chandrasekhar (ed.), *'A Dirty, Filthy Book': The Writings of Charles Knowlton and Annie Besant on Reproductive Physiology and Birth Control—an Account of the Bradlaugh-Besant Trial* (Berkeley, Calif., 1981), 211.

evolutionists, since the theory of reincarnation was a religious explanation for what Darwin had already explained scientifically: the gradual improvement of the species.

Other women in the early twentieth century were also writing about their mystic feelings as the product of same-sex relationships. H.D. describes her vision of writing on the wall at great length in *Tribute to Freud*. The vision occurred in 1920, during a trip to Greece with her lover, Winifred Ellermann ('Bryher').

I knew that this experience, this writing-on-the-wall before me . . . could not be shared with anyone except the girl who stood so bravely there beside me. This girl had said without hesitation, 'Go on.' It was she really who had the detachment and the integrity of the Pythoness of Delphi . . . we were 'seeing' it together, for without her, admittedly, I could not have gone on.[45]

Here, the mystic vision is the product of a shared gaze between women, a shared revelation. Although Bryher does not actually see the writing, they are 'seeing' it together, and their intimacy is the condition without which the vision could not survive.

H.D.'s account of this episode shares some important features with Gwen St. Aubyn's description of her vision of the white light quoted earlier. Both experiences seem to occur on the boundary between intimacy and isolation, between love and solitude. An event is shared, but silently, and apparently without the conscious awareness of one of the spectators that anything is happening. This kind of communality is central to *The Waves*, discussed in the next chapter; but it is central also, as we have seen, to the writing of biographies: always a celebration of an intimacy of which one of the participants is almost always unaware. However, all biographies, as we have seen, necessarily engage with mourning—the end of intimacy —as well as with intimacy itself, and that engagement is played out in Sackville-West's biographies also.

Sackville-West spends many pages of *The Eagle and the Dove* describing what happened to St Teresa of Avila after her death. As for all subjects of biographies, death never quite seemed to be accomplished; and in Teresa's case, her resur-

[45] H. D., *Tribute to Freud* (Manchester, 1985), 48–9.

rection was literalized in the events of her life themselves. Teresa's corpse resisted decay and gave off a penetrating fragrance that seems to have intoxicated her followers. So many parts of her body were removed as religious relics that only a horribly mutilated semblance remained.

They had taken the right foot, and some fingers from the hand that was still raised in benediction; some ribs had been torn away from the side; pieces of flesh had been torn off for distribution among the crowd. Most ghastly of all, the head had been severed from the trunk, and ... lay on a cushion ... Part of the jaw had been taken, and the left eye was now an empty socket ... The heart, Teresa's warm heart, had been ripped out.[46]

Sackville-West's biography displays a fascination with dismemberment and resurrection. Biography as mourning becomes in Sackville-West's hands a ghoulish study *of* mourning; the worshippers need to possess parts of Teresa in a way that recalls Woolf's desire to possess Sackville-West through writing *Orlando*. *The Eagle and the Dove* describes a literal claiming of the dead; and there is even an image of resurrection, describing Teresa's corpse over two years after her death: 'Such, then, was the somewhat macabre spectacle offered to the Bishop of Avila and his suite at San José on that January morning—a withered and mummified image, the colour of dates, which could be propped upright by a hand placed between the shoulders.'[47] St Teresa could be made to walk again. The image echoes Vanessa Bell, writing about their mother's story told by Virginia Woolf in *To the Lighthouse*: 'It is almost painful to have her so raised from the dead'.[48] *The Eagle and the Dove* enacts within its pages the processes of biography itself.

Writing biography—and being *in* a biography—means living in a limbo between death and life; between the public and the private. Hillis Miller, writing about *Mrs Dalloway*, suggests that stream of consciousness writing moves on exactly that limit. The indirect style means that the novel constantly

---

[46] Sackville-West, *The Eagle and the Dove*, 99.   [47] Ibid. 97.
[48] Vanessa Bell to Virginia Woolf, repr. in an appendix to L, iii. 572, 11 May 1927.

invades the characters' privacy. The narrator seems to know everything about them, without their being aware of her or his intervention. But Miller also reads the novel as a story about resurrection through intense recollection: 'the revivification of the past performed by the characters becomes in its turn another past revivified, brought back from the dead, by the narrator.'[49] The stream of consciousness method, moving as it does on the border between public and private, deliberately confusing memory and perception, is conventionally taken to be a product of new developments in psychological theory: the phrase 'stream of consciousness' is traced back to William James. But it has an alternative genealogy in writing about mysticism.

Most critics find the earliest use of the phrase 'stream of consciousness' in William James's *Principles of Psychology* (1890).

Consciousness, then, does not appear to itself chopped up in bits. Such words as 'chain' or 'train' do not describe it fitly as it presents itself in the first instance. It is nothing jointed; it flows. A 'river' or a 'stream' are the metaphors by which it is most naturally described. In talking of it hereafter, let us call it the stream of thought, of consciousness, or of subjective life.[50]

The first use of the phrase in literary criticism was in May Sinclair's 1918 review of Dorothy Richardson's *Pilgrimage*, and her source is generally taken to have been William James.[51] But the phrase 'stream of consciousness' occurs in exactly that form (as opposed to James's more fragmented use of it) in Evelyn Underhill's *Mysticism* (1911), a book in which she acknowledges help from May Sinclair. It is used in an account of 'popular psychology': 'popular psychology . . . represents the subliminal self as an imprisoned angel, a mystic creature possessed of supernatural powers.' In fact, Underhill maintains, Robert Louis Stevenson was more accurate in *Dr Jekyll*

---

[49] J. Hillis Miller, '*Mrs Dalloway*: Repetition as the Raising of the Dead', in J. Hillis Miller, *Fiction and Repetition: Seven English Novels* (Oxford, 1982), 188.

[50] Quoted in Shirley Rose, 'The Unmoving Center: Consciousness in Dorothy Richardson's *Pilgrimage*', *Contemporary Literature*, 10 (1969), 367.

[51] See May Sinclair, 'The Novels of Dorothy Richardson', *Egoist*, 5 (1918), 57–9. Shirley Rose for example, assumes that James was Sinclair's source.

and Mr Hyde: the unconscious contains 'all those "uncivil-ised" instincts and vices, those remains of the ancestral savage which education has forced out of the stream of con-sciousness'.[52] Given Sinclair's familiarity with *Mysticism*, it seems at least as likely that this was the source of her famous phrase; and if this is so, we can take mysticism as at least as involved as psychology in the genesis of modern literary method.

As post-Freudians, we feel some surprise at Underhill's account of 'popular psychology'; for us, the unconscious is full of things we are trying to forget. But Underhill is referring not to Freudian psychology, but to the parlour games and occult healing groups that were still popular even at the time of Ouspensky's visit to London in 1921.[53] William James describes the 'mind-cure' method in *Varieties of Religious Experi-ence*: the subject effects a cure on him- or herself through auto-suggestion. It was this belief in the interaction of mind and body on which Katherine Mansfield relied when she entered the Fontainebleau Institute. The popular psychology against which Underhill and Freud were arguing assumed that powers of telepathy could be harnessed so that one mind could act on another, or on itself, to effect dramatic changes. Healing, especially in the context of the war wounded, was a dominant social concern.

The mind-cure's model of the relation between mind and body bears strong resemblance to Bergson's conception of the subject–object relation and modes of perception. In *Creative Evolution* (translated 1911) he describes how the intuitive mind sees objects as a crystallization of possible actions to be performed on them; for him, perception is anticipatory, always implying the influence of the perceiving subject on the perceived object. 'An intellect bent upon the act to be performed and the reaction to follow, feeling its object so as to get its mobile impression at every instant, is an intellect that teaches something of the absolute.'[54] This fluid intellect is in opposition to the mind that divides and reifies; and it is this forward-looking, flowing intellect which is usually taken as the

[52] Both quotations are from Underhill, *Mysticism*, 62.
[53] See Moore, *Gurdjieff and Katherine Mansfield*, for descriptions of these.
[54] Bergson, *Creative Evolution*, p. xi.

psychological justification of stream of consciousness writing. Proust, for example, read widely in Bergson's work. In *Mrs Dalloway*, Virginia Woolf uses stream of consciousness to explore all the different areas of social concern with which the technique was linked: psychology and the unconscious in Septimus's insanity, healing and its perversion in Drs Bradshaw and Holmes, and mysticism in the epiphanic moments around which it is structured, and on the most famous of which it ends.

One consequence of Bergson's sense of the interrelation of minds with each other and with the world of objects is that subject–object boundaries become blurred. Ouspensky, drawing on Kant, maintains that 'we know nothing about things *separately from us*.'[55] 'Everything that we accept as a property of the world, we call objective; and everything that we accept as a property of our psyche, we call subjective.'[56] Our knowledge of the outside world is gained by 'projecting outside of ourselves the causes of our sensations'.[57] Wyndham Lewis, in his scathing appraisal of Bergsonism, *Time and Western Man* (1927), comments that the object of the time-philosophers has to be lived: 'it has to be subject and object at once'.[58] Mrs Ramsay, in *To the Lighthouse*, has first-hand experience of this: 'It was odd, she thought, how if one was alone, one leant to things, inanimate things; trees, streams, flowers; felt they expressed one; felt they became one; felt they knew one, in a sense were one; felt an irrational tenderness thus (she looked at that long steady light) as for oneself' (p. 87). This conjunction of subjective and objective, so characteristic of the fictional innovations of the time, encouraged the development of similar experiments in the writing of biography. Fiction and non-fiction in the period, often read and analysed as though they were separate enterprises, were in fact part of a general response to changes in psychology and mystic philosophy.

However, the dynamic subject–object interaction of which Bergson wrote presents a problem for literary representation. Mrs Ramsay's Bergsonian feelings about inanimate things

[55] Ouspensky, *Tertium Organum*, 14.   [56] Ibid. 13.
[57] Ibid.   [58] Wyndham Lewis, *Time and Western Man* (London, 1927), 180.

almost rule out any possibility of action of the subject on the object, because subject and object are insufficiently differentiated. The identity of the perceiving mind with the object of perception would seem also to rule out representation (exactly the mystics' problem—they can never find the right words). Bergson is concerned with the relation of consciousness to representation:

Representation is stopped up by action. The proof of this is, that if the accomplishment of the act is arrested or thwarted by an obstacle, consciousness may reappear. It was there, but neutralized by the action which fulfilled and thereby filled the representation ... The inadequacy of act to representation is precisely what we here call consciousness.[59]

In the Bergsonian world, consciousness is produced when the mind goes ahead of, or exceeds the body; when it wants to do something the body is not yet adapted to perform. It is the space of frustration, of enforced hesitation, even of paralysis; it was what Teresa experienced standing rigid against a wall, when no one, not even herself, could bring her to move her limbs. The equation of the mystic trance with the inception of consciousness that emerged from Woolf's autobiography is theoretically confirmed by Bergson's work.

It is this kind of self alienation that Sackville-West explores in *Solitude*. As an examination of frustration, *Solitude* is, in Bergsonian and in mystic terms, an examination of consciousness itself. Sackville-West's agnosticism is peculiarly painful. She desperately desires faith, but cannot believe. In Bergsonian terms, she cannot accomplish the act (belief) that would destroy the need for representation (the articulation of her desire to believe):

> God, integrator of this strange concern,
> Give us a sign. Regard, O God, our need.
> Give us a sign. We die without your heed.[60]

The torment of her agnosticism is expressed in an image of the coincidence of pain and pleasure which she may have derived from St Teresa:

[59] Bergson, *Creative Evolution*, 151.   [60] Sackville-West, *Solitude*, p. 46.

> Then with fresh fiery consciousness comes pain,
> Dreaded and welcome, quickening and rash.
> I burn, consumed; and resurrect, half-slain.[61]

The contradiction of 'dreaded and welcome' represents for Sackville-West a radical uncertainty: the uncertainty of agnosticism. For earlier souls, this seems to have posed less of a problem. Caroline Stephen, Virginia Woolf's Quaker aunt, claimed that 'agnosticism with mystery at the heart of it seems another description of the "rational mysticism" which is my favourite expression of my own ground'.[62] But Sackville-West, remembering the wound in St. Teresa's side, is herself torn; and her turning to the asexual Joan, in whom there was literally no rupture and spiritually no doubt, is an attempt to find a solution to her own conflicts.

The danger of the mystic experience was that it often felt like a violation. Occult healing, for example, could be simply a transfer of pain and identity. May Sinclair explored this possibility in a compelling short story called 'The Flaw in the Crystal' (1911), later to be reprinted in a collection, *Uncanny Stories* (1923). In 'The Flaw in the Crystal' Agatha Verrall lives quietly in the country waiting for the periodic visits of her lover, with whom her relationship is purely platonic. She has a strange gift of healing.

You shut your eyes and ears, you closed up the sense of touch, you made everything dark around you and withdrew into your innermost self; you burrowed deep into the darkness there till you got beyond it; you tapped the Power, as it were, underground at any point you pleased and turned it in any direction.[63]

Agatha experiences herself as a fragile container for this darkness, a 'crystal vessel'. But she decides finally that it is her body and its desires which are her undoing. In order to help a friend whose husband is insane, she starts healing him, but when her friend tells her husband what is going on, the husband, Harding Powell, begins to predominate in Agatha's unconscious; gradually she becomes aware that she is going insane. 'It was her sanity, not his own, that he walked in. Or

---

[61] Sackville-West, *Solitude*, p. 36.

[62] Caroline Stephen, *The Vision of Faith and Other Essays* (Cambridge, 1911), p. cxi.   [63] Sinclair, 'The Flaw in the Crystal', 85.

else what she saw was the empty shell of him. *He* was in her.'[64] The power, which allows minds to meet, also dissolves their boundaries; it destroys 'those innermost walls of personality that divide and protect, mercifully, one spirit from another'.[65] Agatha finally decides that the crystal of her body is flawed, and that is why her mind is vulnerable; so she gives up the flaw (her desire for her lover) by leaving him, and becomes perfect again.

'The Flaw in the Crystal' dramatizes many of the implications of mystic philosophy and its concomitant, Bergsonism. The interpenetration of minds (or mind and world—Agatha has an ecstatic vision of the life or substance of things), the potential of that interpenetration for healing, and the physical and sexual aspects of mysticism are all woven into the narrative. The kind of fusion that is being explored is similar to the fusion actually *sought* by Woolf in the writing of Orlando, where she attempted to take over Sackville-West's memory and identity. In the case of *Orlando* it was a purely textual manœuvre (although Woolf presumably regretted the fact that her approaches were no longer sexual). Sackville-West, less sceptical, moved in spiritual circles where the fusion of minds was acknowledged as a possible effect of faith.

The intensity of Sackville-West's unformulated belief, and the sharpness of her doubt, were realized in the extraordinary beauty of her garden. It was the setting of her poem of agnosticism, *Solitude*, and the subject of her last long poem, *The Garden*. This poem was written during the Second World War, and, as we saw in the lyric poetry discussed in the Introduction, the pastoral setting was conceived as a retreat from the harsh facts of political life at the time. In a world of destruction and impermanence, Sackville-West seeks something that will last (p. 14):

> Daring to find a world in a lost world,
> A little world, a little perfect world,
> With owlet vision in a blinding time.

But retreat was not always possible and, continuing the images of vision, Sackville-West describes the experience of the

---

[64] Ibid. 117.   [65] Ibid. 122.

blackout as something not unlike the mystics' 'negative way' (pp. 21–2):

> Darkness is greater light, to those who see;
> Solitude greater company to those
> Who hear the immaterial voices; those
> Who dare to be alone.

This life of wintry contemplation is balanced by a life of imaginative action, as the gardener plans her planting for the spring. In winter (pp. 25–6):

> Here may we dream of different beauty seen,
> Desired though not fulfilled, that final beauty
> Denied to all our scheming as we know
> Too well, yet still delude ourselves in vision
> Unreasonable, in pathetic faith
> As the advancing soul, abashed, disheartened,
> Loses itself in night to reach a day
> Resplendent after darkness,—so in Winter
> The gardener sees what he will never see.

Gardening in winter is seen as an effort of desire; and the public burgeoning of the garden is always something at once less than, and in excess of, the vision. Less than, because it disappoints (Sackville-West writes of the Box of the Dead, labels from dead and dying plants); more than, because the flowers when they bloom have a life and beauty that the gardener never gave them (p. 17).

> Sowing us, you sowed more than you knew
> And something not ourselves has done the rest.

As the gardener watches, the body of her garden comes to spiritual life (p. 18):

> Hint of the secret synthesis that lies
> So surely round some corner of our road;
> That deepest canon of our faith, the prize
> We look for but shall never realise;
> Suspected cipher that implies a code.

The growth of the garden demonstrates the mystery of life and its spiritual secrets; but even those who are not so spiritually aware gain pleasure from the colours and the fragrances. Beholders can respond to the flesh or the spirit, as they choose: to the practical or to the mystical side of the gardener's world. The garden's flowering is the public fulfilment of a private fantasy: the space of Sackville-West's reserve and intimacy is the piece of ground on which her visitors gaze. In some sense her garden was her mystic vision, alleviating the discomfort of her agnosticism. She relied on its survival, writing against T. S. Eliot that 'I will believe in April while I live, / I will believe in Spring' (G, p. 64). It was her private belief, the only one she was sure of, and, as Jane Brown says, in contrast to her other published works, all inspired by or dedicated to a person or place, 'she wrote *The Garden* for herself'.[66] In the daily routines of weeding and cutting she found peace, and in her nurturing of Sissinghurst she created a pastoral setting for her retreat into the companionship of Gwen St. Aubyn. Sissinghurst garden, with all that it implies of the everyday—routine work, domesticity —is as much of a demonstration of Sackville-West's mysticism as is her poetry. Poised as it is between dailiness and dreaming, it offered Sackville-West an appropriately ambiguous expression of her painful and conflicted faith.

[66] Jane Brown, *Vita's Other World: A Gardening Biography of Vita Sackville-West* (Harmondsworth, 1985), 143.

CHAPTER 6

'By what Name shall we Call Death?':
Virginia Woolf's *The Waves*

TELLING other people's stories—writing biographies—is an engagement with the limits of the self. Story-telling alleviates frustration, apparently extending the boundaries of who we are, and of who we might be. In finding a suitable narrative for Joan of Arc's life, Sackville-West was encouraging herself to feel that there might, one day, be an appropriate story for her own: one to comfort, to shelter, and to explain. Narratives imply that the chaos of identity can momentarily make sense.

Woolf also sought shelter in story-telling. In *The Waves*, published in 1931 (the same year as *All Passion Spent*), Bernard and the others are haunted by the fear of a world without coherence, of a world or self that escapes narrative. 'If there are no stories, what end can there be, or what beginning?' (p. 223). Phrases and little sequences protect: Bernard speaks of 'the shelter from phrases' (p. 239). *The Waves* desperately and courageously confronts the instinct for making stories, and asks why we do it, what it achieves. It explores the nature both of solitude and of intimacy, showing its six characters developing each other's identity and their own, telling stories that are simultaneously theirs and someone else's, testing the limits of the individual life narrative. They are constantly comparing themselves with each other. Susan, watching Jinny arrive in the restaurant, thinks how exposed Jinny's presence makes her feel:

And I, though I pile my mind with damp grass, with wet fields, with the sound of rain on the roof and the gusts of wind that batter at the house in winter and so protect my soul against her, feel her derision steal round me, feel her laughter curl its tongues of fire around me and light up unsparingly my shabby dress, my square-tipped finger-nails, which I at once hide under the table-cloth. (p. 99)

Susan measures herself against Jinny and Jinny's incandescent physical presence in an attempt to construct herself in relation to her friend. In the same way, Sackville-West searched for a clue to her own identity in the life stories of mystics who had gone before her; in the same way Sackville-West and Woolf together explored the recounting and the claiming of narratives as a gesture of intimacy.

The Waves, then, is Woolf's book of friendship. It is also her book of fear: fear that the self will dissolve without the support of other presences, other forms. 'To be myself (I note) I need the illumination of other people's eyes, and therefore cannot be entirely sure what is my self' (p. 95). Bernard, like Susan, lives in the light of other's lives, and when that light is withdrawn, he faces the darkness of self-dispersal. 'How can I proceed now, I said, without a self, weightless and visionless, through a world weightless, without illusion?' (p. 238). His sense of weightlessness is also one of insubstantiality, of a lack of boundary. He can no longer measure himself against the standards of others: he is at once infinite and non-existent.

The failure of illusion is the failure of stories. Bernard is desperately afraid there may be no such thing as narrative sequence: 'And sometimes I begin to doubt if there are stories. What is my story? What is Rhoda's? What is Neville's?' (p. 118). Left alone he is haunted by the thought that linguistic sequence may simply not exist; and the absence of linguistic sequence means that identity is impossible. Bernard longs for the stories of others: he longs for the shelter that narrative provides.

Woolf's preoccupations in *The Waves* are close to those of Sackville-West, in spite of the difference in texture of their prose. Sackville-West, as we saw, needed convention and structure in both her life and her fiction to allow her to abandon them within certain strict limits. Within those limits her sense of herself and of life's energy was boundless. With Trefusis she experienced a passion which seemed to defy limitation. Nigel Nicolson describes it as 'a bond of flesh' which so 'so compelling that it became almost a spiritual, not a bodily, necessity, exacting so close and tremulous an intimacy that nothing existed for them outside' (*PM*, 152). Lady Slane gathers herself together in the solitude of her Hampstead home; Sackville-West felt surest of who she was in solitude; or in the shared privacy of sexual desire. Sackville-West's sense that she was dispersed in the presence of others, that she became simply a collection of scraps and patches, meant that it was in solitude that she was most aware of her own identity. She had a sure sense of her own territory: she knew how to claim it and to maintain it.

But it was not so for Woolf. When solitary, she felt far from alone. Her mental and emotional landscapes echoed with voices whose very existence brought terror, or ecstasy, because it was unclear whose they were. During one of her breakdowns, she heard the birds speaking Greek, a language whose alien nature she had stressed in her essay 'On Not Knowing Greek'.[1] Her suicide note (one of several) described her invasion by speech: 'I begin to hear voices, and I can't concentrate.'[2] She was used to *speaking* her own books (Louie Mayer, her cook, described hearing her every morning in her bath, talking in a hurried monotone),[3] and the voices in her head destroyed the silence that produced her books, drove her from that border-country between writing and speech to which Louie Mayer listened in such bewilderment.

Woolf—apparently insubstantial (Sackville-West referred to that 'fragile body' (Sackville-West to Nicolson, 27 Sept. 1928)) —feared possession: the 'being possessed' that the uncontrolled, demonic voices implied. Sackville-West, seen by Woolf as having all the physical robustness that Woolf herself lacked (a 'real woman' (*D*, iii. 52, 21 Dec. 1925)), feared *dis*possession, being excluded from her home. This difference, among others, led to a fundamental divergence in the narrative techniques of their fiction. The aristocratic confidence that Woolf so admired in Sackville-West ('her capacity I mean to take the floor in any situation' (*D*, iii. 52, 21 Dec. 1925)) is reflected in the effortless omniscience of her narrators, their untroubled relations with the stories they tell. For Woolf that confidence was artistically deadening, and bound up with the fullness—the repletion—of Sackville-West's erotic presence.

[1] See Quentin Bell, *Virginia Woolf: A Biography*, 2 vols. (London, 1972), i. 90; and Virginia Woolf, 'On Not Knowing Greek', in *The Common Reader I* (London, 1984; 1st edn. 1925), 23–38.
[2] Bell, *Virginia Woolf*, ii. 226.
[3] Joan Russell Noble (ed.), *Recollections of Virginia Woolf* (London, 1972), 189.

Vita very free & easy, always giving me great pleasure to watch, & recalling some image of a ship breasting a sea, nobly, magnificently, with all sails spread, & the gold sunlight on them. As for her poetry . . . She never breaks first ground. She picks up what the tide rolls to her feet. For example, she follows, with simple instinct, all the inherited tradition of furnishing, so that her home is gracious, glowing, stately, but without novelty or adventure . . . [Their lives] will grow freely & fully round them both; their fruit will ripen, & their leaves golden; & the night will be indigo blue, with a soft gold moon. They lack only what we have—some cutting edge; some invaluable idiosyncrasy, intensity, for which I would not have all the sons & all the moons in the world. (*D*, iii. 146, 4 July 1927)

Woolf's slip—conscious or unconscious—of 'sons' for 'suns' connects motherhood with the fullness of being that is Sackville-West's sexual glory.

Woolf's feeling of imminent failure, derived, at least in part, from her childlessness ('let me watch the wave rise. I watch. Vanessa. Children. Failure. Yes; I detect that. Failure failure. (The wave rises)' (*D*, iii. 110, 15 Sept. 1926)) makes her hesitant about her right to possess anything. Feeling that her 'incomprehensible and quite negligible femininity' (*L*, i. 329, 6 May 1908, to Clive Bell) is precarious—that she does not adequately inhabit her own female body—Woolf envies Sackville-West's certainties. Besides her erotic confidence, she is sure that in a just world she would have inherited Knole. For Woolf, the possession at stake is not a house but language; and unlike Sackville-West, she is uncertain whether or not she has a right to it. Sackville-West, for all her moods of self-deprecation, was astonishingly fluent: her manuscripts contain hardly any crossings out. But for Woolf, the question is posed continually, in a variety of voices and accents: can she *write*? can *she* write? The 'she' is both specific and general: a worry about her own particular ability, and a patriarchal imperative to all woman ('there would always have been that assertion —you cannot do this, you are incapable of doing that—to protest against, to overcome').[4]

---

[4] Virginia Woolf, *A Room of One's Own* (Oxford 1992; 1st edn. 1929), 70.

If women's possession of their language is continually disputed, then women's narrative constructions of themselves are always precarious. The instability of the narrative subject becomes a crisis of personal identity. Woolf's exploration of the subject's relation to its own stories has a terrible urgency about it, what Jean Guiguet calls 'anguish'.[5] *The Waves* was awkward to write, and Woolf complains continually in her diary of her lack of pleasure in it: 'I wish I enjoyed it more. I don't have it in my head all day like The Lighthouse & Orlando' (*D*, iii. 275, 26 Dec. 1929). A part of her difficulty was with the form: 'the abandonment of Orlando & Lighthouse is much checked by the extreme difficulty of the form' (*D*, iii. 300, 9 Apr. 1930). The problem is with the status of the monologues: are they written? spoken? heard? unheard? This ambiguity is built into the history of the book's conception. Originally it was going to be somewhere between autobiography and biography: 'I am now & then haunted by some semimystic very profound life of a woman, which shall all be told on one occasion' (*D*, iii. 118, 23 Nov. 1926). This haunting is behind *Orlando* as well as behind *To the Lighthouse*: it materializes eventually in the soliloquies of *The Waves*.

Woolf did not think of *The Waves* simply as a novel. She called it a 'playpoem', an 'abstract mystical eyeless book' (*D*, iii. 203, 7 Nov. 1928). Another of her early plans was for a dialogue (*D*, iii. 139, 18 June 1927). The form that she finally adopted was radically innovative in terms of the fiction of her own day: long soliloquies, apparently 'spoken' by each character in turn, and yet not constructed as responses to each other. They take place in parallel, almost chorically, somewhere on the border between speech and silence. Just so did Woolf speak her own books to herself in the bath.

Orlando and *The Waves* were closely linked in Woolf's mind. The day on which she records 'the conception last night between 12 & one of a new book' (*Orlando*) also marks her decision to 'rest my head before starting the very serious, mystical poetical work which I want to come next' (*D*, iii. 131, 14 Mar. 1927). A marginal note reads 'Orlando leading to The

[5] Jean Guiguet, *Virginia Woolf and her Works*, trans. J. Stewart (London, 1965), 397.

waves (July 8th 1933)'. The two works, often thought to be at the extremes of her *œuvre*—the lightweight romp and the philosophical prose poem—were for her phases of the same cycle, and as she wrote *Orlando* she continued to muse on *The Waves*. The impersonality of *The Waves* (Eric Warner calls it a move towards a more 'impersonal art')[6] is the obverse of the intense, if concealed, personal relevance of *Orlando*. Guiguet goes so far as to say that only Sackville-West can understand *Orlando*: 'for her it has its meaning; for us it offers only signs'.[7] This is ironic, given the popularity of Orlando and the bafflement of many readers when faced with *The Waves*. Woolf herself wrote of *The Waves* that it was 'a difficult book' (*D*, iii. 296, 11 Mar. 1930), and critic Mark Hussey calls it 'anti-reading . . . hostile to reading'.[8] It makes few concessions to the imperfections of the reader's memory. Despite its insistence on the recollections of the characters, the book itself is very hard to remember. Reading it is to experience a kind of amnesia which throws into sharper relief the detailed powers of recall of the characters. The reader is denied any easy sense of sequence; and because all the voices have the same status, he or she is denied any feeling of a centre, or of an organizing perspective. Bernard is as close as the text gets to a central point of view, but he has no self, and feels he exists only in relation to the others: 'I am not one person; I am many people; I do not altogether know who I am—Jinny, Susan, Neville, Rhoda, or Louis; or how to distinguish my life from theirs' (*W*, 230). *The Waves* is structured around the void, the experience of dismemberment that is, in the terms of *The Waves*, all we have of identity. The centrifugal pull of the stories of others leads us to question whether there was ever such a thing as a story of our own. On 23 September 1925 Woolf wrote to Sackville-West:

Do keep it up—your belief that I achieve things. I assure you, I have need of all your illusions after 6 weeks of lying in bed, drinking milk, now and then turning over and answering a letter . . . what I was

[6] Eric Warner, *Virginia Woolf: The Waves* (Cambridge, 1987), 28.
[7] Guiguet, *Virginia Woolf*, 397.
[8] Mark Hussey, *The Singing of the Real World: The Philosophy of Virginia Woolf's Fiction* (Columbus, Ohio, 1986), 87.

going to say was to beg for more illusions. I can assure you, if you'll make me up, I'll make you. (*L*, iii. 214)

This relatively flippant remark eventually issues in the full-scale illusion of *Orlando*, in which Woolf made Sackville-West up with a vengeance. Bernard almost exactly echoes Woolf's words to Sackville-West during a passage about Neville: 'let me then create you. (You have done as much for me.)' (*W*, 68). And as Sackville-West did, Neville feels taken over: 'I cannot talk to him of Percival. I cannot expose my absurd and violent passion to his sympathetic understanding. It too would make a "story"' (*W*, 39). The offer of a story —being 'made up' by someone—is also a gesture of possession, one of the misalliances of intimacy. *The Waves* reflects on the implications of the writing of *Orlando*. No wonder then that Woolf felt they were conceived simultaneously.

Even while writing the novel, Woolf was not sure it was her own. In a now famous passage in her diary she wrote:

I wrote the words O Death fifteen minutes ago, having reeled across the last ten pages with some moments of such intensity & intoxication that I seemed only to stumble after my own voice, or almost, after some sort of speaker (as when I was mad). I was almost afraid, remembering the voices that used to fly ahead. (*D*, iv. 10, 7 Feb. 1931)

The link with her madness that Woolf makes indicates the passion with which she negotiates her life *as* writing. Susan and Edwin Kenney have provocatively demonstrated that her breakdowns were a negotiation, with herself and others, of her identity, part of a struggle to define the terms of her own life.[9] Like madness, writing for Woolf was an intoxication, an invasion by voices, some that are your own, and some that are not. Finding her way through this Babel was the task of Woolf's life: identifying and reproducing both voices and stories.

For writing, and that fearful intensity, were Woolf's existence. As Hussey points out, 'her day was a schedule of different writings'.[10] She lived at the intersection of her various

---

[9] Susan M. Kenney and Edwin J. Kenney Jr, 'Virginia Woolf and the Art of Madness', *Massachusetts Review*, 23 (1982), 161–85.
[10] Hussey, *The Singing of the Real World*, p. xiii.

writing practices; and even within each one, could never be sure whose voice—whose language—was being written. *The Waves* explores what it means to construct the self in language. The soliloquies allude to many possible contexts for speaking the self, without confining themselves to any exclusively. They could be letters, biography, autobiography, monologue, dialogue, or the stream of thought. But the book, for all its concern with identity, is not concerned to present the six speakers as people. 'Odd, that they (The Times) shd. praise my characters when I meant to have none' (*D*, iv. 47, 8 Oct. 1931). But if *The Waves* is not about characters, this is because it is about what it is like to *be* a character or a person. In her early thoughts about the book, Woolf refers to it, as we have seen, as 'an abstract mystical eyeless book: a playpoem' (*D*, iii. 203, 7 Nov. 1928). Bernard has a sense of his own existence only when others stimulate him to speak, or to write:

I only come into existence when the plumber, or the horse-dealer, or whoever it may be, says something which sets me alight. Then how lovely the smoke of my phrase is, rising and falling, flaunting and falling, upon red lobsters and yellow fruit, wreathing them into one beauty. But observe how meretricious the phrase is—made up of what evasions and old lies. Thus my character is in part made of the stimulus which other people provide, and is not mine, as yours are. (*W*, 109)

Bernard only knows he exists when he is creating phrases and linguistic sequences, and for that sense of connection, emotional and semantic, he needs the presence of others. His identity is made up of phrases to which they have inspired him.

In his final soliloquy his identity is merged with those of the others: 'this is not one life; nor do I always know if I am man or woman' (*W*, 234). As he sums up his life, he uses images drawn from the soliloquies of the others:

The wax—the virginal wax that coats the spine melted in different patches for each of us. The growl of the boot-boy making love to the tweeny among the gooseberry bushes; the clothes blown out hard on the line; the dead man in the gutter; the apple tree, stark in the moonlight; the rat swarming with maggots; the lustre dripping blue—our white wax was streaked and stained by each of these differently. Louis was disgusted by the nature of human flesh; Rhoda by our cruelty; Susan could not share; Neville wanted order; Jinny love; and so on. We suffered terribly as we became separate bodies. (*W*, 202)

All these images echo earlier passages: Susan's 'he was blind as a bull, and she swooned in anguish, only little veins streaking her white cheeks red' (*W*, 18); Neville's 'the apple-tree leaves became fixed in the sky; the moon glared; I was unable to lift my foot up the stair. He was found in the gutter' (*W*, 17–18). The wax with which each is covered as a newborn is marked—'streaked'—differently by experience. The image is of streaks of placental blood, the flush of sexual excitement, or ink on the page. In order to experience himself as a separate being, Bernard sometimes feels that he must reject narrative and sequence altogether. Stories are always linked to other stories; they can never guarantee the distinctness of the individual, muddied as they are with the confusions of intimacy and of hostility. Bernard needs the inarticulate sounds of basic needs—food and sex—to be sure that he is, in fact, a separate body. 'I begin to long for some little language such as lovers use, broken words, inarticulate words, like the shuffling of feet on the pavement. I begin to seek some design more in accordance with those moments of humiliation and triumph that come now and then undeniably' (*W*, 199–200). Stories can destroy as well as save you: it is only in the unmediated expression of a primal demand that the self can be sure it exists. 'What is the use of painfully elaborating these consecutive sentences when what one needs is nothing consecutive but a bark, a groan?' (*W*, 209–10). Yet barks and groans can also kill, and it is the labour of dissembling and reassembling that in the end keeps the subject alive. Bernard's life is an effort: 'it is the effort and the struggle, it is the perpetual warfare, it is the shattering and piecing together—this is the daily battle, defeat or victory, the absorbing pursuit' (*W*, 225). The self is simply a field of conflict and reconciliation, an area of articulate and inarticulate energies.

The continual reworking of material in *The Waves* has the effect of holding off the end. Closure is conceivable only as confrontation: 'against you I will fling myself, unvanquished and unyielding, O Death!' (p. 248). Five years before writing those words, Woolf had had 'my new vision of death; active, positive, like all the rest, exciting; & of great importance—as an experience. "The one experience I shall never describe" I said to Vita yesterday' (*D*, iii. 117, 23 Nov. 1926). Bernard's experience of death is necessarily in the future tense, and the image is one of a fight against annihilation: 'it is death against whom I ride with my spear couched and my hair flying back like a young man's, like Percival's, when he galloped in India' (*W*, 247). It is death, as well as Percival, around which the six have gathered all along.

Although they gather around death, the effect of the narrative for Woolf was to keep death at bay. The Kenneys point out that for Woolf, this was, at times, the only reason to survive: 'at times it seemed to her that life itself was nothing but an intolerably long and meaningless anticipation of death . . . It is not surprising that she . . . finally chose it over possible madness; for death, whatever else it does, puts an end to dreadful anticipation.'[11] The claustrophobic endlessness of *The Waves* is in defiance of a silent future. *The Waves* is obsessed by death as it is by the relations between people. Where *Orlando*, offered in place of biography, actually keeps Sackville-West's death away, *The Waves*—offered in place of autobiography?—perhaps kept Woolf's death, and all other deaths, at bay. In her diary she notes that the idea for *The Waves* came to her during a long, and not entirely happy, summer at Rodmell. She sometimes woke in the middle of the night:

Woke up perhaps at 3. Oh its beginning its coming—the horror —physically like a painful wave swelling about the heart—tossing me up. I'm unhappy unhappy! Down—God, I wish I were dead. Pause. But why am I feeling this? Let me watch the wave rise. I watch. Vanessa. Children. Failure. Yes; I detect that. Failure failure. (The wave rises). Oh they laughed at my taste in green paint! Wave crashes. I wish I were dead! I've only a few years to live I hope. I cant face this horror any more—(this is the wave spreading out over me). (*D*, iii. 110, 15 Sept. 1926)

The experience is one of annihilation, of being engulfed by the waves of her own despair. Thinking of the children who

---

[11] Kenney and Kenney, 'Virginia Woolf', 181.

guarantee Vanessa's identity, she feels in comparison negligible and out of control. Measuring herself against others only confirms her own inadequacies. The longing to die is a relinquishment of the struggle to preserve the self against all the forces that constantly threaten to dismantle it: solitude, feelings of failure, an inability to grasp one's own identity.

Twelve days later she is beginning to reassess the experience as something positive. 'One goes down into the well & nothing protects one from the assault of truth. Down there I cant write or read; I exist however. I am' (*D*, iii. 112, 28 Sept. 1926). A few years later she would transform this feeling into Bernard's experience of himself as an inarticulate howl or cry, far from all writing and reading. She and Bernard share emotional images: 'It is this that is frightening & exciting in the midst of my profound gloom, depression, boredom, whatever it is: One sees a fin passing far out' (*D*, iii. 113, 30 Sept. 1926). Bernard's version is 'One of those silences which are now and again broken by a few words, as if a fin rose in the wastes of silence; and then the fin, the thought, sinks back into the depths, spreading round it a little ripple of satisfaction, content' (*W*, 228). Bernard's experience of the loss of self is directly linked to Woolf's solitude that summer at Rodmell, and the writing of *The Waves* was a confrontation with despair, an attempt to keep herself going for a little longer in the face of feelings of self- dispersal and dissolution. *The Waves* was a victory over the desire for suicide: 'I have netted that fin in the waste of waters which appeared to me over the marshes out of my window at Rodmell' (*D*, iv. 10, 7 Feb. 1931).

It is not only suicide that is held off by the writing of *The Waves*. Critic Eric Warner comments that action too is kept at bay by the verbal tense of the book.

Collapsing all movement and activity into the pure present removes the sense of felt duration of the actions, and thus suspends the sense of a precise location in time. The result is that a sense of actual participation in the world is diminished; action is effectively reconstituted as speech.[12]

The simple present of the text—the speakers' declarations of their own actions or emotions—makes the entire work

[12] Warner, *Virginia Woolf*, 44.

a pseudo-performative (I sit down, I put down my glass), although the verbs used rarely are actual performatives. This usage postpones accomplishment, as it postpones ending: verbs are not adequate substitutes for achieved actions. For Woolf the pseudo-performative represented a postponement of the decision to die. *The Waves* engages with the power of the human subject to make decisions about its own survival. This engagement is enacted at a formal level, so that the characters, as we have seen, are continually being dispersed. Woolf, rewriting it, commented that 'this is the most concentrated work I have ever done' (*D*, iv. 28, 30 May 1931).

Fiction can apparently bring the dead back to life. The Kenneys note that Thoby's was the only one of the numerous deaths in Woolf's family not to precipitate one of her nervous breakdowns. Part of the reason for this was her absorption in *The Voyage Out* during the period of his illness and death. But she also constructed a false narrative of his survival after he was already dead. In her letters to the ailing Violet Dickinson, she pretended that Thoby was still alive, in order to spare her friend a shock that she was as yet too weak to withstand. Woolf's imagination is vivid and detailed. Three days after his death she wrote: 'there isnt much change. His temp. is up to 104 again this afternoon, but otherwise his pulse is good, and he takes milk well' (*L*, i. 249, 23? Nov. 1906). A week later he is having 'whey, and chicken broth' (*L*, i. 253, 28 Nov. 1906); nearly two weeks after that he 'will be up by Christmas' (*L*, i. 259, 10 Dec. 1906). Yet death, of course, was on her mind. While keeping Thoby alive in her letters, she contemplated the killing of Rachel in *The Voyage Out*. The anxiety of writing a novelistic fiction of death simultaneously with the epistolary fiction of Thoby's survival, is neutralized in the shift from masculine to feminine (Thoby to Rachel).

The Waves is sometimes seen as a stage in Woolf's work of mourning for Thoby. Woolf wrote after finishing the novel: 'I have been sitting these 15 minutes in a state of glory, & calm, & some tears, thinking of Thoby & if I could write Julian Thoby Stephen 1881–1906 on the first page' (*D*, iv. 10, 7 Feb. 1931). As she wrote the last words of *The Waves*, and imagined Bernard meeting death with defiance, she thought of all those for whom defiance had not been enough. Originally she was going to call *The Waves* 'The Moths', and her essay, 'The Death of the Moth', demonstrates the association she made between moths and dying. 'Just as life had been strange a few minutes before, so death was now as strange. The moth having righted himself now lay most decently and uncomplainingly composed. O yes, he seemed to say, death is stronger than I am.'[13] This resignation is in stark contrast to the end of *The Waves*, when Bernard, 'unyielding', refuses death. Jean Guiguet notes that the image of the moth carried for Woolf a feeling of imminent death, and he suggests that the substitution of waves for moths represented a decision to emphasize rhythm rather than annihilation in the overall structure of the book.[14] The endless recurrence of the waves is a defiance of death and ending. Woolf wanted *The Waves* to be written not to a 'plot', that would have an end, but to a 'rhythm', that would not (*D*, iii. 316, 2 Sept. 1930). The waves, drawing back only to reappear, serve as symbols of deprivation and recovery, as images of the fictional working through of death.

If *The Waves* is preoccupied with death, it is also concerned with reproduction. The depression that drove Woolf to write it was partly a response to her own childlessness, and Susan is a powerful study of maternity and the instinct (if we can call it that) to mother.

Woolf had already written extensively about motherhood in *To the Lighthouse*. Mrs Ramsay was explicitly conceived with her own mother, Julia Stephen, in mind (Woolf to Vanessa Bell, *L*, iii. 383, 25 May 1927); but she also felt that there was much of Vanessa Bell herself in Mrs Ramsay: 'something of Nessa leaked in', she wrote to Roger Fry on 27 May 1927 (*L*, iii. 386). However, Sackville-West was also an important maternal presence for Woolf:

There is her maturity & full breastedness: her being so much in full sail on the high tides, where I am coasting down backwaters; her capacity I mean to take the floor in any company, to represent her country, to visit Chatsworth, to control silver, servants, chow dogs; her motherhood (but she is a little cold & offhand with her boys)

---

[13] Virginia Woolf, 'The Death of the Moth', in *Collected Essays*, 4 vols. (London, 1966–7), i. 361.   [14] Guiguet, *Virginia Woolf*, 397.

her being in short (what I have never been) a real woman. (*D*, iii. 52, 21 Dec. 1925)

Woolf's sense of her own inadequacies—her childlessness, her failure as a writer—easily surfaced in relation to Sackville-West, so that the fears that *The Waves* was written to conquer were associated with her reactions to Sackville-West, as well as to Vanessa Bell. Both took the place of a mother to her: Sackville-West 'lavishes on me the maternal protection which, for some reason, is what I have always most wished from everyone. What L. gives me, & Nessa gives me, & Vita, in her more clumsy external way, tries to give me' (*D*, iii. 52, 21 Dec. 1925). Her account of motherhood in *The Waves* has the spectre of many figures behind it, and Sackville-West is among them. The reassurance Woolf derived from their intimacy was continually compromised by her feeling that she herself was somehow perpetually dispersed. Sackville-West's emotional withdrawal, and the retaliatory writing of *Orlando*, did nothing fundamentally to remove that precariousness.

Their physical awareness of each other was important for the emotional economy that produced *The Waves*. Sackville-West's knowledge of Woolf's disturbed past made her very tender towards her. Sackville-West wrote to Harold Nicolson on 17 August 1926:

One's love for Virginia is a very different thing: a mental thing, a spiritual thing if you like, an intellectual thing, and she inspires a feeling of tenderness which I suppose is because of her funny mixture of hardness and softness,—the hardness of her mind, and her terror of going mad again. She makes me feel protective. . . . I am scared to death of arousing physical feelings in her, because of the madness. I don't know what effect it would have, you see; and that is a fire with which I have no wish to play.

Sackville-West felt there was a disjunction between Woolf's mind and her body. On 27 September 1928, she wrote to Harold Nicolson: 'she is very very sweet, and I feel extra-ordinarily protective towards her—The combination of that brilliant brain and that fragile body is very loveable—so independent in all mental ways, so dependent in all practical ways.' Woolf's body and its fragility represented for Sackville-West the difficulties of Woolf's past. Sackville-West—not usually so scrupulous—avoided sexual contact with Woolf because she was frightened of what she might resurrect. Explaining to Nicolson that sleeping with Woolf would be playing with fire, she added an account of Woolf's sexual history: 'she has never lived with anyone but Leonard, which was a terrible failure, and was abandoned quite soon' (Sackville-West to Nicolson, 17 Aug. 1926). Sackville-West could not predict what Woolf's responses would be: she might not respond at all, or she might respond too much, with illness. Even Sackville-West, who delighted in the unpredictability of the sexual, and who used it to destabilize her own life, in particular with Violet Trefusis, found Woolf's history —that vulnerable, dependent body—unattractive finally: 'so you see I am sagacious,—though probably I would be less sagacious if I were more tempted, which is at least frank!' (Sackville-West to Nicolson, 17 Aug. 1926). Sackville-West's attitudes, presumably derived partly from Woolf's own account of herself, confirmed Woolf's sense of her own insubstantiality: a delicate, unreliable body. In contrast, Sackville-West's flamboyance seemed to guarantee her sexual solidity.

Long before *Orlando*, Woolf felt that Sackville-West summarized English history.

If I were she, I should merely stride, with 11 Elk hounds, behind me, through my ancestral woods. She descends from Dorset, Buckingham, Sir Philip Sidney, and the whole of English history, which she keeps, stretched in coffins, one after another, from 1300 to the present day, under her dining room floor. (*L*, iii. 150, 26 Dec. 1924, to Jacques Raverat)

Woolf's attraction to Sackville-West was also an attraction to aristocracy, to Englishness, to wealth: all the social privileges about which later, in *Three Guineas*, she was to express so much ambivalence. Sackville-West's body was far from simply a physical entity: it was an excuse to make phrases, to weave fantasies, to tell stories. The legs that would play such a major role in *Orlando* are important even at this early stage of their relationship: 'Her real claim to consideration, is, if I may be so coarse, her legs. Oh they are exquisite—running like slender pillars up into her trunk, which is that of a breastless cuirassier (yet she has 2 children) but all about her is virginal, savage, patrician' (*L*, iii. 150, 26 Dec. 1924, to Jacques Raverat). Woolf was fascinated by Sackville-West's conjunction of maternity and pseudo-virginity: her evasion of sexual relations with men and her retreat into a world of gardens and women. It was important to Woolf, as we have seen, that Sackville-West was a 'real woman', fully realized. Sackville-West's physical confidence encouraged Woolf to playful, transgressive fantasies: 'I have a perfectly romantic and no doubt untrue vision of you in my mind—stamping out the hops in a great vat in Kent—stark naked, brown as a satyr, and very beautiful' (*L*, iii, 198, 24 Aug. 1925). Her responses to Sackville-West satisfied both the desire to make phrases and the desire to make love. *Orlando* was a perfect crystallization of the energy that was flowing between them.

But Sackville-West's sexual independence, while inspiring Woolf to transports of desire and of story-telling, could also, as we have seen, threaten Woolf's precarious sense of her self. There was something greedy and deadening about Sackville-West.

Isn't there something obscure in you? There's something that doesn't vibrate in you: It may be purposely—you don't let it: but I see it with other people, as well as with me: something reserved, muted—God knows what . . . It's in your writing too, by the bye. The thing I call central transparency—sometimes fails you there too. (*L*, iii. 302, 19 Nov. 1926)

The price of Sackville-West's opacity, her substantiality, was a lack of the exaggerated sensitivity from which Woolf suffered. Sackville-West narcissistically recognized the justice of Woolf's demands:

Damn the woman, she has put her finger on it. There *is* something muted. What is it, Hadji [Harold]? Something that doesn't vibrate, something that doesn't come alive. I brood and brood; feel that I grope in a dark tunnel, persuaded that somewhere there is light, but never can find the way to emerge. It makes everything I do (i.e. write) a little unreal; gives the effect of having been done from the outside. (Sackville-West to Nicolson, 20 Nov. 1926)

This lack of intensity, of emotional resonance, meant that Sackville-West was always a little detached, both from herself and from others. As we saw in Chapter 4, she always kept some of herself apart, not allowing her whole being to respond. This gave her the stability that Woolf loved; but it also gave her a certain stubbornness, which caused her, in the end, to abandon Woolf in search of a more passionate partner. Protectiveness could turn quickly to impatience, boredom to hostility.

In *The Waves* Woolf explored what it might mean to be so sure of who you were and what you wanted. The character she used for these reflections, Susan, has something of Sackville-West and something of Vanessa Bell also. Woolf often balanced her own childlessness against her literary creativity. 'I scarcely want children of my own now,' she wrote in December 1927. 'This insatiable desire to write something before I die, this ravaging sense of the shortness & feverishness of life, make me cling, like a man on a rock, to my one anchor' (*D*, iii. 167, 20 Dec. 1927). In *The Waves* the writerly passion and concomitant awareness of death is displaced into Susan's feelings about her children, almost as a way of exploring what might have happened to Woolf's energy, had she, like Vanessa Bell, chosen (or been allowed) to direct at least some of it into raising a family.

Susan, walking with her son in the fields, feels her childhood conflicts resolved, her 'violent passions . . . rewarded by security, possession, familiarity' (*W*, 158). Her relation to the things around her mirrors Sackville-West's relation to the series of gardens with which she lived:

I have had peaceful, productive years. I possess all I see. I have grown trees from the seed. I have made ponds in which goldfish hide under the broad-leaved lilies. I have netted over strawberry beds and lettuce beds, and stitched the pears and the plums into white bags to keep them safe from the wasps. I have seen my sons and daughters, once netted over like fruit in their cots, break the meshes and walk with me, taller than I am, casting shadows on the grass. (*W*, 158)

Susan's maternity is symbolized as an identification with the natural world: 'I shall lie like a field bearing crops in rotation' (*W*, 108). She is coextensive with the landscape around her, nurturing and protecting its fruits as she nurtures and protects her own children. But nurturing is also identified with capture: netting the fruits, netting the children. It is a defensive act, keeping them safe. Susan herself is sometimes overcome by the lassitude of struggle and possession: 'I am sick of the body, I am sick of my own craft, industry and cunning, of the unscrupulous ways of the mother who protects, who collects under her jealous eyes at one long table her own children, always her own' (*W*, 159).

Susan's 'bestial and beautiful passion' (*W*, 108) is linked to an exchange of letters between Vanessa Bell and Virginia Woolf a couple of years before the writing of *The Waves*. Woolf and Bell saw motherhood as at once possessive and ruthless. Woolf wrote to Bell in 1927: 'I slightly distrust or suspect the maternal passion. It is obviously immeasurable and unscrupulous. You would fry us all to cinders to give Angelica a days pleasure, without knowing it. You are a mere tool in the hands of passion' (*L*, iii. 366, 21 Apr. 1927). Vanessa Bell responded on 3 May with a letter describing the capture of a huge moth—'half-a-foot across'—in her house at Cassis, and its preservation in a bottle of chloroform. She continues: 'I wish you would write a book about the maternal instinct. . . . Of course it is one of the worst of the passions, animal and remorseless. But how can one help yielding to these instincts if one happens to have them?' (Berg Collection, New York Public Library) The letter closes: 'the moths die around me'. Images of moths frame this letter about maternity. Maybe 'The Moths' (later *The Waves*) was the book on mothers that Bell was asking for.

The mother's care—washing and feeding, or Susan's netting—acquaints the child with disease and death: the threats to the body. Woolf remembered her own mother as constantly in mourning. Describing her, forty-four years after her death, she wrote:

Severe; with a background of knowledge that made her sad. She had her own sorrow waiting behind her to dip into privately. Once when she had set us to write exercises I looked up from mine and watched her reading—the Bible perhaps; and, struck by the gravity of her face, told myself that her first husband had been a clergyman and that she was thinking, as she read what he had read, of him. This was a fable on my part; but it shows that she looked very sad when she was not talking. (SP, 96)

Woolf's mother had had a short first marriage of legendary happiness, and Woolf believed that she had been permanently marked by the loss of her first husband. For Woolf, her

mother was always widow as well as wife. She thought she saw a
man sitting by her mother's death-bed, and Mark Spilka has
interpreted this as an indication of Woolf's obsession with her
mother's own grieving.[15]

Woolf's feeling seems to be confirmed in those of her
mother's papers that have survived. Jean O. Love, after reading all the letters between Julia and Leslie Stephen, comes to
the conclusion that the death of her first husband did indeed
leave Julia Stephen with a 'persisting melancholia and suicidal
ideas that turned her into a "chronic" mourner'.[16] She notes
that not only did Julia never conclude her work of mourning
(Woolf remarks on the tirelessness with which her mother
worked in the service of others, particularly the ill and dying,
and suggests that her mother died of overwork (SP, 133)), but
also continued to foster a genuine and deeply felt death-wish
for years after Herbert Duckworth's death.

Yet Woolf also remembered her at the centre of an active
and busy household. 'Can I remember ever being alone with
her for more than a few minutes? Someone was always inter-
rupting' (SP, 97). After Julia Stephen's death, the busyness
that Woolf remembered in her is re-experienced as a spectral
elusiveness. Woolf wrote to Sackville-West after sending her *To
the Lighthouse*: 'I don't know if I'm like Mrs Ramsay: as my
mother died when I was 13 probably it is a child's view of her:
but I have some sentimental delight in thinking that you like
her [sic]. She has haunted me' (*L*, iii. 374, 13 May 1927).
Woolf became, like her mother, haunted. Her mother's legacy
to her—in spite of her own energy—was one of mourning:
femininity as mourning, and daughterhood as mourning.

The Waves shows Susan similarly preoccupied by contradictory feelings about life and death. Woolf takes Julia
Stephen's lack of concentration on her children ('she was
living on such an extended surface that she had not time, nor
strength, to concentrate, except for a moment . . . upon me'
(SP, 96)) as evidence both of her life-force, and of a certain
reserve. Susan's ordering of her life and body around her chil-

[15] Mark Spilka, *Virginia Woolf's Quarrel with Grieving* (Lincoln, Nebr., 1980),
78ff.
[16] Jean O. Love, *Virginia Woolf: Sources of Madness and Art* (Berkeley, Calif.,
1977), 65.

dren, seems to owe more to Woolf's impressions of Vanessa Bell as a mother, than to her memories of her own mother. But Susan's maternity is all the same, like Julia Stephen's, shadowed by the anticipation of death. Her reaction to Percival's death—who loved her—is not to grieve for him but to fear for her baby: 'sleep, sleep, I say, warning off with my voice all who rattle milk-cans, fire at rooks, shoot rabbits, or in any way bring the shock of destruction near this wicker cradle, laden with soft limbs, curled under a pink coverlet' (*W*, 142). The passionate protectiveness of Susan's maternity *is* her mourning of Percival: collecting together the living in an attempt to keep away their deaths. She exemplifies not the nature of grief, but the mother's relation to death. Bernard's question, 'by what name are we to call death?' is answered by his call for 'a little language such as lovers use, words of one syllable such as children speak when they come into the room and find their mother sewing and pick up some scrap of bright wool, a feather, or a shred of chintz' (*W*, 246). The language of death that he seeks is the language that children speak in response to the work of mothering; but mothers too have their own 'little language', the 'howl', the 'cry' of some 'wilder, darker violence' with which Susan, howling like a child, would 'fell down with one blow any intruder, any snatcher, who should break into this room and wake the sleeper' (*W*, 142). For the naming of children, as Sackville-West had reason to know (Chapter 3), is peculiarly the province of mothers: it marks their claim on their child. Naming death—those who will die—is the destiny of all mothers whose children are mortal. And living with death—the death of the self and the death of the mother—was Woolf's lifelong task.

Afterword

ON 31 March 1941 Sackville-West wrote to Harold Nicolson that she had just had news of Woolf's suicide. As soon as Nicolson received the letter he hurried down to Sissinghurst to be with her. 'My dearest I know that Virginia meant something to you which nobody else can ever mean and that you will feel deprived of a particular sort of haven which was a background comfort and strength' (Nicolson to Sackville-West, 2 Apr. 1941). By the time of Woolf's death the two women had faded into the background of each other's lives; and yet, as Nicolson pointed out, they continued to provide each other with an image of safety and of power. With Woolf's death that image was erased and silenced: 'Virginia leaves an irreplaceable blank in my life' (Sackville-West to Nicolson, 3 Apr. 1941). Sackville-West's life would no longer resonate through the very different timbre of Woolf's. Instead all intensities were damped down, deprived of an answer or an echo.

What remained of their love was silence. When Nicolson came down to Kent to be with Sackville-West he did not mention Woolf. 'There was nothing that could be said. I just wanted to be with you' (Nicolson to Sackville-West, 3 Apr. 1941). It was silences of this kind that had sustained the women's intimacy all along, allowing it to flourish in the unspoken places that escaped the conversation and companionship provided by Woolf's and Sackville-West's marriages. When Sackville-West informed Nicolson of the state of affairs between herself and Woolf (in the letter quoted in the Introduction), it was to reassure, rather than to include him. The women's erotic and emotional connection fluctuated according to its own momentum and according to the amount of space and energy each woman was, at various moments, willing to give it. Jane Marcus has pointed out the various strategies Woolf used, in *A Room of One's Own*, to signal, rather than to speak, female desire: allusion, question marks, ellipses.[1] Women's sexuality is experienced in the silences of the heterosexual text. Women together hear what marriage cannot say. For Woolf and Sackville-West lesbian possibility was one of the many things marriage was designed to allow. Their intimacy did not subvert the conjugal institution: it existed within it.

We are beginning to see that institutions are no more identical to themselves than are texts: that institutions, in fact, are texts with lapses, silences, always allowing the possibility of their own disappearance. If in Woolf's and Sackville-West's lives marriage was a euphemism for a series of incompatible and contradictory feelings, then their lives were simultaneously a denial and an acknowledgement of what marriage was conventionally taken to be. It was in the play between denial and acknowledgement that the feeling of marriage—the feeling of being married—flourished.

What then of the institution of lesbianism? Similarly, Woolf and Sackville-West both were and were not lesbian. In *Am I that Name?* Denise Riley wonders what it means to say or feel: 'I am a woman.'[2] Evoking particular moments when 'being a woman' becomes suddenly apparent (the onset of menstruation, being whistled at in the street), she suggests that even at these moments the transitivity of 'being a woman' is at best (or at worst) provisional.[3] And how much more provisional the transitivity of 'being a lesbian'? 'While there is indeed a phenomenology of inhabiting a sex, the swaying in and out of it is more like ventures among descriptions than like returns to a founding sexed condition.'[4] The coincidence of self (body? mind? soul?) and description can only ever be momentary. Identity is rarely felt or lived as such, as an experience of being identical to oneself.

It is with suspensions and provisionalities of these kinds that lesbian studies is now working. The willingness to forgo the

[1] Jane Marcus, 'Sapphistory: The Woolf and the Well', in Karla Jay and Joanne Glasgow (ed.), *Lesbian Tests and Contexts: Radical Revisions* (New York, 1990), 168.

[2] Denise Riley, *'Am I That Name?': Feminism and the Category of 'Women' in History* (London, 1988), 96–7.

[3] Ibid.   [4] Ibid. 97–8.

'risk of essence'[5] is politically and emotionally controversial. But it reaches back, of course, to the foundations of twentieth-century theories of subjectivity: to Freud, whose subject was never identical to itself, always harbouring otherness in the unconscious; and to Lacan ('when the subject appears somewhere as meaning, he [sic] is manifested elsewhere as "fading", as disappearance').[6] To claim a sexual identity is implicitly to challenge the idea that identity itself is always in crisis. To 'mean' something as a woman or as a lesbian is also to 'mean' nothing. The appearance of a significant relation to one or other 'description' is an appearance only: fleeting, and implying disorder.

The relations of Woolf and Sackville-West to each other, to the institutions of marriage, lesbianism, literature, class, are not questions of identity. Rather they may well be, as Catharine Stimpson has argued, metaphorical relations: relations whose identity means nothing more nor less than the coincidence of two concepts in the field of language.

For 'lesbianism' might signify a critique of heterosexuality; a cry for the abolition of the binary oppositions of modern sexuality; a demand for the release of women's self-named desires; a belief that such release might itself be a sign of a rebellious, subtle, raucous textuality. 'Lesbianism' might represent a space in which we shape and reshape our psychosexual identities, in which we are metamorphic creatures.[7]

It was indeed in erotic relation to each other, and to other women, past and present, that Woolf and Sackville-West shaped and reshaped who they were, what they wanted, who they had been: found themselves in continual suspension.

This provisionality was made possible by the failure of the institution (marriage) through which they related to one another, actually to represent their relations. Close friendships between wives, yes; actively sexual relationships, no. The

---

[5] Stephen Heath, 'Difference', *Screen*, 19 (1978), 99.

[6] Jacques Lacan, 'The Subject and the Other: Aphanisis', in Jacques-Alain Miller (ed.), *The Four Fundamental Concepts of Psycho-Analysis*, trans. Alan Sheridan (New York, 1981), 218.

[7] Catharine R. Stimpson, 'Afterword: Lesbian Studies in the 1990s', in *Lesbian Texts and Contexts*, 380.

situation was a little like that described by Joanne Glasgow for lesbians in the Catholic Church:

If sex is by definition what happens between men or between men and women, if for women its reality is defined by intercourse, then . . . lesbians were indeed innocent. And from all the evidence, it seems clear that their sexuality was seen as innocent by the church. Lesbian sexuality did not exist as a Catholic reality.[8]

The religious and legal contexts from which marriage derived most of its force, in Woolf's and Sackville-West's time (and presumably still today), simply did not recognize their feelings. Within this silence both women found tremendous and transgressive freedom.

But absolute silence is a kind of death. As I have shown, different kinds of writing and of text allowed the exploration of feelings and of metaphors that were neither spoken nor sanctioned by the governing institutions within which the women lived. Fictional, biographical, and autobiographical texts allowed the 'ventures among descriptions', the risk of metaphor, of which Denise Riley speaks. These ventures were undertaken with a peculiar intensity and excitement—even trepidation—when both terms of the metaphor were women. Indeed, a metaphorical relation between man and woman is hard to imagine: for metaphor holds out the lure and the threat of sameness, rather than of difference. Metaphorical writing of all kinds was the way in which Woolf and Sackville-West related to the world, to each other, and to themselves. As they wrote their way into and out of conscious and unconscious 'descriptions', they performed exactly that task for which Woolf said Chloe and Olivia would one day be famous: the acknowledgement of 'those unrecorded gestures, those unsaid or half-said words, which form themselves, no more palpably than the shadows of moths on the ceiling, when women are alone.'[9] Chloe, their lives and writing demonstrate, *did* like Olivia: and, presumably, she always will.

---

[8] Joanne Glasgow, 'What's a Nice Lesbian Like You Doing in the Church of Torquemada? Radclyffe Hall and Other Catholic Converts', in *Lesbian Texts and Contexts*, 251.

[9] Virginia Woolf, *A Room of One's Own* (Oxford, 1992; 1st edn. 1929), 110.

Vita Sackville-West

Victoria Mary Sackville-West (Vita) was born on 9 March 1892, at Knole, Kent. Her mother, Victoria, Lady Sackville, was the illegitimate daughter of Lionel, Lord Sackville, and a Spanish flamenco dancer, Pepita da Oliva. Lady Sackville married her cousin Lionel, who became Lord Sackville in 1910. She was a passionate and extravagantly charming woman, with whom Sackville-West had a stormy relationship until Lady Sackville's death in 1936. Sackville-West was her only child, and she was brought up at the family home at Knole, a vast estate with, so the story goes, 365 rooms, 52 staircases, and 7 courtyards. Sackville-West loved Knole intensely, and never ceased to regret that her sex barred her from inheriting it (it passed laterally to her uncle when her father died in 1928). She started writing in childhood, and continued to do so, prolifically, throughout her life. The year 1910 saw a highly public lawsuit brought against the family by Lady Sackville's brother, Henry, who sought to prove his legitimacy and his claim to the title. He lost his case, but the trial was deeply distressing to Sackville-West's family.

In 1913, Sackville-West married a young diplomat, Harold Nicolson (later to become an MP), and spent the first few months of the marriage in Constantinople, where Nicolson was posted. Their two sons, Ben and Nigel, were born in 1914 and 1917 (Sackville-West had a stillborn son in 1915). Although the first years of her marriage were very happy, Sackville-West had always been attracted to women (during her engagement she was involved with Rosamund Grosvenor), and in 1918 she began a passionate relationship with a childhood friend, Violet Keppel (later Trefusis). Sackville-West finally returned to Nicolson, after several traumatic years and repeated periods in France with Trefusis, and the Sackville-West Nicolson marriage survived as a deep and stable friendship which lasted until Sackville-West's death. Sackville-West continued to sleep with women throughout her life, among them Virginia Woolf (whom she met in 1922), Mary Campbell, Evelyn Irons, and Hilda Matheson. Sackville-West developed a passion for gardening from the earliest years of her marriage, and, after acquiring Sissinghurst Castle in 1930, created with Harold Nicolson the beautiful gardens that are still in existence today (Sissinghurst is now owned by the National

Trust). Sackville-West wrote gardening notes for the *Observer* for many years, and became a well-known reviewer and broadcaster. But after 1930 she came to London less and less, writing and gardening at Sissinghurst during the week, and joined there by Nicolson at weekends. In the early summer of 1962 she died of cancer at Sissinghurst.

Sackville-West wrote in a much wider variety of literary genres than Woolf, who concentrated on the novel and the review. Sackville-West published four collections of poetry, twelve novels, four long poems, three collections of short stories, two travel books, and six biographies (one of her mother and grandmother). As well as these, she edited Lady Anne Clifford's diary, wrote a history of her family and of Knole, translated Rilke, and wrote for the National Trust. Her interests were eclectic, and she was a highly regarded and popular writer (*The Land* won the Hawthornden Prize in 1927, and *The Edwardians* (1930) was a best seller). As far as the literary establishment of her day was concerned, she was far better established and more widely respected as an author than Virginia Woolf.

Virginia Woolf

Virginia Woolf was born Adeline Virginia Stephen in 1882, the third of four children. Her father, Leslie Stephen, began to edit the *Dictionary of National Biography* in the year of her birth. Before that he had resigned his Fellowship at Trinity Hall in Cambridge when he lost his faith, and made a name for himself as a Victorian man of letters. Woolf's mother Julia Stephen had three children by her first husband, Herbert Duckworth, who died tragically young. Woolf, like Sackville-West, was educated at home, along with her sister Vanessa, and brothers Thoby and Adrian. Summers were spent at the family house at St. Ives in Cornwall.

Her adolescence was dominated by illness and death: her mother died in 1895, and her half-sister Stella in 1897. Woolf had her first mental breakdown at the age of 13, following the death of her mother. After that she would suffer recurring bouts of mental illness throughout her life, experiencing severe and prolonged attacks in 1904, 1912–15, and 1940–1.

In 1904 Leslie Stephen died, after a long and painful illness, and Woolf moved to Bloomsbury with her brothers and sister, but in 1906 Thoby died of typhoid. By this time Woolf had become close to Thoby's Cambridge friends, and in 1912 she married one of them, Leonard Woolf. The first years of her marriage saw a serious breakdown, but by 1917 she was well enough to buy a printing press, with Leonard Woolf, and to set up the Hogarth Press. Her first novel, *The Voyage Out*, was published in 1915. From then on she divided her time between writing, reviewing, and helping to run the Press. She spent the summer months in Sussex at Rodmell, and the rest of the year in London. Throughout her life she was cautious about provoking another breakdown, and she avoided a serious attack until the year of her death two years after the outbreak of the Second World War. She drowned herself in the Ouse at Rodmell in 1941.

Woolf is probably the best-known modernist woman writer. Her novels include *The Voyage Out* (1915), *Night and Day* (1919), *Jacob's Room* (1922), *Mrs Dalloway* (1925), *To the Lighthouse* (1927), *Orlando* (1928), *The Waves* (1931), *The Years* (1937), and *Between the Acts* (1941). She also wrote many critical and review essays, two works of feminist non-fiction (*A Room of One's Own* (1929) and *Three Guineas* (1938)), and a biography of Roger Fry. She is famous for her copious diaries and letters, all of which have now been published.

Bibliography

The place of publication is London, unless stated otherwise.

V. SACKVILLE-WEST

Constantinople: Eight Poems, 1915
Poems of West and East, 1917
Heritage, 1919
The Dragon in Shallow Waters, 1921
Orchard and Vineyard, 1921
The Heir, 1922
Knole and the Sackvilles, 1922
Grey Wethers, 1923
The Diary of the Lady Anne Clifford, ed. V. Sackville-West, 1923
Challenge (New York, 1924)
Seducers in Ecuador, 1924
The Land, 1926
Passenger to Teheran, 1926
Aphra Behn, 1927
Twelve Days, 1928
King's Daughter, 1929
Andrew Marvell, 1929
The Edwardians, 1930
Sissinghurst, 1931
Invitation to Cast Out Care, 1931
Rilke: Duino Elegies, trans. by V. Sackville-West and Edward Sackville-West, 1931
All Passion Spent, 1931
Vita Sackville-West's Poetry, 1931
The Death of Noble Godavary and Gottfried Kunstler, 1932
Thirty Clocks Strike the Hour (New York, 1932)
Family History, 1932
Collected Poems, 2 vols.; i. 1933 (ii never appeared)
The Dark Island, 1934
Saint Joan of Arc, 1936
Pepita, 1937
Some Flowers, 1937
Solitude, 1938
Country Notes, articles from *New Statesman*, 1939

Country Notes in Wartime, articles from *New Statesman* and *Nation,* 1940
English Country Houses, 1941
Selected Poems, 1941
Grand Canyon, 1942
The Eagle and the Dove: A Study in Contrasts, St. Teresa of Avila, St. Thérèse of Lisieux, 1943
The Women's Land Army, 1944
Another World Than This, poetry compiled by V. Sackville-West and Harold Nicolson, 1945
The Garden, 1946
Nursery Rhymes, 1947
Devil at Westease (New York, 1947)
In Your Garden, articles from the *Observer,* 1951
In Your Garden Again, articles from the *Observer,* 1953
The Easter Party, 1953
More for Your Garden, articles from the *Observer,* 1955
'Virginia Woolf and *Orlando',* the *Listener,* 53 (1955), 157–8
Even More for Your Garden, articles from the *Observer,* 1958
A Joy of Gardening (New York, 1958)
Daughter of France: The Life of Anne Marie Louise d'Orléans, 1959
No Signposts in the Sea, 1961
Faces: Profiles of Dogs, 1961
Dearest Andrew: Letters from V. Sackville-West to Andrew Reiber, 1951–1962, ed. Nancy MacKnight, 1980
The Letters of Vita Sackville-West to Virginia Woolf, ed. Louise DeSalvo and Mitchell A. Leaska, 1985

VIRGINIA WOOLF

The Voyage Out, 1915
Night and Day, 1919
Monday or Tuesday, 1921
Jacob's Room, 1922
Mr. Bennett and Mrs. Brown, Hogarth Essays, 1924
The Common Reader, 1925
Mrs Dalloway, 1925
To the Lighthouse, 1927
Orlando: A Biography, 1928
A Room of One's Own, 1929
The Waves, 1931
A Letter to a Young Poet, Hogarth Letters, No. 8, 1932
The Common Reader, 2nd ser., 1932

The Years, 1937
Three Guineas, 1938
Flush: A Biography, 1940
Roger Fry: A Biography, 1940
Between the Acts, 1941
The Death of the Moth and Other Essays, 1942
A Haunted House and Other Short Stories, 1943
The Moment and Other Essays, 1947
The Captain's Death Bed and Other Essays, 1950
A Writer's Diary, ed. Leonard Woolf, 1953
Virginia Woolf and Lytton Strachey: Letters, ed. Leonard Woolf and
   James Strachey, 1956
Granite and Rainbow: Essays, 1958
Contemporary Writers, ed. Jean Guiguet, 1963
Collected Essays, 4 vols., 1966–7
Mrs. Dalloway's Party: A Short Story Sequence, ed. Stella McNichol, 1973
The Letters of Virginia Woolf, ed. Nigel Nicolson and Joanne Traut-
   mann, 6 vols., 1975–80
Books and Portraits, ed. Mary Lyon, 1977
The Diary of Virginia Woolf, ed. Anne Olivier Bell with Andrew
   McNeillie, 5 vols., 1977–84
Moments of Being: Unpublished Autobiographical Writings, ed. Jeanne
   Schulkind, 1978
Virginia Woolf: Women and Writing, ed. Michèle Barrett, 1979

OTHER WORKS CONSULTED

ABEL, ELIZABETH, '(E)merging Identities: The Dynamics of Female
   Friendship in Contemporary Fiction by Women', *Signs*, 6 (1981),
   413–35.
—— (ed.), *Writing and Sexual Difference* (Brighton, 1982).
ACKLAND, VALENTINE, *For Sylvia: An Honest Account* (1985).
ALEXANDER, JEAN, *The Venture of Form in the Novels of Virginia Woolf* (Port
   Washington, 1974).
ALPERS, ANTHONY, *The Life of Katherine Mansfield* (Oxford, 1982).
ALSOP, SUSAN MARY, *Lady Sackville: A Biography* (1978).
AMES, CAROL, 'Nature and Aristocracy in V. Sackville-West', *Studies in
   the Literary Imagination*, 11 (1978), 11–25.
ANNAN, NOEL, *Leslie Stephen: His Thought and Character in Relation to his
   Time* (1951).
APTER, T. E., *Virginia Woolf: A Study of her Novels* (1979).
ARMSTRONG, CHRISTOPHER, *Evelyn Underhill (1875–1941)* (1975).

ASCHER, CAROL, DESALVO, LOUISE, and RUDDICK, SARA (eds.), *Between Women* (Boston, 1984).

AUGUSTINE, *Confessions*, trans. by R. S. Pine-Coffin (Harmondsworth, 1961).

BAJEMA, CARL J. (ed.), *Eugenics Then and Now* (Strondberg, Pa., 1976).

BAKER, MICHAEL, *Our Three Selves: A Life of Radclyffe Hall* (1985).

BAKER, SUSAN W. 'Biological Influences on Human Sex and Gender', in Catharine R. Stimpson and Ethel Spector Person (ed.), *Women: Sex and Sexuality* (Chicago, 1980), 175–91.

BALDANZA, FRANK, '*Orlando* and the Sackvilles', *PMLA* 70/1 (1955), 274–9.

BARNES, DJUNA, *Nightwood* (New York, 1937).

BASHAM, DIANA, *The Trial of Woman: Feminism and the Occult Sciences in Victorian Literature and Society* (1991).

BAZIN, NANCY TOPPING, *Virginia Woolf and the Androgynous Vision* (New Brunswick, NJ, 1973).

BEAUMAN, NICOLA, *A Very Great Profession: The Woman's Novel 1914–39* (1983).

BEER, GILLIAN, *Darwin's Plots: Evolutionary Narrative in Darwin, George Eliot, and Nineteenth-Century Fiction* (1983).

—— 'Hume, Stephen, and Elegy in *To the Lighthouse*', *Essays in Criticism*, 34 (1984), 33–55.

—— 'The Body of the People in Virginia Woolf', in Sue Roe (ed.) *Women Reading Women's Writing* (Brighton, 1987), 83–114.

BEERBOHM, MAX, *Lytton Strachey: The Rede Lecture, 1943* (Cambridge, 1943).

BELL, QUENTIN, *Virginia Woolf: A Biography*, 2 vols. (1972).

BENNETT, JOAN, *Virginia Woolf: Her Art as a Novelist* (Cambridge, 1945).

BENSTOCK, SHARI (ed.), *The Private Self: Theory and Practice of Women's Autobiographical Writing* (1988).

BERGONZI, BERNARD, *The Myth of Modernism and Twentieth-Century Literature* (Brighton, 1986).

BERGSON, HENRI, *Creative Evolution*, trans. Arthur Mitchell (1911).

BERNIKOW, LOUISE, *The World Split Open: Four Centuries of Women Poets in England and America, 1552–1950* (New York, 1974).

BESANT, ANNIE, *An Autobiography* (1893).

—— 'Theosophy and the Law of Population', 1896, repr. in S. Chandrasekhar (ed.), *'A Dirty, Filthy Book': The Writings of Charles Knowlton and Annie Besant on Reproductive Physiology and Birth Control—an Account of the Bradlaugh–Besant Trial* (Berkeley, Calif., 1981), 203–12.

BLACKER, C. P., *Eugenics: Galton and After* (1952).

BLACKSTONE, BERNARD, *Virginia Woolf: A Commentary* (1949).

BLAIN, VIRGINIA, 'Narrative Voice and the Female Perspective in Virginia Woolf's Early Novels', in Patricia Clements and Isobel Grundy (ed.), *Virginia Woolf: New Critical Essays* (1983), 115–36.

BLOCK, JEANNE H., *Sex Role Identity and Ego Development* (San Francisco, 1984).

BOLL, T. E. M., *Miss May Sinclair, Novelist, a Biographical and Critical Introduction* (Rutherford, NJ, 1973).

BOWLBY, RACHEL, *Virginia Woolf: Feminist Destinations* (Oxford, 1988).

—— 'Still Crazy after all these Years', in Teresa Brennan (ed.), *Between Feminism and Psychoanalysis* (1989), 40–59.

BRADFORD, GAMALIEL, *Samuel Pepys: The Soul of a Man* (1924).

—— 'Confessions of a Biographer', in *Wives* (New York, 1925), 3–14.

BREWSTER, DOROTHY, *Virginia Woolf* (1963).

BRITTAIN, VERA, *Radclyffe Hall: A Case of Obscenity* (1968).

—— *Testament of Youth: An Autobiographical Study of the Years 1900–1925*, (1979; 1st edn. 1933).

—— *Testament of Friendship: The Story of Winifred Holtby*, (1980; 1st edn. 1940).

BROWN, JANE, *Vita's Other World: A Gardening Biography of Vita Sackville-West* (Harmondsworth, 1985).

BRUSS, ELIZABETH W., *Autobiographical Acts: The Changing Situation of a Literary Genre* (Baltimore, 1976).

BRYHER, WINIFRED ELLERMANN, 'A Good Pasture Needs Many Grasses', *Life and Letters Today*, 30 (1941), 195–7.

BURKE, CAROLYN G., 'Report from Paris: Women's Writing and the Women's Movement', *Signs*, 3 (1978), 843–55.

—— 'Gertrude Stein, the Cone Sisters, and the Puzzle of Female Friendship', in Elizabeth Abel (ed.), *Writing and Sexual Difference* (Chicago, 1982), 221–42.

BUTLER, JUDITH, *Gender Trouble: Feminism and the Subversion of Identity* (1990).

CARPENTER, EDWARD, *The Intermediate Sex: A Study of Some Transitional Types of Men and Women* (1909).

CARRINGTON, NOEL, *Carrington: Paintings, Drawings and Decorations* (Oxford, 1978).

Carrington: Letters and Extracts from her Diaries, ed. David Garnett (1970).

CARROLL, BERNICE A., 'To Crush Him in Our Own Country: The Political Thought of Virginia Woolf', *Feminist Studies*, 4 (1978), 99–131.

CARRUTHERS, MARY, 'Imagining Women: Notes towards a Feminist Poetic', *Massachusetts Review*, 20 (1979), 281–307.

CASTLE, TERRY, 'Sylvia Townsend Warner and the Counterplot of Lesbian Fiction', *Textual Practice*, 4 (1990), 213–35.

CAWS, MARY ANN, *Women of Bloomsbury: Virginia, Vanessa and Carrington* (1990).

CHESLER, PHYLLIS, *Women and Madness* (1974).

CHODOROW, NANCY, *The Reproduction of Mothering: Psychoanalysis and the Sociology of Gender* (Berkeley, Calif., 1978).

CIXOUS, HÉLÈNE, 'The Laugh of the Medusa', in Elaine Marks and Isabelle de Courtivron (eds.), *New French Feminisms* (New York, 1981), 245–64

CLIFFORD, JAMES L. (ed.), *Biography as an Art: Selected Criticism 1560–1960* (1962).

—— and GEORGE E. MARCUS (ed.), *Writing Culture: The Poetics and Politics of Ethnography* (Berkeley, Calif., 1986).

COCKBURN, CLAUD, *Bestseller: The Books that Everyone Read 1900–1939* (1972).

COCKSHUT, A. O. J., *The Art of Autobiography in Nineteenth and Twentieth Century England* (New Haven, Conn., 1984).

COE, RICHARD N., *When the Grass was Taller: Autobiography and the Experience of Childhood* (New Haven, Conn., 1984).

COLETTE, *La Naissance du jour* (Paris, 1928).

CONWAY, JILL, 'Stereotypes of Femininity in a Theory of Sexual Evolution', in Martha Vicinus (ed.), *Suffer and Be Still: Women in the Victorian Age* (Bloomington, Ind., 1972), 140–54.

COOK, BLANCHE WIESEN, ' "Women Alone Stir my Imagination": Lesbianism and the Cultural Tradition', *Signs*, 4 (1979), 718–39.

DAICHES, DAVID, *Virginia Woolf* (1945).

DARWIN, CHARLES, *The Descent of Man and Selection in Relation to Sex* (1901; 1st edn. 1871).

—— *The Origin of Species by Means of Natural Selection: On the Preservation of Favoured Races in the Struggle for Life* (Harmondsworth, 1985; 1st edn. 1859).

—— and HUXLEY T. H., *Autobiographies*, ed. Gavin de Beer (Oxford, 1983).

DARWIN, FRANCIS, *Life and Letters of Charles Darwin*, 3 vols. (1887).

DELAFIELD, E. M., *The Heel of Achilles* (1921).

DE MAN, PAUL, 'Autobiography as De-Facement', *Modern Language Notes*, 94 (1979), 919–30.

DESALVO, LOUISE, A., 'Lighting the Cave: The Relationship between Vita Sackville-West and Virginia Woolf', *Signs*, 8 (1982), 195–214.

—— 'Every Woman is an Island: Vita Sackville-West, the Image of the City, and the Pastoral Idyll', in Susan Merrill Squier (ed.), *Women Writers and the City: Essays in Feminist Literary Criticism* (Knoxville, Tenn., 1984), 97–114.

—— *Virginia Woolf: The Impact of Childhood Sexual Abuse on her Life and Work* (1989).

DIBATTISTA, MARIA, *Virginia Woolf's Major Novels: The Fables of Anon* (New Haven, Conn., 1980).

DINNERSTEIN, DOROTHY, *The Rocking of the Cradle and the Ruling of the World* (1978).

DONAHUE, DELIA, *The Novels of Virginia Woolf* (Rome, 1977).

DOWLING, DAVID, *Bloomsbury Aesthetics and the Novels of Virginia Woolf* (1985).

DUNN, JANE, *A Very Close Conspiracy: Vanessa Bell and Virginia Woolf* (1990).

DUSINBERRE, JULIET, *Alice to the Lighthouse: Children's Books and Radical Experiments in Art* (1987).

EDEL, LEON, *Literary Biography: The Alexander Lectures 1955–56* (1957).

ELLIS, HAVELOCK, *Studies in the Psychology of Sex*, 2nd edn., 6 vols. (Philadelphia, 1923–4).

FADERMAN, LILLIAN, *Surpassing the Love of Men: Romantic Friendship and Love between Women from the Renaissance to the Present* (New York, 1981).

FEIT-DEIHL, JOANNE, 'Come Slowly—Eden: An Exploration of Women Poets and their Muse', *Signs*, 3 (1978), 572–87.

FLEISHMAN, AVROM, *Virginia Woolf: A Critical Reading* (Baltimore, 1971).

FONTAINE, CORALYN, 'Teaching the Psychology of Women: A Lesbian-Feminist Perspective', in Margaret Cruikshank (ed.), *Lesbian Studies: Present and Future* (Old Westbury, NY, 1982), 70–80.

FORRESTER, VIVIANE, *Virginia Woolf* (Paris, 1973).

FORSTER, E. M., *Virginia Woolf: The Rede Lecture, 1941* (Cambridge, 1942).

FREEDMAN, RALPH (ed.), *Virginia Woolf: Revaluation and Continuity* (Berkeley, Calif., 1980).

FREUD, SIGMUND, *Standard Edition of the Complete Psychological Works*, viii. *Jokes and their Relation to the Unconscious*, ed. and trans. James Strachey (24 vols.; 1966–74).

—— *Standard Edition of the Complete Psychological Works*, xix. 'The Dissolution of the Oedipus Complex', 171–9.

—— *Standard Edition of the Complete Psychological Works*, xxii. 'Femininity', in *New Introductory Lectures on Psychoanalysis*, 112–35.

FURBANK, P. N., *Unholy Pleasure, or the Idea of Social Class* (Oxford, 1985).

GALTON, FRANCIS, *Inquiries into Human Faculty and Its Development* (1883).

—— *Memories of my Life* (1908).

GALTON, FRANCIS, *Hereditary Genius: An Inquiry into its Laws and Consequences* (1914; 1st edn. 1869).

GARNER, SHIRLEY NELSON, KAHANE, CLAIRE, and SPRENGNETHER, MADELON (ed.), *The (M)other Tongue: Essays in Feminist Psychoanalytic Interpretation* (Ithaca, NY., 1985).

GASCHE, RODOLPHE, 'Introduction', *Modern Language Notes*, 93 (1978), 573–4.

GEDDES, PATRICK and THOMSON, J. ARTHUR, *The Evolution of Sex* (1889).

GERMAN, HOWARD and KAEHELE, SHARON, 'The Dialectic of Time in *Orlando*', *College English*, 24 (1962), 35–41.

GILBERT, SANDRA, 'Life Studies, or Speech after Long Silence—Feminist Criticism Today', *College English*, 40 (1979), 849–63.

—— 'Costumes of the Mind: Transvestism as Metaphor in Modern Literature', *Critical Inquiry*, 7 (1980), 391–417.

GILLESPIE, DIANE F., 'Virginia Woolf and the Reign of Error', *Research Studies*, 43 (1975), 222–34.

GILLIGAN, CAROL, *In a Different Voice: Psychological Theory and Women's Development* (Cambridge, Mass., 1982).

GIROUARD, MARK, *Life in the English Country House: A Social and Architectural History* (New Haven, Conn., 1978).

GITTINGS, ROBERT, *The Nature of Biography* (1978).

GLASGOW, JOANNE, 'What's a Nice Lesbian Like You Doing in the Church of Torquemada? Radclyffe Hall and Other Catholic Converts', in Karla Jay and Joanne Glasgow (ed.), *Lesbian Texts and Contexts: Radical Revisions* (New York, 1990), 241–54.

GLENDINNING, VICTORIA, *Vita: The Life of V. Sackville-West* (New York, 1983).

GORDON, LYNDALL, *Virginia Woolf: A Writer's Life* (Oxford, 1984).

GORSKY, SUSAN RUBINOW, *Virginia Woolf* (Boston, 1978).

GRAHAM, JOHN, 'The "Caricature Value" of Parody and Fantasy in *Orlando*', *University of Toronto Quarterly*, 30 (1961), 345–66.

—— 'Point of View in *The Waves*: Some Services of the Style', *University of Toronto Quarterly*, 39 (1970), 193–211.

GRAHAM, J. W., 'A Negative Note on Bergson and Virginia Woolf', *Essays in Criticism*, 6 (1956), 70–4.

GREEN, DAVID, '*Orlando* and the Sackvilles: Addendum', *PMLA* 71/1 (1956), 268–9.

GUBAR, SUSAN, 'The Birth of the Artist as Heroine: Reproduction, the Künstlerroman, and the Fiction of Katherine Mansfield', in Carolyn G. Heilbrun and Margaret R. Higonnet (eds.), *The Representation of Women in Fiction* (Baltimore, 1983), 19–59.

GUIGUET, JEAN, *Virginia Woolf and her Works*, trans. J. Stewart (1965).

GUSDORF, GEORGES, 'Conditions and Limits of Autobiography', 1956, trans. James Olney, repr. in James Olney (ed.), *Autobiography: Essays Theoretical and Critical* (Princeton, NJ, 1980), 28–48.

HAFLEY, JAMES, *The Glass Roof: Virginia Woolf as Novelist* (New York, 1954).

HALL, RADCLYFFE, *The Well of Loneliness* (1982; 1st edn. 1928).

HALL, RUTH, *Marie Stopes: A Biography* (1977).

—— (ed.), *Dear Dr. Stopes: Sex in the 1920s* (Harmondsworth, 1978).

HANKIN, C. A., *Katherine Mansfield and her Confessional Stories* (1983).

HANSCOMBE, GILLIAN, *The Art of Life: Dorothy Richardson and the Development of Feminist Consciousness* (1982).

—— and SMYERS, VIRGINIA L., *Writing for their Lives: The Modernist Women 1910–1940* (1987).

HARPER, HOWARD, *Between Language and Silence: The Novels of Virginia Woolf* (Baton Rouge, La., 1982).

HART, FRANCIS R., 'Notes for an Anatomy of Modern Autobiography', *New Literary History*, 1 (1970), 485–511.

HARTMAN, GEOFFREY, 'Virginia's Web', *Chicago Review*, 45 (1961), 20–32.

HAVARD-WILLIAMS, PETER and MARGARET, 'Mystical Experience in Virginia Woolf's *The Waves*', *Essays in Criticism*, 4 (1954), 71–84.

H. D., *Tribute to Freud*, (Manchester, 1985; 1st edn. 1956).

HEATH, STEPHEN, 'Difference', *Screen*, 19 (1978), 50–112.

—— *The Sexual Fix* (1982).

HEILBRUN, CAROLYN, *Toward a Recognition of Androgyny*, 1964 (New York, 1982).

—— *Writing a Woman's Life* (1989).

—— and STIMPSON, CATHARINE, 'Theories of Feminist Criticism: A Dialogue', in Josephine Donovan (ed.), *Feminist Literary Criticism* (Lexington, K., 1976), 61–73.

HOFFMANN, CHARLES G., 'Fact and Fantasy in *Orlando*: Virginia Woolf's Manuscript Revisions', *Texas Studies in Language and Literature*, 10 (1978), 435–44.

HOBHOUSE, JANET, *Everybody who was Anybody: A Biography of Gertrude Stein* (New York, 1975).

HOLROYD, MICHAEL, *Lytton Strachey: A Biography* (Harmondsworth, 1971).

—— *Lytton Strachey and the Bloomsbury Group: His Work, Their Influence* (Harmondsworth, 1971).

HOLTBY, WINIFRED, *Virginia Woolf* (1932).

—— *Virginia Woolf: A Critical Memoir* (1942).

HUNTING, CONSTANCE, 'The Technique of Persuasion in *Orlando*', *Modern Fiction Studies*, 2 (1956), 17–23.

HUSSEY, MARK, *The Singing of the Real World: The Philosophy of Virginia Woolf's Fiction* (Columbus, Oh., 1986).

HYNES, SAMUEL, *The Edwardian Turn of Mind* (Princeton, NJ, 1968).

JACKSON, ROSEMARY, *Fantasy: The Literature of Subversion* (1981).

JACOBUS, MARY (ed.), *Women Writing and Writing about Women* (1979).

—— *Reading Woman: Essays in Feminist Criticism* (New York, 1986).

JAMES, WILLIAM, *The Varieties of Religious Experience* (Harmondsworth, 1982; 1st edn. 1902).

JARDINE, ALICE, 'Gynesis', *Diacritics*, 12 (1982), 54–65.

JARDINE, LISA, *Still Harping on Daughters: Women and Drama in the Age of Shakespeare* (Brighton, 1983).

JAY, PAUL, *Being in the Text: Self-Representation from Wordsworth to Roland Barthes* (Ithaca, NY, 1984).

JEFFREYS, SHEILA, *The Spinster and her Enemies: Feminism and Sexuality 1880–1930* (1985).

JELINEK, ESTELLE C. (ed.), *Women's Autobiography: Essays in Criticism* (Bloomington, Ind., 1980).

JOHNSON, BARBARA, 'My Monster/My Self', *Diacritics*, 12 (1982), 2–10.

JOHNSON, EDGAR, *One Mighty Torrent: The Drama of Biography* (New York, 1955; 1st edn. 1937).

JONES, GRETA, *Social Darwinism and English Thought: The Interaction between Biological and Social Theory* (Brighton, 1980).

JULLIAN, PHILIPPE and PHILLIPS, JOHN, *Violet Trefusis: A Biography* (1976).

KALCIK, SUSAN, '"... Like Ann's Gynecologist or the Time I was almost Raped": Personal Narratives in Women's Rap Groups', *Journal of American Folklore*, 88 (1975), 3–11.

KAPLAN, CORA, *Sea Changes: Culture and Feminism* (1986).

KATZ, PHYLLIS A., 'The Development of Female Identity', in Claire B. Kopp (ed.), *Becoming Female: Perspectives on Development* (New York, 1979), 3–28.

KELLERMANN, FREDERICK, 'A New Key to Virginia Woolf's *Orlando*', *English Studies*, 59 (1978), 138–50.

KELLY, ALICE VAN BUREN, *The Novels of Virginia Woolf: Fact and Vision* (Chicago, 1973).

KENNEY, SUSAN M. and EDWIN J. JR, 'Virginia Woolf and the Art of Madness', *Massachusetts Review*, 23 (1982), 161–85.

The Selected Melanie Klein, ed. Juliet Mitchell (Harmondsworth, 1986).

KNOPP, SHERRON E., '"If I saw you would you kiss me?": Sapphism and the Subversiveness of Virginia Woolf's *Orlando*', in Joseph Bristow (ed.), *Sexual Sameness: Textual Difference in Lesbian and Gay Writing* (London, 1992).

KRAFFT-EBING, RICHARD VON, *Psychopathia Sexualis* (New York, 1925; 1st edn. 1882).

LACAN, JACQUES, 'The Subject and the Other: Aphanisis', in Jacques

Alain Miller (ed.), *The Four Fundamental Concepts of Psycho-Analysis*, trans. Alan Sheridan (New York, 1981), 216–29.

—— 'God and the *Jouissance* of Woman. A Love Letter', trans. Jacqueline Rose, in Juliet Mitchell and Jacqueline Rose (ed.), *Feminine Sexuality: Jacques Lacan and the Ecole Freudienne* (1982), 137–48.

LEASKA, MITCHELL A., *The Novels of Virginia Woolf: From Beginning to End* (1977).

LEAVIS, Q. D., *Fiction and the Reading Public* (1939).

LEE, HERMIONE, *The Novels of Virginia Woolf* (1977).

LEE, SIDNEY, 'National Biography', *Cornhill*, NS, 24 (1896), 258–77.

—— *Queen Victoria* (1902).

—— *The Principles of Biography* (Cambridge, 1911).

LEJEUNE, PHILIPPE, *Le pacte autobiographique* (Paris, 1975).

Lesbian History Group, *Not a Passing Phase: Reclaiming Lesbians in History 1840–1985* (1989).

LEWIS, WYNDHAM, *Time and Western Man* (1927).

LILIENFELD, JANE, ' "The Deceptiveness of Beauty": Mother Love and Mother Hate in *To the Lighthouse*', *Twentieth Century Literature*, 23 (1977), 345–76.

—— 'Reentering Paradise: Cather, Colette, Woolf and their Mothers', in Cathy M. Davidson and E. M. Broner (ed.), *The Lost Tradition: Mothers and Daughters in Literature* (New York, 1979), 160–75.

LITTLE, JUDY, *Comedy and the Woman Writer: Woolf, Spark and Feminism* (Lincoln, Nebr., 1983).

LOMBROSO, CESARE, *The Female Offender* (1895).

—— *Criminal Man According to the Classification of Cesare Lombroso*, summarized by Gina Lombroso Ferrero, intr. by Cesare Lombroso (1911).

—— and FERRERO, GINA, *La Femme Criminelle et la prostituée*, trans. L. Meille (Paris, 1896).

LONGAKER, MARK, *Contemporary Biography* (Philadelphia, 1934).

LOVE, JEAN O., *Virginia Woolf: Sources of Madness and Art* (Berkeley, Calif., 1977).

—— '*Orlando* and Its Genesis: Venturing and Experimenting in Art, Love and Sex', in Ralph Freedman (ed.), *Virginia Woolf: Revaluation and Continuity* (Berkeley, Calif., 1980), 189–218.

LUDWIG, EMIL, *Goethe: The History of a Man*, trans. Ethel Colburn Mayne (1928).

McLAURIN, ALLEN, 'Virginia Woolf and Unanimism', *Journal of Modern Literature*, 9 (1982), 115–22.

MAJUMDAR, ROBIN and McLAURIN, ALLEN (ed.), *Virginia Woolf: The Critical Heritage* (1975).

The Collected Stories of Katherine Mansfield (Harmondsworth, 1981).

The Letters and Journals of Katherine Mansfield: A Selection, ed. C. K. Stead (Harmondsworth, 1977).

MARCUS, JANE (ed.), *New Feminist Essays on Virginia Woolf* (London, 1981).

—— (ed.), *Virginia Woolf: A Feminist Slant* (Lincoln, Nebr., 1983).

—— (ed.), *Virginia Woolf and Bloomsbury: A Centenary Celebration* (1987).

—— 'Sapphistory: The Woolf and the Well', in Karla Jay and Joanne Glasgow (ed.), *Lesbian Texts and Contexts: Radical Revisions* (New York, 1990), 164–79.

MARDER, HERBERT, *Feminism and Art: A Study of Virginia Woolf* (1968).

MARKS, ELAINE, 'Lesbian Intertextuality', in George Stambolian and Elaine Marks (eds.), *Homosexualities and French Literature* (Ithaca, NY, 1979), 353–77.

MAUROIS, ANDRÉ, *Ariel: A Shelley Romance*, trans. Ella d'Arcy (1924).

—— *Disraeli: A Picture of the Victorian Age*, trans. Hamish Miles (1927).

—— *Aspects of Biography* (Cambridge, 1929).

—— *Byron*, trans. Hamish Miles (1930).

MEISEL, PERRY, *The Absent Father: Virginia Woolf and Walter Pater* (New Haven, Conn., 1980).

MEPHAM, JOHN, 'Mourning and Modernism', in Patricia Clements and Isobel Grundy (ed.), *Virginia Woolf: New Critical Essays* (1983), 137–56.

MILLER, D. A., *The Novel and the Police* (Berkeley, Calif., 1988).

MILLER, J. HILLIS, '*Mrs. Dalloway*: Repetition as the Raising of the Dead', in J. Hillis Miller, *Fiction and Repetition: Seven English Novels* (Oxford, 1982), 176–202.

MILLER, NANCY K., 'Women's Autobiography in France: For a Dialectics of Identification', in Sally McConnell-Ginet, Ruth Borker, and Nelly Furman (ed.), *Women and Language in Literature and Society* (New York, 1980), 258–73.

MILLETT, KATE, *Flying* (1974).

MINOW, MAKIKO, 'Versions of Female Modernism: Review-Article', *News from Nowhere*, 7 (1989), 64–9.

MINOW-PINKNEY, MAKIKO, *Virginia Woolf and the Problem of the Subject: Feminine Writing in the Major Novels* (Brighton, 1987).

MITCHELL, JULIET, *Psychoanalysis and Feminism: Freud, Laing, and Women* (1974).

Modern Language Notes, issue 'Autobiography and the Problem of the Subject', 93 (1978).

MOI, TORIL, *Sexual/Textual Politics: Feminist Literary Theory* (1985).

MOODY, A. D., *Virginia Woolf* (Edinburgh, 1963).

MOORE, G. E., *Principia Ethica* (Cambridge, 1903).

MOORE, JAMES, *Gurdjieff and Katherine Mansfield* (1980).

MOORE, MADELINE, *The Short Season between Two Silences: The Mystical and the Political in the Novels of Virginia Woolf* (Boston, 1984).

MULFORD, WENDY, *This Narrow Place: Sylvia Townsend Warner and Valentine Ackland: Life, Letters and Politics, 1930–1951* (1988).

NEFF, REBECCA, 'New Mysticism in the Writing of May Sinclair and T. S. Eliot', *Twentieth-Century Literature*, 26 (1980), 82–100.

NICOLSON, HAROLD, *Tennyson: Aspects of his Life, Character and Poetry* (1923).

—— *Byron: The Last Journey, April 1823–April 1824* (1924).

—— *Swinburne* (1926).

—— *Some People* (1927).

—— *The Development of English Biography* (1927).

—— *Diaries and Letters*, ed. Nigel Nicolson, 3 vols. (1966–8).

NICOLSON, NIGEL, *Portrait of a Marriage* (1973).

NOBLE, JOAN RUSSELL (ed.), *Recollections of Virginia Woolf* (1972).

NOVAK, JANE, *The Razor Edge of Balance: A Study of Virginia Woolf* (Miami, Fla., 1975).

OLNEY, JAMES, *Metaphors of Self: the Meaning of Autobiography* (Princeton, NJ, 1972).

—— *Autobiography: Essays Theoretical and Critical* (Princeton, NJ, 1980).

OUSPENSKY, P. D., *Tertium Organum: The Third Canon of Thought*, trans. Nicholas Bessaraboff and Claude Bragdon, 2nd edn. (London, 1923).

OWEN, ALEX, *The Darkened Room: Women, Power and Spiritualism in Late Victorian England* (1989).

Personal Narratives Group (ed.), *Interpreting Women's Lives: Feminist Theory and Personal Narratives* (Bloomington, Ind., 1989).

PHILIPSON, MORRIS, 'Virginia Woolf's *Orlando*: Biography as a Work of Fiction', in Dora B. Weiner and William R. Keylor (eds.), *From Parnassus: Essays in Honor of Jacques Barzun* (New York, 1976), 237–48.

PHILLIPS, CHARLES JAMES, *History of the Sackville Family* (1930).

PILLING, JOHN, *Autobiography and Imagination: Studies in Self-Scrutiny* (1981).

PIPPETT, AILEEN, *The Moth and the Star* (Boston, 1955).

POMEROY, ELIZABETH W., 'Within Living Memory: Vita Sackville-West's Poems of Land and Garden', *Twentieth-Century Literature*, 28 (1982), 269–89.

POOLE, ROGER, *The Unknown Virginia Woolf* (Cambridge, 1978).

PORESKY, LOUISE, *The Elusive Self: Psyche and Spirit in Virginia Woolf's Novels* (1981).

POWYS, JOHN COWPER, *Dorothy M. Richardson* (1931).

RAITT, SUZANNE, 'Fakes and Femininity: Vita Sackville-West and her Mother', in Isobel Armstrong (ed.), *New Feminist Discourses* (1992).

RANTAVAARA, IRMA, *Virginia Woolf's 'The Waves'* (Helsinki, 1960).

RICE, THOMAS JACKSON, *Virginia Woolf: A Guide to Research* (1984).

RICH, ADRIENNE, *On Lies, Secrets and Silence: Selected Prose 1966–1978* (New York, 1979).

RICHARDSON, DOROTHY, *Pilgrimage*, 4 vols. (1979; 1st edn. 1915–35).

RICHTER, HARVENA, 'Hunting the Moth: Virginia Woolf and the Creative Imagination', in Ralph Freedman (ed.), *Virginia Woolf: Revaluation and Continuity* (Berkeley, Calif., 1980), 13–28.

RICHTER, MELVIN, *The Politics of Conscience: T. H. Green and his Age* (1964).

RIGNEY, BARBARA HILL, *Madness and Sexual Politics in the Feminist Novel: Studies in Brontë, Woolf, Lessing and Atwood* (Madison, Wis., 1978).

RILEY, DENISE, *'Am I That Name?': Feminism and the Category of 'Women' in History* (1988).

ROBINSON, LILLIAN S., *Sex, Class and Culture* (Bloomington, Ind., 1978).

ROGAT, ELLEN HAWKES, 'The Virgin in the Bell Biography', *Twentieth Century Literature*, 20 (1974), 96–113.

ROSE, JACQUELINE, *The Haunting of Sylvia Plath* (1991).

ROSE, PHYLLIS, *Woman of Letters: A Life of Virginia Woolf* (Oxford, 1978).

ROSE, SHIRLEY, 'The Unmoving Center: Consciousness in Dorothy Richardson's *Pilgrimage*', *Contemporary Literature*, 10 (1969), 366–82.

ROSENBAUM, S. P., 'The Philosophical Realism of Virginia Woolf', in S. P. Rosenbaum (ed.), *English Literature and British Philosophy* (1971), 316–56.

—— *The Bloomsbury Group, A Collection of Memoirs, Commentary and Criticism* (1975).

ROSENBERG, JOHN, *Dorothy Richardson, the Genius they Forgot: A Critical Biography* (1973).

RUDDICK, SARA, 'Learning to Live with the Angel in the House', *Women's Studies*, 4 (1977), 181–200.

—— 'Private Brother, Public World', in Jane Marcus (ed.), *New Feminist Essays on Virginia Woolf* (1981), 185–215.

RULE, JANE, *Lesbian Images* (1975).

ST. AUBYN, GWEN, *The Family Book* (1934).

—— *Towards a Pattern* (1940).

ST. TERESA OF AVILA, *The Life of St. Teresa of Avila*, 1562–5, trans. E. Allison Peers (1979).

ST. THÉRÈSE OF LISIEUX, *Story of a Soul: The Autobiography of St. Thérèse of Lisieux*, trans. John Clarke, 2nd edn. (Washington, DC, 1976; 1st edn. 1893–6).

SCHAEFER, JOSEPHINE O'BRIEN, *The Three-Fold Nature of Reality in the Novels of Virginia Woolf* (1965).

SCOTT, JOHN, *The Upper Classes: Property and Privilege in Britain* (1982).

SCOTT-JAMES, ANN, *Sissinghurst: The Making of a Garden* (1974).

SEARLE, G. R., *Eugenics and Politics in Britain, 1900–1914* (Leyden, 1976).

SEDGWICK, EVE KOSOFSKY, *The Epistemology of the Closet* (Hemel Hempstead, 1991).

SHAPIRO, STEPHEN A., 'The Dark Continent of Literature: Autobiography', *Comparative Literature Studies*, 5 (1968), 421–54.

SHEPPARD, RICHARD, 'The Crisis of Language', in Malcolm Bradbury and James McFarlane (ed.), *Modernism* (Harmondsworth, 1976), 323–36.

SHOWALTER, ELAINE, *A Literature of Their Own: British Women Novelists from Brontë to Lessing* (1978).

—— *The New Feminist Criticism: Essays on Women, Literature and Theory* (New York, 1985).

SHUMAKER, WAYNE, *English Autobiography: Its Emergence, Materials, and Form* (Berkeley, Calif., 1954).

SIMMONS, CHRISTINA, 'Companionate Marriage and the Lesbian Threat', *Frontiers*, 4 (1979), 54–9.

SINCLAIR, MAY, *The Helpmate* (1907).

—— *A Defence of Idealism* (1917).

—— *The Tree of Heaven* (1917).

—— 'The Novels of Dorothy Richardson', *Egoist*, 5 (1918), 57–9.

—— *The New Idealism* (1922).

—— *Uncanny Stories* (1923).

SMITH-ROSENBERG, CARROLL, 'The Female World of Love and Ritual: Relations between Women in Nineteenth-Century America', *Signs*, 1 (1975), 1–29.

SMYTH, CHARLES, 'A Note on Historical Biography and Mr. Strachey', *Criterion*, 8 (1929), 647–60.

SMYTH, ETHEL, *Impressions that Remained*, 2 vols. (1919).

—— *A Final Burning of Boats Etc.* (1928).

—— *Female Pipings in Eden* (1933).

—— *Beecham and Pharaoh* (1935).

—— *As Time Went On* (1936).

—— *What Happened Next* (1940).

SNIDER, CLIFTON, '"A Single Self": A Jungian Interpretation of Virginia Woolf's *Orlando*', *Modern Fiction Studies*, 25 (1979), 263–8.

SNITOW, ANN, STANSELL, CHRISTINE, and THOMPSON, SHARON (ed.), *Desire: The Politics of Sexuality* (1984).

SPACKS, PATRICIA MEYER, 'Reflecting Women', *Yale Review*, 63 (1973), 26–42.

SPACKS, PATRICIA MEYER, *Imagining a Self: Autobiography and Novel in Eighteenth Century England* (Cambridge, Mass., 1976).

—— 'Women's Stories, Women's Selves', *Hudson Review*, 30 (1977), 29–46.

SPALDING, FRANCES, *Vanessa Bell* (1983).

SPATER, GEORGE and PARSONS, IAN, *A Marriage of True Minds, An Intimate Portrait of Leonard and Virginia Woolf* (1977).

SPENGEMANN, WILLIAM C., *The Forms of Autobiography: Episodes in the History of a Literary Genre* (New Haven, Conn., 1980).

SPILKA, MARK, *Virginia Woolf's Quarrel with Grieving* (Lincoln, Nebr., 1980).

SPRAGUE, CLAIRE (ed.), *Virginia Woolf: A Collection of Critical Essays* (Englewood Cliffs, NJ, 1971).

SQUIER, SUSAN, 'Mirroring and Mothering: Reflections on the Mirror Encounter Metaphor in Virginia Woolf's Works', *Twentieth Century Literature*, 27 (1981), 272–88.

—— *Virginia Woolf and London: The Sexual Politics of the City* (Chapel Hill, NC, 1985).

—— 'Tradition and Revision in Woolf's *Orlando*: Defoe and "The Jessamy Brides"', *Women's Studies*, 12 (1986), 167–78.

STANTON, DOMNA C. (ed.), *The Female Autograph* (New York, 1985).

STEIN, GERTRUDE, *Composition as Explanation* (1926).

—— *Four Saints in Three Acts: An Opera to be Sung* (New York, 1934).

—— *Everybody's Autobiography* (1938).

STEPHEN, CAROLINE, *The Vision of Faith and Other Essays* (Cambridge, 1911).

STEPHEN, LESLIE, 'National Biography', in *Studies of a Biographer*, 2 vols. (1898), i. 1–36.

—— *The Mausoleum Book*, ed. Alan Bell (Oxford, 1977).

STEVENS, MICHAEL, *V. Sackville-West: A Critical Biography* (1973).

STEWART, GARRETT, 'Catching the Stylistic D/Rift: Sound Defects in Woolf's *The Waves*', *English Literary History*, 54 (1987), 421–61.

STEWART, JACK F., 'Historical Impressionism in *Orlando*', *Studies in the Novel*, 5 (1973), 63–85.

STIMPSON, CATHARINE R., 'The Androgyne and the Homosexual', *Women's Studies*, 2 (1974), 237–48.

—— 'Zero Degree Deviancy: The Lesbian Novel in English', *Critical Inquiry*, 8 (1981), 363–80.

—— 'Afterword: Lesbian Studies in the 1990s', in Karla Jay and Joanne Glasgow (ed.), *Lesbian Texts and Contexts* (New York, 1990), 377–82.

STOPES, MARIE, *Married Love: A New Contribution to the Solution of Sex Difficulties* (1918).

—— *Contraception: Its Theory, History and Practice* (1923).

STRACHEY, LYTTON, *Eminent Victorians* (1918).

—— *Queen Victoria* (1971; 1st edn. 1921).

—— *Books and Characters: French and English* (1922).

—— *Elizabeth and Essex: A Tragic History* (1928).

—— *Portraits in Miniature and Other Essays* (1931).

STUBBS, PATRICIA, *Women and Fiction: Feminism and the Novel 1880–1920* (1981).

SWINDELLS, JULIA, *Victorian Writing and Working Women* (Cambridge, 1985).

THAKUR, N. C., *The Symbolism of Virginia Woolf* (Oxford, 1965).

THOMPSON, SYLVIA, *Third Act in Venice* (1936).

TODOROV, TZVETAN, *The Fantastic: A Structural Approach to a Literary Genre*, trans. Richard Howard (Ithaca, NY, 1975).

TRAUTMANN, JOANNE, *The Jessamy Brides: The Friendship of Virginia Woolf and V. Sackville-West* (Philadelphia, 1973).

TREFUSIS, VIOLET, *Don't Look Round* (1952).

—— *Broderie Anglaise*, trans. Barbara Bray (1985).

—— *Violet to Vita: The Letters of Violet Trefusis to Vita Sackville-West, 1910–21*, ed. Mitchell A. Leaska and John Phillips (1989).

TROMBLEY, STEPHEN, *All that Summer she was Mad: Virginia Woolf and her Doctors* (1981).

UNDERHILL, EVELYN, *Mysticism: A Study in the Nature and Development of Man's Spiritual Consciousness* (1911).

—— *Practical Mysticism* (1914).

—— *Poetry* (1932).

VUARNET, JEAN-NOEL, *Extases féminines* (Paris, 1980).

WARNER, ERIC (ed.), *Virginia Woolf: A Centenary Perspective* (1984).

—— *Virginia Woolf: The Waves* (Cambridge, 1987).

WATSON, SARA RUTH, *V. Sackville-West* (New York, 1972).

WEEKS, JEFFREY, *Coming Out: Homosexual Politics in Britain, from the Nineteenth Century to the Present* (1977).

WEINTRAUB, KARL JOACHIM, *The Value of the Individual: Self and Circumstance in Autobiography* (Chicago, 1978).

WELLS, H. G., *An Experiment in Autobiography* (1934).

WILLIAMS, RAYMOND, *The Country and the City* (1985; 1st edn. 1973).

WILSON, COLIN, *Poetry and Mysticism* (1970).

WILSON, J. J., 'Why is *Orlando* Difficult?', in Jane Marcus (ed.), *New Feminist Essays on Virginia Woolf* (1981), 170–84.

WOOLF, LEONARD, *Sowing: An Autobiography of the Years 1880–1904* (1960).

—— *Growing: An Autobiography of the Years 1904–1911* (1961).

—— *Beginning Again: An Autobiography of the Years 1911–1918* (1964).

WOOLF, LEONARD, *Downhill All the Way: An Autobiography of the Years 1919–1939* (1967).

—— *The Journey not the Arrival Matters: An Autobiography of the Years 1939–1969* (1969).

ZEGGER, H. D., *May Sinclair* (Boston, 1976).

ZWERDLING, ALEX, *Virginia Woolf and the Real World* (Berkeley, Calif., 1986).

Index